CONCEPTS OF BUSINESS ENVIRONMENT

CONCEPTS OF BUSINESS ENVIRONMENT

A. Rohtagi

CYBER TECH PUBLICATIONS
4264/3, Ansari Road, Daryaganj, New Delhi-110002 (India)
Ph.: 011-23244078, 011-43559448 Fax: 011-23280028
E-Mail: cyberpublicationsdelhi@yahoo.com
Website: www.cybertechpublications.com

CONCEPTS OF BUSINESS ENVIRONMENT

A. Rohtagi

First Edition 2011

Published by :

G.S. Rawat for **Cyber Tech Publications**
4264/3, Ansari Road, Daryaganj, New Delhi-110002 (India)
Ph.: 011-23244078, 011-43559448 Fax: 011-23280028
E-Mail: cyberpublicationsdelhi@yahoo.com
Website: www.cybertechpublications.com

CONTENTS

Preface

IThe present book comes amid renewed optimism against the background of a much more encouraging regional business environment that is better now than it has been for years. Many Indian countries are experiencing an economic resurgence. Between 2001 and 2006, growth in gross domestic product (GDP) on the continent averaged 4.9 percent annually. In 2006, the continent grew by more than 5.5 percent, and in 2007, the rate is expected to increase further to the highest growth rate registered for decades. Moreover, the cost of doing business is coming down in most countries as an increasing number of them are implementing critical reforms, placing India among the top three reforming continents-ahead of Latin America and the Middle East.

This economic progress opens the door to greater wealth creation and better standards of living for the people of India. Continued policy and institutional reform remain central to ensuring that Indian countries stay on a higher growth trajectory. Those responsible for economic management will have to be aware of the continued need for action and not give in to complacency as a result of the recent cushion of growth. While the timing is propitious for reform, new policies should be introduced in a prioritized and sequenced way, and attention must be given to the political economy of reform as care must be taken to balance the interests of winners and losers that any program of reform engenders. This Book is intended as a tool for Indian decision makers from private and public circles. It measures the business climate potential for sustainable growth and prosperity and as such should be used to stimulate private-public dialogue on the issues at stake. The private sector can play a vital role in the process of reform. As a stakeholder, business can support and advocate competitiveness-enhancing reforms with their governments while highlighting the benefits of a more competitive economy for creating jobs and increasing wealth for all. For their part, governments will want to emphasize a sound business climate as a catalyst for long-term growth and prosperity. This Book is an ongoing collaboration among the three institutions. This year it examines many aspects of India's business environment and, more generally, themes that will boost the prosperity of nations, including detailed assessments of the drivers of productivity and employment growth; the competitiveness and investment climate in India's four largest economies, which together account for slightly more than half of the continent's output; the effect of gender disparities on employment and competitiveness; and the role of new technologies in fostering a more dynamic business environment.

The Book also includes detailed competitiveness and investment climate profiles, providing a comprehensive summary of the drivers of investment and competitiveness in each of the countries included in the Book.

— *Author*

1

Introduction

Business activity is a fundamental and universal feature of human existence and yet the concept of 'business' is difficult to define with any degree of precision. Dictionary defini-tions tend to describe it as being concerned with buying and selling or with trade and commerce, or the concern of profit-making organisations, and clearly all of these would come within the accepted view of business. Such a restricted view, however, would exclude large parts of the work of government and its agencies and the activities of non-profit-making organisations-a perspective it would be hard to sustain in a climate in which business methods, skills, attitudes and objectives are being increasingly adopted by these organisations. It is this broader view of business and its activities which is adopted below and which forms the focus of an investigation into the business environment.

THE BUSINESS ORGANISATION AND ITS ENVIRONMENT: A MODEL OF BUSINESS ACTIVITY

Most business activity takes place within an organisational context and even a cursory investigation of the business world reveals the wide variety of organisations involved, ranging from the small local supplier of a single good or service to the multibillion dollar international or multinational corporation producing and trading on a global scale. Given this rich organisational diversity most observers of the business scene tend to differentiate between organisations in terms of their size, type of product and/or market, methods of finance, scale of operations, legal status and so on. Nissan, for example, would be characterised as a major multinational car producer and distributor trading on world markets, while a local builder is likely to be seen as a small business operating at a local level with a limited market and relatively restricted turnover.

While such distinctions are both legitimate and informative, they can conceal the fact that all business organisations are ultimately involved in the same basic activity, namely, the transformation of inputs (resources) into outputs (goods or services).

In essence, all organisations acquire resources-including labour, premises, tech-nology, finance, materials-and transform these resources into the goods or services required by their customers. While the type, amount and combination of resources will vary according to the needs of each organisation and may also vary over time, the simple process described above is common to all types of business organisation and provides a useful starting-point for investigating business activity and the environment in which it takes place.

A more detailed analysis of business resources and those internal aspects of organisa-tions which help to transform inputs into output can be found. The need, here, is simply to appreciate the idea of the firm as a transformation system and to recognise that in producing and selling output most organisations hope to earn sufficient revenue to allow them to maintain and replenish their resources, thus permitting them to produce further output which in turn produces further inputs. In short, inputs help to create output and output creates inputs. Moreover, the output of one organisation may represent an input for another, as in the case of the firm produc-ing capital equipment or basic materials or information or ideas. This interrelationship between business organisations is just one example of the complex and integrated nature of business activity and it helps to highlight the fact that the fortunes of any single business organisation are invariably linked with those of another or others-a point clearly illustrated in many of the examples cited in the text.

The Firm in its Environment

The simple model of business activity described above is based on the systems approach to management. One of the benefits of this approach is that it stresses that organisations are entities made up of interrelated parts which are inter-twined with the outside world-the 'external environment' in systems language. This environment comprises a wide range of influences-economic, demographic, social, political, legal, technological, etc.-which affect business activity in a variety of ways and which can impinge not only on the transformation process itself, but also on the process of resource acquisition and on the creation and consumption of output.

In examining the business environment, a useful distinction can be made between those external factors which tend to have a more immediate effect on the day-to-day operations of a firm and those which tend to have a more general influ-ence.

The immediate or operational environment for most firms includes suppliers, competitors, labour markets, financial institutions and customers, and may also include trading organisations, trade unions and possibly a parent company. In con-trast the general or contextual environment comprises those macroenvironmental factors such as economic, political, socio-cultural, technological and legal influ-ences on business which affect a wide variety of businesses and which can emanate not only from local and national sources but also from international and suprana-tional developments.

This type of analysis can also be extended to the different functional areas of an organisation's activities such as marketing or personnel or production or finance, as illustrated in Figure 1.4. Such an analysis can be seen to be useful in at least two ways. First, it emphasises the influence of external factors on specific activities within the firm and in doing so underlines the importance of the interface between the internal and external environments. Second, by drawing attention to this interface, it highlights the fact that, while business organisations are often able to exercise some degree of control over their internal activities and processes, it is often very difficult, if not impossible, to control the external environment in which they operate.

Environmental influences on a firm's marketing system

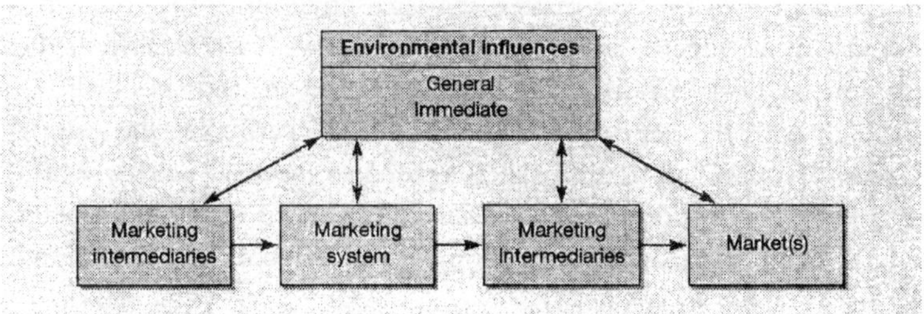

THE GENERAL OR CONTEXTUAL ENVIRONMENT

While the external factors referred to above form the subject-matter of the rest of the book, it is useful at this point to gain an overview of the business environment by highlighting some of the key environmental influences on business activity. In keeping with the distinction made between general and more immediate influ-ences, these are discussed separately below. In this section we examine what are frequently referred to as the 'PESTLE' factors (i.e. political, economic, socio-cultural, technological, legal and ethical influences). A 'PESTLE' (or 'PEST') analysis can be used to analyse a firm's current and future environment as part of the strategic management process.

The Political Environment

A number of aspects of the political environment clearly impinge on business activ-ity. These range from general questions concerning the nature of the political system and its institutions and processes, to the more specific questions relating to government involvement in the working of the economy and its attempts to influence market structure and behaviour.

Government activities, both directly and indirectly, influence business activity and government can be seen as the biggest business enterprise at national or local level. Given the trend towards the globalisation of markets and the existence of international trading organisations and blocs, international politico-economic influences on business activity represent one key feature of the business environment. Another is the influence of public, as well as politi-cal, opinion in areas such as environmental policy and corporate responsibility.

The Economic Environment

The distinction made between the political and economic environment-and, for that matter, the legal environment-is somewhat arbitrary. Government, as indi-cated above, plays a major role in the economy at both national and local level and its activities help to influence both the demand and supply side. Nevertheless there are a number of other eco-nomic aspects related to business activity which are worthy of consideration. These include various structural aspects of both firms and markets and a comparison of economic theory and practice.

THE SOCIAL, CULTURAL AND DEMOGRAPHIC ENVIRONMENT

Both demand and supply are influenced by social, cultural and demographic factors. Cultural factors, for example, may affect the type of products being produced or sold, the markets they are sold in, the price at which they are sold and a range of other variables. People are a key organisational resource and a fundamental part of the market for goods and services.

Accordingly, socio-cultural influences and develop-ments have an important effect on business operations, as do demographic changes.

The Technological Environment

Technology is both an input and an output of business organisations as well as being an environmental influence on them. Investment in technology and innova-tion is frequently seen as a key to the success of an enterprise and has been used to explain differences in the relative competitiveness of different countries. It has also been responsible for significant developments in the internal organi-sation of businesses in the markets for economic resources.

The Legal Environment

Businesses operate within a framework of law which has a significant impact on various aspects of their existence. Laws usually govern, among other things, the status of the organisation, its relationship with its customers and sup-pliers and certain internal procedures and activities. They may also influence market structures and behaviour. Since laws emanate from government (including supranational governments) and from the judgments of the courts, some understanding of the relevant institutions and processes is desirable.

The Ethical Environment

Ethical considerations have become an increasingly important influence on busi-ness behaviour, particularly among the larger, more high profile companies. One area where this has been manifest is in the demand for firms to act in a more socially responsible way and to consider the impact they might have on people, their communities and the natural environment.

THE IMMEDIATE OR OPERATIONAL ENVIRONMENT

An organisation's need for resources makes it dependent to a large degree on the suppliers of those resources, some of whom operate in markets which are structured to a considerable extent. Some aspects of the operation of resource markets or indeed the activities of an individual supplier can have a fundamental impact on an organisation's success and upon the way in which it structures its internal procedures and processes. By the same token, the success of suppliers is often intimately connected with the decisions and/or fortunes of their customers. While some organisations may seek to gain an advantage in price, quality or deliv-ery by purchasing resources from overseas, such a decision can engender a degree of uncertainty, particularly where exchange rates are free rather than fixed. Equally, organisations may face uncertainty and change in the domestic mar-kets for resources as a result of factors as varied as technological change, government intervention or public opinion (e.g. conservation issues).

Customers

Customers are vital to all organisations and the ability both to identify and to meet consumer needs is seen as one of the keys to organisational survival and prosperity-a point not overlooked by politicians, who are increasingly using business tech-niques to attract the support of the electorate. This idea of consumer sovereignty-where resources are allocated to produce output to satisfy customer demands-is a central tenet of the market economy and is part of an ideology whose influence has become all pervasive in recent years. Understanding the many factors affecting both individual and market demand, and the ways in which firms organ-ise themselves to satisfy that demand is a vital component of a business environment that is increasingly market led.

Competitors

Competition-both direct and indirect-is an important part of the context in which many firms operate and is a factor equally applicable to the input as well as the output side of business. The effects of competition, whether from domestic organisations or from overseas firms, is significant at the macro as well as the micro level and its influence can be seen in the changing structures of many advanced industrial economies. How firms respond to these competitive challenges and the attitudes of gov-ernments to anti-competitive practices is a legitimate area of concern for students of business.

Analysing the Business Environment

In a subject as all encompassing as the business environment it is possible to iden-tify numerous approaches to the organisation of the material. One obvious solution would be to examine the various factors mentioned above, devoting separate chap-ters to each of the environmental influences and discussing their impact on business organisations. While this solution has much to recommend it-not least of which is its simplicity-the approach adopted below is based on the grouping of environmental influences into four main areas, in the belief that this helps to focus attention on key aspects of the business world, notably contexts, firms and their markets and issues of significance to entrepreneurs and to society as a whole.

In Part Two consideration is given to the political, economic, social, cultural, demographic, legal and resource contexts within which businesses function. In addition to examining the influence of political and economic systems, institutions and processes on the conduct of business, this section focuses on the macroeco-nomic environment and on those broad social influences which effect both consumers and key organisational resources, particularly labour, technology and raw materials. The legal system and the influence of law in a number of critical areas of business activity is also a primary concern and one which has links with Part Three.

In Part Three, attention is focused on three central structural aspects: legal struc-ture, size structure and industrial structure. The chapter on legal structure examines the impact of different legal definitions on a firm's operations and considers possi-ble variations in organisational goals based on legal and other influences. The focus then shifts to how differences in size can affect the organisation (e.g. access to capi-tal, economies of scale) and to an examination of how changes in scale and/or direction can occur, including the role of government in assisting small-business development and growth. One of the consequences of changes in the component elements of the economy is its effect on the overall structure of industry and commerce-a subject which helps to highlight the impact of international compe-tition on the economic structure of many advanced industrial economies. Since government is a key actor in the economy, the section concludes with an analysis of government involvement in business and in particular its influence on the supply as well as the demand side of the economy at both national and local level.

In Part Four, the aim is to compare theory with practice by examining issues such as pricing, market structure and foreign trade. The analysis of price theory illustrates the degree to which the theoretical models of economists shed light on the operation of business in the 'real' world. Similarly, by analysing basic models of market structure, it is possible to gain an understanding of the effects of competi-tion on a firm's behaviour and to appreciate the significance of both price and non-price decisions in the operation of markets.

The analysis continues with an examination of external markets and the role of government in influencing both the structure and operation of the market-place. The chapter on international markets looks at the theoretical basis of trade and the development of overseas markets in practice, particularly in the con-text of recent institutional, economic and financial developments (e.g. the Single Market, globalisation, the Euro). The section concludes with an investigation of the rationale for government intervention in markets and a review of government action in three areas, namely, privatisation and deregulation, competition policy and the operation of the labour market.

Finally, in Part Five, consideration is given to three aspects of business which are highly topical. One of these-corporate responsibility towards the natural environ-ment-raises fundamental questions about the moral dimension of business activity, a subject often overlooked by writers and commentators on the business scene. A second, on the subject of technology, looks in detail at the impact of new technology on organisations and on market development and examines the increasingly important issue of 'e-business'.

The concluding chapter in this section-and, appropriately, in the book as a whole-emphasises the continuing need for organisations to monitor change in the business environment and examines a number of frameworks through which such an analysis can take place. In seeking to make sense of their environment, businesses need access to a wide range of information, much of which is available from published material, including government sources. Some of the major types of information available to students of business and to business organisations-including statistical and other forms of information-are considered in the final part of this chapter.

CENTRAL THEMES

A number of themes run through the text and it is useful to draw attention to these at this point.

Interaction with the Environment

Viewed as an open system, the business organisation is in constant interaction with its environment. Changes in the environment can cause changes in inputs, in the transformation process and in outputs and these in turn may engender further changes in the organisation's environment. The internal and external environ-ments should be seen as interrelated and interdependent, not as separate entities.

Interaction between Environmental Variables

In addition to the interaction between the internal and external environments, the various external influences affecting business organisations are also frequently interrelated. Changes in interest rates, for example, may affect consumer confi-dence and this can have an important bearing on business activity. Subsequent attempts by government to influence the level of demand could exacerbate the sit-uation and this may lead to changes in general economic conditions, causing further problems for firms. The combined effect of these factors could be to create a turbulent environment which could result in uncertainty in the minds of man-agers. Failure to respond to the challenges (or opportunities) presented by such changes could signal the demise of the organisation or at best a significant decline in its potential performance.

The Complexity of the Environment

The environmental factors identified above are only some of the potential variables faced by all organisations. These external influences are almost infinite in number and variety and no study could hope to consider them all. For students of business and for managers alike, the requirement is to recognise the complexity of the exter-nal environment and to pay greater attention to those influences which appear the most pertinent and pressing for the organisation in question, rather than to attempt to consider all possible contingencies.

Environmental Volatility and Change

The organisation's external environment is further complicated by the tendency towards environmental change. This volatility may be particularly prevalent in some areas (e.g. technology) or in some markets or in some types of industry or organisation. As indicated above, a highly volatile environment causes uncertainty for the organisation (or for its sub-units) and this makes decision making more dif-ficult.

Environmental Uniqueness

Implicit in the remarks above is the notion that each organisation has to some degree a unique environment in which it operates and which will affect it in a unique way. Thus, while it is possible to make generalisations about the impact of the external environment on the firm, it is necessary to recognise the existence of this uniqueness and where appropriate to take into account exceptions to the general rule.

Different Spatial Levels of Analysis

External influences operate at different spatial levels-local, regional, national, supranational, international. There are few businesses, if any, today which could justifiably claim to be unaffected by influences outside their immediate market(s).

Two-way Flow of Influence

As a final point, it is important to recognise that the flow of influence between the organisation and its environment operates in both directions. The external environ-ment influences firms, but by the same token firms can influence their environment and this is an acceptable feature of business in a democratic society which is operat-ing through a market-based economic system.

SYNOPSIS

In the process of transforming inputs into output, business organisations operate in a multifaceted environment which affects and is affected by their activities. This environment tends to be complex and volatile and comprises influences which are of both a general and an immediate kind and which operate at different spatial levels.

Understanding this environment and its effects on business operations is of vital impor-tance to the study and practice of business.

SUMMARY OF KEY POINTS

- Business activity is essentially concerned with transforming inputs into outputs for consumption purposes.
- All businesses operate within an external environment which shapes their operations and decisions.
- This environment comprises influences which are both operational and general.
- The operational environment of business is concerned with such factors as cus-tomers, suppliers, creditors and competitors.
- The general environment focuses on what are known as the PESTLE factors.
- In analysing a firm's external environment attention needs to be paid to the interac-tion between the different environmental variables, environmental complexity, volatility and change and to the spatial influences.
- While all firms are affected by the environment in which they exist and operate, at times they help to shape that environment by their activities and behaviour.

A SHOCK OF THE SYSTEM

For the most part changes in a firm's (or industry's or sector's) external environ-ment tend to be relatively predictable and this can aid business planning. Economic indicators, for example, usually signal the onset of a recession (or recov-ery) well before it occurs and this provides businesses with time to consider not only how they are likely to be affected by economic change, but also what steps they can take to minimise any potential threat to the organisation (or maximise any opportunity). On occasions, however, the business environment can change dramatically and unexpectedly for the worse, leaving some firms to face rapidly deteriorating trading conditions often without any contingency plans in place.

Such a situation occurred on Tuesday 11 September 2001 when terrorist attacks on the World Trade Center and the US Department of Defense rapidly sent shock waves through the global economic system, engulfing a wide range of firms and industries in all countries. The most immediate and obvious manifestation of the crisis was seen in the airline industry where the major airline operators suddenly found people unwilling to fly, thereby significantly exacerbating the problems already being experienced as a result of increased competition and recession in some of their markets. In the United States carriers such as United, Delta and Continental announced tens of thousands of redundancies and further job losses were announced by British Airways, Virgin and Air Canada. Elsewhere in Europe both Swissair and Sabena went into receivership and other operators signalled a period of retrenchment.

The knock-on effect of the reduction in air travel also impacted on two allied industries: aircraft manufacturing and tourism. Again this found expression in falling demand and the inevitable loss of jobs. Companies such as Airbus Industrie, Boeing and Bombardier slimmed down their workforces and additional job losses occurred in supplier organisations including Rolls-Royce and in travel, tourism and allied industries such as hotels, catering and car hire. For a company such as Disney, for instance, the impact on visitor numbers at its theme parks in America and Europe was immediately felt and numerous other organisations and holiday destinations rapidly experienced the effect of the decline in overseas tourists in the immediate aftermath of the attack.

While it was suggested at the time by a number of observers that some busi-nesses might have been taking advantage of the crisis to slim down their workforces, there seems little doubt that the attack had a significant economic as well as human and psychological impact. Mercifully such shocks to the system tend to be few and far between and even when they occur some enterprising firms will find they provide unexpected business opportunities.

2

Business Organisations: The Internal Environment

The systems approach to the study of business organisations stresses the interaction between a firm's internal and external environments. Key aspects of the internal context of business include the organisation's structure and functions and the way they are configured in pursuit of specified organisational objectives. If the enterprise is to remain successful, constant attention needs to be paid to balancing the different influences on the organisation and to the requirement to adapt to new external circumstances. This responsibility lies essentially with the organisation's management, which has the task of blending people, technologies, structures and environments.

LEARNING OUTCOMES

Having read this chapter you should be able to:

- outline the broad approaches to organisation and management, paying particular attention to the systems approach
- identify alternative organisation structures used by business organisations
- discuss major aspects of the functional management of firms
- illustrate the interaction between a firm's internal and external environments

INTRODUCTION

The internal features of business organisations have received considerable attention by scholars of organisation and management, and a large number of texts have been devoted to this aspect of business studies. In the discussion below, the aim is to focus on three areas of the internal organisation that relate directly to a study of the business environment: approaches to understanding organisations, organisation structures, and key functions within the enterprise. Further insight into these aspects and into management and organisational behaviour generally can be gained by con-sulting the many specialist books in this field, a number of which are mentioned at the end of this chapter.

A central theme running through any analysis of the internal environment is the idea of 'management', which has been subjected to a wide variety of definitions. As used in this context, management is seen both as a system of roles fulfilled by individuals who manage the organisation (e.g. entrepreneur, resource manager, co-ordinator, leader, motivator, organiser) and as a process which enables an organisation to achieve its objectives. The essential point is that management should be seen as a function of organisations, rather than as a controlling element, and its task is to enable the organi-sation to identify and achieve its objectives and to adapt to change. Managers need to integrate the various influences on the organisation-including people, technology, sys-tems and the environment-in a manner best designed to meet the needs of the enterprise at the time in question and be prepared to institute change as and when cir-cumstances dictate.

APPROACHES TO ORGANISATION AND MANAGEMENT

An important insight into the principles which are felt to underlie the process of management can be gained by a brief examination of organisational theories. These theories or approaches-some of which date back to the late nineteenth century-represent the views of both practising managers and academics as to the factors that determine organisational effectiveness and the influences on individuals and groups within the work environment. Broadly speaking, these approaches can be broken down into three main categories: the classical approach, the human rela-tions approach, and the systems approach. Since the last of these encompasses the model presented in Chapter 1, particular attention is paid to this perspective.

The Classical Approach

Classical theories of organisation and management mostly date from the first half of the twentieth century and are associated with the work of writers such as Taylor, Fayol, Urwick and Brech. In essence, the classicists basically viewed organisations as formal structures established to achieve a particular number of objectives under the direction of management. By identifying a set of principles to guide managers in the design of the organisational structure, the proponents of the classical view believed that organisations would be able to achieve their objectives more effectively. Fayol, for example, identified fourteen principles which included the division of work, the scalar chain, centralisation and the unity of command-features which also found expression in Weber's notion of 'bureaucracy'. Urwick's rules or principles similarly emphasised aspects of organisation structure and operations-such as specialisation, co-ordination, authority, responsibility and the span of control-and were presented essentially as a code of good management practice.

Within the classical approach special attention is often given to two important sub-groupings, known as 'scientific management' and 'bureaucracy'. The former is associated with the pioneering work of F. W. Taylor (1856-1915) who believed that scientific methods could be attached to the design of work so that productivity could be increased. For Taylor, the systematic analysis of jobs (e.g. using some form of work study technique) was seen as the key to finding the best way to perform a particular task and thereby of achieving significant productivity gains from individ-uals which would earn them increased financial rewards. In Taylor's view, the responsibility for the institution of a scientific approach lay with management, under whose control and direction the workers would operate to the mutual bene-fit of all concerned.

The second sub-group, bureaucracy, draws heavily on the work of Max Weber (1864-1920) whose studies of authority structures highlighted the importance of 'office' and 'rules' in the operation of organisations. According to Weber, bureau-cracy-with its system of rules and procedures, specified spheres of competence, hierarchical organisation of offices, appointment based on merit, high level of spe-cialisation and impersonality-possessed a degree of technical superiority over other forms of organisation, and this explained why an increasing number of enter-prises were becoming bureaucratic in structure. Over 50 years after Weber's studies were first published in English, bureaucratic organisation remains a key feature of many enterprises throughout the world and is clearly linked to increasing organisa-tional size and complexity. Notwithstanding the many valid criticisms of Weber's work, it is difficult to imagine how it could be otherwise.

The Human Relations Approach

Whereas the classical approach focuses largely on structure and on the formal organisation, the human relations approach to management emphasises the importance of people in the work situation and the influence of social and psycho-logical factors in shaping organisational behaviour. Human relations theorists have primarily been concerned with issues such as individual motivation, leadership, communications and group dynamics and have stressed the significance of the informal pattern of relationships which exist within the formal structure. The fac-tors influencing human behaviour have accordingly been portrayed as a key to achieving greater organisational effectiveness, thus elevating the 'management of people' to a prime position in the determination of managerial strategies.

The early work in this field is associated with Elton Mayo (1880-1949) and with the famous Hawthorne Experiments, conducted at the Western Electric Company (USA) between 1924 and 1932. What these experiments basically showed was that individuals at work were members of informal (i.e. unofficial) as well as formal groups

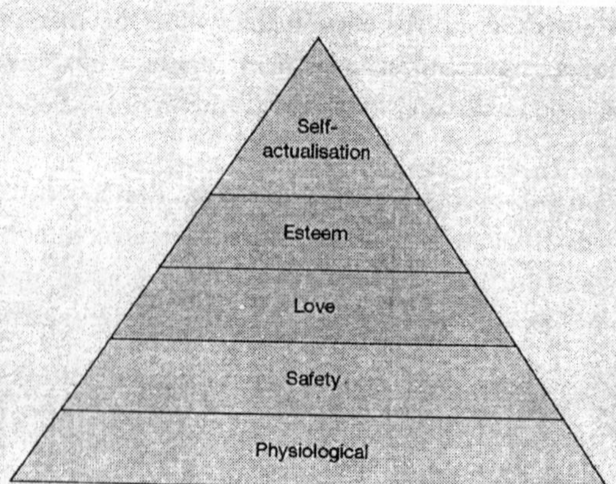

Figure 2.1

A hierarchy of needs and that group influences were fundamental to explaining individual behaviour. Later work by writers such as Maslow, McGregor, Argyris, Likert and Herzberg contin-ued to stress the importance of the human factor in determining organisational effectiveness, but tended to adopt a more psychological orientation, as exemplified by Maslow's 'hierarchy of needs' and McGregor's 'Theory X and Theory Y'. Maslow's central proposition was that individuals seek to satisfy specific groups of needs, rang-ing from basic physiological requirements (e.g. food, sleep, sex), through safety, love and esteem, to self-actualisation (i.e. self-fulfilment); progressing systematically up the hierarchy as each lower-level need is satisfied. To McGregor indi-viduals at work were seen by management as either inherently lazy (Theory X) or committed to the organisation's objectives and often actively seeking responsibility (Theory Y). These perceptions consequently provided the basis for different styles of management, which ranged from the coercive to the supportive.

McGregor's concern with management styles is reflected in later studies, includ-ing Ouichi's notion of 'Theory Z'. According to Ouichi one of the key factors in the success of Japanese manufacturing industries was their approach to the man-agement of people. Theory Z organisations were those which offered workers long-term (often lifetime) employment, a share in decision making, opportunities for training, development and promotion, and a number of other advantages which gave them a positive orientation towards the organisation. For Ouichi, the key to organisational effectiveness lay in the development of a Japanese-style Theory Z environment, adapted to western requirements.

The Systems Approach

More recent approaches to organisation and management have helped to integrate previous work on structures, people and technology, by portraying organisations as socio-technical systems interacting with their environment. Under this approach-which became popular in the 1960s-organisations were seen as complex systems of people, tasks and technologies that were part of and interacted with a larger environment, comprising a wide range of influences. This environ-ment was frequently subject to fluctuations, which on occasions could become turbulent (i.e. involving rapid and often unpredictable change). For organisations to survive and prosper, adaptation to environmental demands was seen as a neces-sary requirement and one which was central to the process of management.

The essence of the systems approach has been described in Chapter 1, but is worth repeating here. Organisations, including those involved in business, are open systems, interacting with their environment as they convert inputs into output. Inputs include people, finance, materials and information, provided by the envi-ronment in which the organisation exists and operates. Output comprises such items as goods and services, information, ideas and waste, discharged into the envi-ronment for consumption by 'end' or 'intermediate' users and in some cases representing inputs used by other organisations.

Systems invariably comprise a number of sub-systems through which the process of conversion or transformation occurs. Business organisations, for exam-ple, usually have sub-systems which deal with activities such as production, marketing, accounting and human resource management and each of these in turn may involve smaller sub-systems (e.g. sales, quality control, training) which collec-tively constitute the whole. Just as the organisation as a system interacts with its environment, so do the sub-systems and their component elements, which also interact with each other. In the case of the latter, the boundary between sub-sys-tems is usually known as an 'interface'.

While the obvious complexities of the systems approach need not be discussed, it is important to emphasise that most modern views of organisations draw heavily on the work in this area, paying particular attention to the interactions between people, technology, structure and environment and to the key role of management in directing the organisation's activities towards the achievement of its goals. Broadly speaking, management is seen as a critical sub-system within the total organisation, responsible for the co-ordination of the other sub-systems and for ensuring that internal and external relationships are managed effectively. As changes occur in one part of the system these will induce changes elsewhere and this will require a management response that will have implications for the organi-sation and for its sub-systems. Such changes may be either the cause or effect of changes in the relationship between the organisation and its environment, and the requirement for managers is to adapt to the new conditions without reducing the organisation's effectiveness.

Given the complex nature of organisations and the environments in which they operate, a number of writers have suggested a 'contingency approach' to organisa-tional design and management (e.g. Lawrence and Lorsch, Woodward, Perrow, Burns and Stalker). In essence, this approach argues that there is no single form of organisation best suited to all situations and that the most appropriate organisa-tional structure and system of management is dependent upon the contingencies of the situation (e.g. size, technology, environment) for each organisation. In some cases a bureaucratic structure might be the best way to operate, while in others much looser and more organic methods of organisation might be more effective. In short, issues of organisational design and management depend on choosing the best combination in the light of the relevant situational variables; this might mean different structures and styles coexisting within an organisation.

ORGANISATION STRUCTURES

Apart from the very simplest form of enterprise in which one individual carries out all tasks and responsibilities, business organisations are characterised by a division of labour which allows employees to specialise in particular roles and to occupy desig-nated positions in pursuit of the organisation's objectives. The resulting pattern of relationships between individuals and roles constitutes what is known as the organi-sation's structure and represents the means by which the purpose and work of the enterprise is carried out. It also provides a framework through which communica-tions can occur and within which the processes of management can be applied.

Responsibility for establishing the formal structure of the organisation lies with management and a variety of options is available. Whatever form is chosen, the basic need is to identify a structure which will best sustain the success of the enter-prise and will permit the achievement of a number of important objectives. Through its structure an organisation should be able to:

- achieve efficiency in the utilisation of resources;
- provide opportunities for monitoring organisational performance;
- ensure the accountability of individuals;
- guarantee co-ordination between the different parts of the enterprise;

- provide an efficient and effective means of organisational communication;
- create job satisfaction, including opportunities for progression; and
- adapt to changing circumstances brought about by internal or external developments.

In short, structure is not an end in itself, but a means to an end and should ideally reflect the needs of the organisation within its existing context and taking into account its future requirements.

Change at Deutsche Bank?

On 17 January 2002 the *Financial Times* carried a report that one of Europe's biggest banks, Deutsche Bank, was poised to announce a change to its management structure. This change would involve a move away from the traditional consensus-driven German board model towards an executive style of management along US lines. According to the *FT*, the incoming head of the bank, Josef Ackermann, intended to create a powerful new executive committee to run the bank's operations and to install a strong chief executive with full control over bank strategy. The executive committee would bring together 'global product heads' from the bank's two divisions and would be chaired by Ackermann himself. Ackermann would also chair a slimmed-down Vorstand (management board) which under national law retains the final say on business matters and is collectively responsible for decision-making.

The essence of structure is the division of work between individuals and the formal organisational relationships that are created between them. These relation-ships will be reflected not only in individual job descriptions, but also in the overall organisation chart which designates the formal pattern of role relation-ships, and the interactions between roles and the individuals occupying those roles. Individual authority relationships can be classified as line, staff, functional and lat-eral and arise from the defined pattern of responsibilities, as follows:

- *Line relationships* occur when authority flows vertically downward through the structure from superior to subordinate (e.g. managers-section leader-staff).
- *Staff relationships* are created when senior personnel appoint assistants who nor-mally have no authority over other staff but act as an extension of their superior.

- *Functional relationships* are those between specialists (or advisers) and line man-agers and their subordinates (e.g. when a specialist provides a common service throughout the organisation but has no authority over the users of the service). The personnel or computing function may be one such service that creates a functional relationship. (Note that specialists have line relationships with their own subordinates.)
- *Lateral relationships* exist across the organisation, particularly between individuals occupying equivalent positions within different departments or sections (e.g. committees, heads of departments, section leaders).

With regard to the division of work and the grouping of organisational activities, this can occur in a variety of ways. These include:

- *By function or major purpose,* associated particularly with departmental structures.
- *By product or service,* where individuals responsible for a particular product or service are grouped together.
- *By location,* based on geographical criteria.
- *By common processes* (e.g. particular skills or methods of operation).
- *By client group* (e.g. children, the disabled, the elderly).

In some organisations a particular method of grouping will predominate; in others there will tend to be a variety of types and each has its own particular advantages and disadvantages. In the discussion below, attention is focused on five main meth-ods of grouping activities in business organisations. Students should attempt to discover what types of structure exist within their own educational institution and the logic (if any) which underlies the choices made.

Functional Organisation

The functional approach to organisation is depicted in Figure 2.2. As its name indi-cates, in this type of structure activities are clustered together by common purpose or function. All marketing activities, for example, are grouped together as a common function, typically within a marketing department. Similarly other areas of activity such as production, finance, personnel and research and development, have their own specialised sections or departments, responsible for all the tasks required of that function.

Figure 2.2: A functional organisation structure

Apart from its obvious simplicity, the functional organisation structure allows individuals to be grouped together on the basis of their specialisms and technical expertise, and this can facilitate the development of the function they offer as well as providing a recognised path for promotion and career development. On the downside, functional specialisation, particularly through departments, is likely to create sectional interests which may operate to the disadvantage of the organisa-tion as a whole, particularly where inequalities in resource allocation between functions become a cause for interfunction rivalry. It could also be argued that this form of structure is most suited to single-product firms and that it becomes less appropriate as organisations diversify their products and/or markets. In such cir-cumstances, the tendency will be for businesses to look for the benefits which can arise from specialisation by product or from the divisionalisation of the enterprise.

Organisation by Product or Service

In this case the division of work and the grouping of activities is dictated by the prod-uct or service provided (see Figure 2.3), such that each group responsible for a particular part of the output of the organisation may have its own specialist in the different functional areas (e.g. marketing, finance, personnel). One advantage of this type of structure is that it allows an organisation to offer a diversified range of prod-ucts, as exemplified by the different services available in National Health Service hospitals (e.g. maternity, orthopaedic, geriatric, and so forth). Its main disadvantage is the danger that the separate units or divisions within the enterprise may attempt to become too autonomous, even at the expense of other parts of the organisation, and this can present management with problems of co-ordination and control.

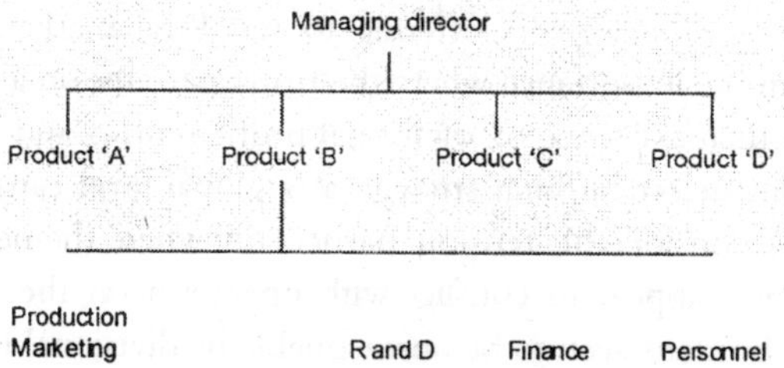

Figure 2.3 : A product-based structure

The Divisional Structure

As firms diversify their products and/or markets-often as a result of merger or takeover-a structure is needed to co-ordinate and control the different parts of the organisa-tion. This structure is likely to be the divisional (or 'multi-divisional') company.

A divisionalised structure is formed when an organisation is split up into a number of self-contained business units, each of which operates as a profit centre. Such a division may occur on the basis of product or market or a combination of the two, with each unit tending to operate along functional or product lines, but with certain key functions (e.g. finance, personnel, corporate planning) provided centrally, usually at company headquarters.

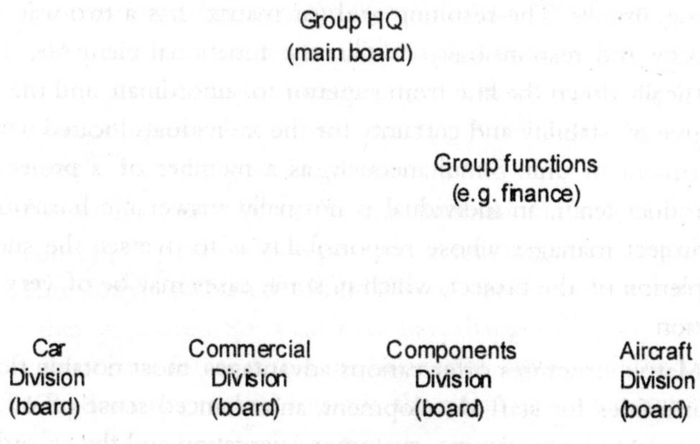

Figure 2.4 : A divisional structure

The main benefit of the multi-divisional company is that it allows each part of what can be a very diverse organisation to operate semi-independently in produc-ing and marketing its products, thus permitting each division to design its offering to suit local market conditions-a factor of prime importance where the firm oper-ates on a multinational basis. The dual existence of divisional profit centres and a central unit responsible for establishing strategy at a global level can, however, be a source of considerable tension, particularly where the needs and aims of the centre appear to conflict with operations at the local level or to impose burdens seen to be unreasonable by divisional managers (e.g. the allocation of central overhead costs).

Much the same kind of arguments apply to the holding company, though this tends to be a much looser structure for managing diverse organisations, favoured by both UK and Japanese companies. Under this arrangement, the different elements of the organisation (usually companies) are co-ordinated and controlled by a parent body, which may be just a financial entity established to maintain or gain control of other trading companies. Holding companies are associated with the growth of firms by acquisition which gives rise to a high degree of product or market diversification. They are also a popular means of operating a multinational organisation.

Matrix Structures

A matrix is an arrangement for combining functional specialisation (e.g. through departments) with structures built around products, projects or programmes. The resulting grid (or matrix) has a two-way flow of authority and responsibility. Within the functional elements, the flow is vertically down the line from superior to subordinate and this creates a degree of stability and certainty for the individuals located within the department or unit. Simultaneously, as a member of a project group or product team, an individual is normally answerable horizontally to the project manager whose responsibility is to oversee the successful completion of the project, which in some cases may be of very limited duration.

Matrix structures offer various advantages, most notably flexibility, opportunities for staff development, an enhanced sense of ownership of a project or programme, customer orientation and the co-ordination of information and expertise. On the negative side, difficulties can include problems of co-ordination and control, conflicting loyalties for staff and uncertain lines of authority. It is not uncommon in an organisation designed on matrix lines for project or programme leaders to be unsure of their authority over the staff from the contributing departments. Nor is it unknown for functional managers to withdraw their co-operation and/or support for projects located outside their immediate sphere of influence.

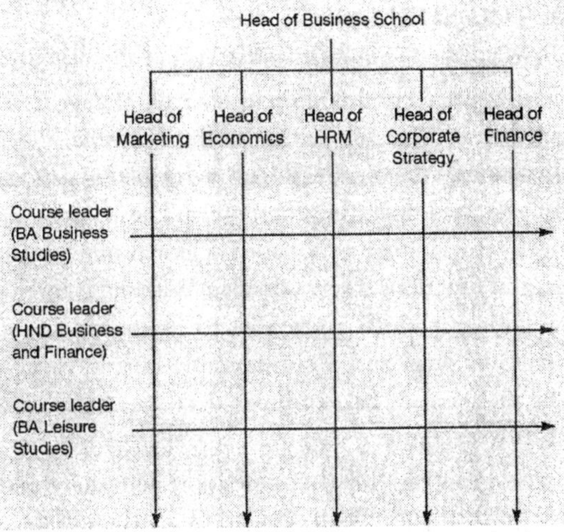

Figure 2.5: A matrix structure in a business school

Project Teams

Despite its flexibility the matrix often has a degree of permanence; in contrast, the project team is essentially a temporary structure established as a means of carrying out a particular task, often in a highly unstable environment. Once the task is com-plete, the team is disbanded and individuals return to their usual departments or are assigned to a new project.

Fashioned around technical expertise rather than managerial rank and often operating closely with clients, project teams are increasingly common in high-tech-nology firms, construction companies and in some types of service industry, especially management consultancies and advertising. Rather than being a replace-ment for the existing structure, they operate alongside it and utilise in-house staff (and in some cases, outside specialists) on a project-by-project basis. While this can present logistical and scheduling problems and may involve some duplication of resources, it can assist an organisation in adapting to change and uncertainty and in providing products to the customer's specifications. Project teams tend to be at their most effective when objectives and tasks are well defined, when the client is clear as to the desired outcome and when the team is chosen with care.

ROYAL DUTCH SHELL

In March 1995 the multinational Anglo-Dutch oil giant, Royal Dutch Shell, announced its intention to radically change its long-admired matrix organisation (see, for example, the *Financial Times,* 30 March 1995). For historical reasons, Shell had developed a structure based on geographically defined operating companies. These operating companies had executives representing national or regional units, business sectors (or divisions) and functions such as finance. Within this three-dimensional matrix, powerful individuals were able to influence the organisation's policies at regional level and a considerable bureaucracy was required to 'police' the matrix and to co-ordinate decisions between the different elements of the structure.

Faced with growing global competition and shareholder pressure for improved performance, Shell decided to restructure the organisation by attacking problems of overstaffing and bureaucracy and by eliminating many of the regional fiefdoms through which the company had come to run its worldwide empire.

Its plan involved shaping the group around five business organisations covering its main activities (e.g. exploration and production, refining and marketing, etc.), with each operating company reporting to and receiving its strategic targets from whichever of the five organisations were relevant to its activities. A new system of business committees was given responsibility for strategic and investment decisions within the different organisations, although executive authority rested with the operating companies. Through this arrangement Shell hoped to retain the sensitivity to local market needs that had traditionally been part of its organisational creed.

In a further effort to improve the company's performance, Shell indicated that more restructuring needed to take place. Part of its blueprint for reshaping itself for the twenty-first century included additional streamlining of its management structure, away from committee-based decision making and towards a system based on American-style chief executives.

Subsequently in October 2004 the company announced the merger of its two elements-Royal Dutch and Shell Transport and Trading-into a single company, to be known as Royal Dutch Shell plc. The new entity comprises an Executive Board, a Supervisory Board, a Board of Management and a Board of Directors for Shell Transport. Members of the Executive Committee are also members of the latter two boards.

THE VIRTUAL ORGANISATION

As indicated above traditional organisations have structures which are designed to facilitate the transformation of inputs into output. Increasingly as the business environment changes, relationships both within and between organisations have needed to become more flexible and this has given rise to such developments as the growth in teleworking and the establishment of dynamic broker/agent net-works involving considerable outsourcing of sub-tasks to 'agents' (e.g. manufacturing, distribution) by the core organisation (the 'broker').

It is fair to say that this demand for greater flexibility has been driven partly by the market and partly by cost considerations and the process of change has been facilitated by rela-tively rapid developments in information technology. One area currently exciting the interest of writers on management and organisation is the concept of the virtual organisation, arguably the ultimate form of organisa-tional flexibility.

In essence a virtual organisation or firm signifies an extremely loose web of essentially freelance individuals or businesses who organise themselves to produce a specific customer product (e.g. an individual holiday package with particular fea-tures unique to the customer).

Without any permanent structure or hierarchy this so-called firm can constantly change its shape and, despite existing across space and time, tends to appear edgeless, with its inputs, outputs and employees increas-ingly dispersed across the linked world of information systems. Given modern forms of communication, the potential exists for a totally electronic-based organi-sation trading in expertise and information with no real-world physical identity. This stands in stark contrast to the traditional view of the firm as an arrangement which adds value by transforming basic economic inputs (e.g. land, labour, capital) into physical outputs or services.

STRUCTURAL CHANGE

Internal change is an important feature of the modern business organisation. In order to remain competitive and meet stakeholder needs, a firm may have to find ways to restructure its organisation as the environment in which it operates changes. Solutions can range from a partial or wholesale shift in the organisation's structural form to strategies for reducing the overall size and shape of the company (e.g. 'downsizing') or a radical redesign of business processes (e.g. 're-engineering').

Whereas business re-engineering normally connotes a root-and-branch reform of the way in which the business operates, downsizing essentially involves shrinking the organisation to make it 'leaner' and 'fitter' and hopefully more 'flexible' in its response to the marketplace. For some companies this means little more than reducing the size of the workforce through natural wastage and/or redundancies, as and when opportunities arise; for others it involves 'delayering' the organisation by removing a tier, or tiers, of management, thus effectively flattening the organisa-tion's hierarchy and helping it to reduce its unit costs of production.

In its most systematic and long-term form, downsizing can be used as a vehicle for cultural change through which an organisation's employees are encouraged to embrace notions of continuous improvement and innovation, and to accept that structural reform is a permanent and natural state of affairs. Under such an approach, retraining and reskilling become vital tools in implementing the chosen strategy and in shaping the organisation to meet the demands of its changing envi-ronment. The danger is, however, that a firm may become too concerned with restructuring as a cure for all its problems, when the real cause of its difficulties lies in its marketplace. Cutting the number of employees, in such a situation, is unlikely to make unattractive products attractive; nor is it likely to boost morale within the organisation.

ASPECTS OF FUNCTIONAL MANAGEMENT

Most organisation structures reflect a degree of functional specialisation, with indi-viduals occupying roles in departments, units or sections which have titles such as Production, Finance, Marketing, Personnel and Research and Development. These functional areas of the internal organisation, and the individuals who are allocated to them, are central to the process of transforming organisational inputs into output. The management of these functions and of the relationships between them will be a key factor in the success of the enterprise and in its ability to respond to external demands for change.

The interdependence of the internal functions can be demonstrated by a simple example. Providing goods and services to meet the market's needs often involves research and development which necessitates a financial input, usually from the capi-tal market or the organisation's own resources. It also requires, as do all the other functions, the recruitment of staff of the right quality, a task which is more often than not the responsibility of the Personnel department. If research and development activities lead to a good idea which the Marketing department is able to sell, then the Production department is required to produce it in the right quantities, to the right specifications and at the time the market needs it. This depends not only on internal scheduling procedures within the Production department, but also on having the right kind of materials supplied on time by the Purchasing department, an appropri-ate system of quality control and work monitoring, machinery that is working and regularly serviced, the finished items packed, despatched and delivered and a multi-tude of other activities, all operating towards the same end.

The extent to which all of these requirements can be met simultaneously depends not only on internal factors, many of which are controllable, but also on a host of external influences, the majority of which tend to be beyond the organisa-tion's control. To demonstrate this interface between the internal and external environments, two key areas of functional management are discussed briefly below-marketing and human resource management. An examination of the other func-tions within the organisation would yield very similar findings.

Human Resource Management (HRM)

People are the key organisational resource; without them organisations would not exist or function. All businesses need to plan for and manage the people they employ if they are to use this resource effectively and efficiently in pursuit of their objectives. In modern and forward-looking organisations this implies a proactive approach to the management of people which goes beyond the bounds of traditional personnel management and involves the establishment of systems for planning, monitoring, appraisal and evaluation, training and development and for integrating the internal needs of the organisation with the external demands of the marketplace. Such an approach is associated with the idea of human resource management.

As in other areas of management, HRM involves a wide variety of activities related to the formulation and implementation of appropriate organisational poli-cies, the provision of opportunities for monitoring, evaluation and change, and the application of resources to the fulfilment of organisational ends. Key aspects of 'people management' include:

- recruitment and selection;
- working conditions;
- training and career development;
- job evaluation;
- employee relations;
- manpower planning; and
- legal aspects of employment.

In most, if not all, cases these will be affected by both internal and external influ-ences (e.g. size of the firm, management style, competition, economic and political developments), some of which will vary over time as well as between organisations.

The provision of these activities within an organisation can occur in a variety of ways and to different degrees of sophistication. Some very small firms may have little in the way of a recognisable HRM function, being concerned primarily with questions of hiring and firing, pay and other working conditions, but not with notions of career development, staff appraisal or job enrichment. In contrast, very large companies may have a specialist HRM or Personnel department, often organ-ised on functional lines and responsible for the formulation and implementation of personnel policies throughout the organisation. Such centralisation provides not only some economies of scale, but also a degree of standardisation and consistency across departments. To allow for flexibility, centralised systems are often combined with an element of decentralisation which permits individual departments or sec-tions to exercise some influence in matters such as the recruitment and selection of staff, working conditions, training and career development.

To illustrate how the different aspects of HRM are influenced by external factors, one part of this function-recruitment and selection of staff-has been chosen. This is the activity within the organisation which seeks to ensure that it has the right quantity and quality of labour in the right place and at the right time to meet its requirements at all levels. To achieve this aim, the organisation initially needs to consider a large number of factors, including possible changes in the demand for labour, the need for new skills and likely labour turnover, before the processes of recruitment and selection can begin. These aspects in turn will be conditioned by a variety of factors such as changes in the demand for the product, the introduction of new technology and social, economic and demographic changes, some of which may not be anticipated or expected by strategic planners.

Once recruitment and selection is ready to begin, a further raft of influences will impinge upon the process, some of which emanate from external sources. In draw-ing up a job specification, for example, attention will normally need to be paid to the state of the local labour market, including skill availability, competition from other employers, wage rates in comparable jobs and/or organisations, and socio-demographic trends. If the quality of labour required is in short supply, an organisation may find itself having to offer improved pay and working conditions simply to attract a sufficient number of applicants to fill the vacancies on offer. Equally, in fashioning its job advertisements and in drawing up the material it sends out to potential applicants, a firm will need to pay due attention to the needs of current legislation in areas such as equal opportunities, race discrimination and employment protection, if it is not to infringe the law.

Among the other external factors the enterprise may need to take into considera-tion in recruiting and selecting staff will be:

- the relative cost and effectiveness of the different advertising media;
- existing relationships with external sources of recruitment (e.g. job centres, schools, colleges, universities);
- commitments to the local community;
- relationships with employee organisations (e.g. trade unions, staff associations); and
- opportunities for staff training and development in local training and educa-tional institutions.

Ideally, it should also pay some attention to possible future changes in the technol-ogy of the workplace, in order to recruit individuals either with appropriate skills or who can be retrained relatively easily with a minimum amount of disruption and expense to the organisation.

The Marketing Function

The processes of human resource management provide a good illustration of the interactions between a firm's internal and external environments. An even better example is provided by an examination of its marketing activities, which are directed primarily, though not exclusively, towards what is happening outside the organisation.

Like 'management', the term 'marketing' has been defined in a wide variety of ways, ranging from Kotler's essentially economic notion of an activity directed at sat-isfying human needs and wants through exchange processes, to the more managerial definitions associated with bodies like the Chartered Institute of Marketing. A common thread running through many of these definitions is the idea that market-ing is concerned with meeting the needs of the consumer in a way which is profitable to the enterprise. Hence, strategic marketing management is normally characterised as the process of ensuring a good fit between the opportunities afforded by the mar-ketplace and the abilities and resources of an organisation operating in it.

This notion of marketing as an integrative function within the organisation-linking the needs of the consumer with the various functional areas of the firm-is central to modern definitions of the term and lies at the heart of what is known as the 'marketing concept'. This is the idea that the customer is of prime importance to the organisation and that the most significant managerial task in any enterprise is first to identify the needs and wants of the consumer and then to ensure that its operations are geared to meeting these requirements profitably. Though it would be true to say that not all organisations subscribe to this view, it is generally accepted that the successful businesses are predominantly those with a customer rather than a production or sales orientation. Equally, the evidence suggests that the need to adopt such a customer-centred approach applies not only to private sector trading organisations, but also increasingly to public sector enterprises and to bodies not established for the pursuit of profits but for other purposes (e.g. charities, political parties, trade unions).

When viewed from a customer perspective, marketing can be seen to comprise a range of activities that go beyond the simple production of an item for sale. These include:

- Identifying the needs of consumers (e.g. through marketing research).
- Designing different 'offerings' to meet the needs of different types of customers (e.g. through market segmentation).
- Choosing products, prices, promotional techniques and distribution channels that are appropriate to a particular market (i.e. designing a 'marketing mix' strategy).
- Undertaking market and product planning.
- Deciding on brand names, types of packages, and methods of communicating with the customer.
- Creating a marketing information system.

As already indicated, in carrying out these activities the firm is brought into con-tact with a range of external influences of both an immediate and indirect kind. This external marketing environment can have a fundamental impact on the degree to which the firm is able to develop and maintain successful transactions with its customers and hence on its profitability and chances of survival.

To illustrate how a firm's marketing effort can be influenced by external factors, the following brief discussion focuses on 'pricing', which is one of the key elements of the 'marketing mix', that is, the set of controllable variables which a business can use to influence the buyer's response, namely, product, price, promotion and place-the 4Ps. Of all the mix elements, price is the only one which generates revenue, while the others result in expenditure. It is therefore a prime determinant of a firm's turnover and profitability and can have a considerable influence on the demand for its products and frequently for those of its competitors.

Leaving aside the broader question of a firm's pricing goals and the fact that prices will tend to vary according to the stage a product has reached in its life cycle, price determination can be said to be influenced by a number of factors. Of these, the costs of production, the prices charged by one's competitors and the price sen-sitivity of consumers tend to be the most significant.

In the case of cost-based pricing, this occurs when a firm relates its price to the cost of buying or producing the product, adding a profit margin or 'mark-up' to arrive at the final selling price. Such an approach tends to be common amongst smaller enterprises (e.g. builders, corner shops) where costs are often easier to esti-mate and where likely consumer reactions are given less attention than the need to make an adequate return on the effort involved. The essential point about this form of price determination is that many of the firm's costs are influenced by exter-nal organisations-including the suppliers of materials, components and energy-and hence pricing will often vary according to changes in the prices of inputs. Only larger organisations, or a group of small businesses operating together, will gener-ally be able to exercise some influence over input prices and even then not all costs will be controllable by the enterprise.

Organisations which take an essentially cost-based approach to pricing will sometimes be influenced by the prices charged by competitors-particularly in markets where considerable competition exists and where the products are largely homogeneous and a buyer's market is evident (e.g. builders during a recession). The competitive approach to pricing, however, is also found in markets where only a few large firms operate and where the need to increase or maintain market share can give rise to virtually identical prices and to fierce non-price competition between the market leaders. In Britain, for instance, a big cross-Channel ferry operator will normally provide the service to customers at the same price as its rivals, differentiating its offering in terms of additional benefits (e.g. on-board entertainment) rather than price. Where this is the case, the external demands of the market rather than costs constitute the primary influence on a firm's decisions, and changes in market conditions (e.g. the actual or potential entry of new firms; changes in a competitor's prices; economic recession) will tend to be reflected in price changes.

This idea of market factors influencing pricing decisions also applies to situations where firms fix their prices according to the actual or anticipated reactions of con-sumers to the price charged for a product-known in economics as the price elasticity of demand. In this case, the customer rather than a firm's competitors is the chief influence on price determination, although the two are often interrelated in that consumers are usually more price sensitive in markets where some choice exists.

Differential levels of price sensitivity between consumers of a product normally arise when a market has distinct segments based on factors such as differences in income or age or location. In such cases a firm will often fix its prices according to the segment of the market it is serving, a process known as 'price discrimination' and one which is familiar to students claiming concessionary fares on public transport.

While the above discussion has been oversimplified and does not take into account factors such as the price of other products in an organisation's product portfolio (e.g. different models of car), it illustrates quite clearly how even one of the so-called controllable variables in a firm's marketing mix is subject to a range of external influences that are often beyond its ability to control. The same argument applies to the other elements of the marketing function and students could usefully add to their understanding of the internal/external interface by examining how the external environment impinges upon such marketing activities as promotion, dis-tribution or market research.

SYNOPSIS

The internal dimension of business organisations constitutes an extensive field of study and one to which students of business devote a considerable amount of time. In seek-ing to illustrate how a firm's internal organisation is influenced by its external environment, emphasis has been placed on a selected number of aspects of a firm's internal operations. Of these, its structure and functions were seen to provide a good illustration of the interface between the internal and external environments. Appreciating the existence of this interface is facilitated by adopting a systems approach to organisational analysis.

SUMMARY OF KEY POINTS

- Management is a key aspect of the internal environment of the business organisation.
- Theories of organisation and management basically fall into three categories: classi-cal theories; human relations approaches; systems approaches.
- The systems view of organisations depicts businesses as open systems interacting with their external environment as they convert inputs into outputs.

- The external environment of the organisation affects all aspects of the business including its structures, functions and processes.
- To carry out their tasks businesses can structure themselves in a variety of ways, including functionally, by product/service, by divisions, in a matrix format or via proj-ect teams. Each has its advantages and disadvantages.
- Structural change tends to be a feature of large modern organisations.
- Within the organisation the different business functions such as marketing, produc-tion, HRM, purchasing and so on are influenced by external factors of both a general and operational kind.
- An examination of the marketing and HRM functions reveals the importance of the wide range of external influences that can impinge upon the day-to-day areas of organisational work.
- Investigations of other functional areas within the organisation would produce a simi-lar picture.

STRUCTURING GLOBAL COMPANIS—CASE STUDY

As the chapter illustrates, to carry out their activities in pursuit of their objectives, virtually all organisations adopt some form of organisational structure. One tradi-tional method of organisation is to group individuals by function or purpose, using a departmental structure to allocate individuals to their specialist areas (e.g. Marketing, HRM and so on). Another is to group activities by product or service, with each product group normally responsible for providing its own functional requirements. A third is to combine the two in the form of a matrix structure with its vertical and horizontal flows of responsibility and authority, a method of organi-sation much favoured in university Business Schools.

What of companies with a global reach: how do they usually organise them-selves?

Writing in the *Financial Times* in November 2000 Julian Birkinshaw, Associate Professor of Strategic and International Management at London Business School, identifies four basic models of global company structure:

- *The International Division*-an arrangement in which the company establishes a separate division to deal with business outside its own country. The International Division would typically be concerned with tariff and trade issues, foreign agents/partners and other aspects involved in selling overseas. Normally the division does not make anything itself, it is simply responsible for interna-tional sales. This arrangement tends to be found in medium-sized companies with limited international sales.

- *The Global Product Division*-a product-based structure with managers responsible for their product line globally. The company is split into a number of global busi-nesses arranged by product (or service) and usually overseen by their own president. It has been a favoured structure among large global companies such as BP, Siemens and 3M.
- *The Area Division*-a geographically based structure in which the major line of authority lies with the country (e.g. Germany) or regional (e.g. Europe) manager who is responsible for the different product offerings within her/his geographical area.
- *The Global Matrix*-as the name suggests a hybrid of the two previous structural types. In the global matrix each business manager reports to two bosses, one responsible for the global product and one for the country/region. As we indi-cated in the previous edition of this book, this type of structure tends to come into and go out of fashion. Ford, for example, adopted a matrix structure in the later 1990s, while a number of other global companies were either streamlining or dismantling theirs (e.g. Shell, BP, IBM).

As Professor Birkinshaw indicates, ultimately there is no perfect structure and organisations tend to change their approach over time according to changing cir-cumstances, fads, the perceived needs of the senior executives or the predispositions of powerful individuals. This observation is no less true of universi-ties than it is of traditional businesses.

3

The Political Environment

INTRODUCTION

In the late 1980s, following a period of difficult negotiations, the British government entered into a collaborative agreement with the governments of Germany, Italy and Spain, to develop and produce a European fighter aircraft (EFA), due to come into service in the later 1990s. This agreement, which involved the participants jointly fund-ing research and development costs, was greeted with delight by firms in Britain's aerospace industry and by their suppliers who welcomed the prospects of a large order of aircraft at a time when defence spending was being restrained. For firms such as GEC Ferranti, BAe, Lucas Aerospace, Rolls-Royce and Smiths Industries, the col-laborative venture offered the prospects of future profits and the opportunity to retain their technological edge. For the communities in which these firms were based, it promised to sustain and possibly create employment during a period of growing eco-nomic uncertainty.

Subsequent indications (in 1992) that the German government would pull out of the venture-on the grounds of escalating costs and a reduced military threat-sent shock waves through the British aerospace industry and threatened to sour relations between the participating governments, the rest of whom wished to continue with the project. In the event, a compromise was reached under which the countries involved agreed to continue with research and development in an effort to produce a cheaper aircraft, to be known as the Eurofighter 2000. Given the problems of German reunification, the German government reserved the right to make a final decision on production at some time in the future. In late 1997 the four countries finally signed an agreement to proceed with production after years of political controversy and delay, thereby triggering a multi-billion-pound contract culminating in delivery of the first aircraft in 2002.

What this simple example illustrates is that business activity takes place both within and across state boundaries and frequently involves governments, whether directly or indirectly. Consequently the political and economic arrangements within the state in which a business is located and/or with which it is trading can have a fundamental impact on its operations-even to the extent of determining whether it is willing or, in some cases able, to trade at all. It is this politico-economic context within which busi-nesses function and the philosophical foundations on which it is based that are the focus of this and the following chapter.

As a prelude to a detailed analysis of the political environment, it is necessary to make a number of general observations regarding political change and uncertainty and its impact on business activity. First, the nature of a country's political system-including its governmental institutions-tends to reflect certain underlying social values and philosophies which help to determine how decisions are made, including decisions about the allocation of resources. Thus, while governments may come and go, the values on which their decisions are based tend to be more enduring and as a result disputes normally centre around 'means' (e.g. sources of revenue), rather than 'ends' (e.g. controlling inflation). While this gives a certain degree of stability to the business environment, this stability cannot be taken for granted, as events in eastern Europe have readily demonstrated. In short, the political environment of business is a dynamic environment, containing elements of both continuity and change, and stu-dents and practitioners of business alike need to be constantly aware of developments in this area, if they are to gain a greater insight into the background of business decision making.

Second, changes in the political environment also emanate from a country's institu-tional arrangements. The tendency in democratic states, for example, to have regular elections, competing political parties offering alternative policies, and a system of pres-sure groups, all help to generate a degree of discontinuity, which renders predictions about the future more uncertain. For a business, such uncertainty can create not only opportunities but also a degree of risk which will often be an important influence on its decisions. Moreover, given that perceptions of such risks (or opportunities) are also normally reflected in the attitudes and behaviour of a country's financial and other mar-kets, this represents a further variable which at times can be critical for an organisation's future prospects. For many businesses, taking steps to maximise oppor-tunities (or to minimise risk) may ultimately make the difference between short-term failure and long-term survival.

Third, it is important to emphasise that political influences are not restricted to national boundaries-a point emphasised by the increasing importance of international and supranational groupings such as the G8 nations, the European Union and the World Trade Organisation, all of which are discussed below. These external politico-economic influences form part of the environment in which a country's governmental institutions take decisions and their impact on domestic policy and on business activity can often be fundamental. No discussion of the business environment would be com-plete without an analysis of their role and impact, particularly in shaping international political and economic relationships.

Fourth, the precise impact of political factors on a business tends to vary to some degree according to the type of organisation involved. Multinational corporations-operating on a global scale-will be more concerned with questions such as the stabil-ity of overseas political regimes than will the small local firm operating in a localised market, where the primary concern will be with local market conditions. That said, there will undoubtedly be occasions when even locally based enterprises will be affected either directly or indirectly by political developments in other parts of the globe-as in the case of an interruption in supplies or the cancellation of a foreign order in which a small business is involved as a subcontractor. In short, while some broad generalisa-tions can be made about the impact of global (or domestic) political developments on an individual organisation, each case is to some extent unique in both space and time, and observers of the business scene need to be cautious and open-minded in their analysis if they are to avoid the twin dangers of over-simplication and empiricism.

Finally, it needs to be recognised that businesses are not merely reactive to changes in the political environment; they can also help to shape the political context in which they operate and can influence government decision makers, often in a way which is beneficial to their own perceived needs. One of the hallmarks of democracy is the right of individuals and groups to seek to influence government, and businesses-both indi-vidually and collectively-have been active in this sphere for centuries. It would be a mistake to underestimate their impact on government policy or on the shaping of values in the established capitalist nations of western Europe and elsewhere.

POLITICAL SYSTEMS

The Nature of Political Activity

All social situations at certain times require decisions to be made between alterna-tive courses of action. Parents may disagree with their offspring about the kind of clothes they wear or how late they stay out at night or how long they grow their hair. Students may challenge lecturers about a particular perspective on an issue or when they should submit a piece of work. The members of the board of directors of a company may have different views about future investment or diversification or the location of a new factory. In all these cases, some solution needs to be found, even if the eventual decision is to do nothing. It is the processes involved in arriv-ing at a solution to a problem, where a conflict of opinion occurs, that are the very essence of political activity.

Politics, in short, is concerned with those processes which help to determine how conflicts are contained, modified, postponed or settled, and as such can be seen as a universal social activity. Hence, individuals often talk of 'office politics' or the 'politics of the board room' or the 'mediating role' played by a parent in the event of a family dispute. For most individuals, however, the term 'politics' tends to be associated with activities at state level, where the resolution of conflict often involves large numbers of people and may even involve individuals in other states. Political activity at this level is clearly qualitatively different from the other social situations mentioned, and given the scale and complexity of the modern state, the problems requiring solutions can often be acute and chronic. Solving those prob-lems tends to be seen, at least in part, as the function of government.

Government as a process is concerned with the pursuit and exercise of power-the power to make decisions which affect the lives of substantial numbers of people, be it at local, regional, national or even international level. Government may also refer to the institutions through which power tends to be formally and legitimately exercised, whether they be cabinets, parliaments, councils, committees or congresses. Whereas the pursuit and exercise of power tends to be an enduring feature of any society, governments are normally transitory, comprising those indi-viduals and/or groups who, at a particular time, have the responsibility for controlling the state, including making laws for 'the good of society'. How govern-ments exercise their power and the ideological foundations on which this is based, helps to indicate the nature of the political system and its likely approaches to the resolution of conflicts.

Authoritarian Political Systems

Broadly speaking, political systems can be seen to range across two extremes, on the one hand 'authoritarian' and on the other 'democratic'. In an authoritarian political system the disposition is to settle conflicts through the enforcement of rules, regulations and orders by an established authority. This authority may be an individual (e.g. a monarch or other powerful individual) or a group of individuals (e.g. a political party or military junta) who may have assumed political power in a variety of ways (e.g. by birth, election or coup). Once in power, the individual or group will tend to act so as to limit the degree of participation by others in the process of decision making, even to the extent of monopolising the process alto-gether and permitting no opposition to occur. Where this is the case, a society is often described as being 'totalitarian' and is perhaps best exemplified by Nazi Germany and Stalinist Russia.

Democratic Political Systems

In contrast, in a democratic political system, the assumption is that as far as possi-ble conflicts should be resolved by rational discussions between the various parties concerned, with the final solution being accepted voluntarily by all participants, even if they disagree. At one extreme, such consultation may involve all individu-als, who have-in theory at least-equal influence over the final outcome (e.g. as in referendums or plebiscites). Given the scale and complexity of modern states, however, such examples of 'pure' or 'direct' democracy tend to be rare and it is invariably the case that the democratic solution to conflict resolution is achieved 'indirectly' through a system of political representation and responsibility. Under such a system, the wishes and views of individuals are said to be represented in an established authority (e.g. a government) that has normally been chosen by the people and which is accountable (responsible) to them at regular intervals through a variety of mechanisms, including regular and free elections. Implicit in this, of course, is the requirement that individuals are able to change this authority and select another individual or group to represent them. Monopolisation of political power by any one individual or group can only occur, therefore, with the expressed consent of the people.

GOVERNMENT IN DEMOCRATIC STATES

Democratic Institutions and Processes

Democracy means far more than just popular government or a system of regular elections; the democratic approach to government implies the existence of a com-plex array of institutions and processes through which the wishes of the people are articulated and carried out. While the specific institutional arrangements tend to vary between states, countries which are held to be democratic invariably have a political system which comprises four common and interlocking elements: an elec-toral system, a party system, a representative assembly and a system for the articulation of sectional interests. The generic roles of these major building blocks of democratic government are discussed below. Location-specific information on how the system operates in a national (i.e. United Kingdom) and a supranational (i.e. European Union) context can be found in the appendices to this chapter. Non-UK readers are encouraged to substitute their own political arrangements for those described in the appendices.

The Electoral System

As indicated above, in a representative democracy the electoral system links the people (the electorate) with government; it is through elections that a country's cit-izens periodically get to choose who will exercise the power to make decisions which will ultimately shape the lives of individuals. Elections, in short, are a vital ingredient of a representative system of government. That said, the fact that elec-tions exist in a particular country is not a sufficient guarantee that it is democratic in the accepted sense of the word.

In order to operate in a way which is normally regarded as democratic, a coun-try's electoral system would need to exhibit a number of features which suggest that the wishes of individual citizens-as expressed through the ballot box-are reasonably reflected in the choice of government. Such features would include:

- a system of regular elections (e.g. every four to five years) based on universal adult suffrage;
- basic freedoms of speech, movement, assembly, etc.;
- freedom from coercion and the absence of illegal electoral practices;
- a secret ballot;
- free media.

Where conditions such as these are absent or are not fully operational, there will always be a suspicion that the electoral outcome may not be a true reflection of the wishes of the people. The act of voting, in other words, needs to be accompanied by a set of legal prescriptions which provide some kind of guarantee that an elec-tion to choose part, if not all, of the government is both free and fair.

To be democratic the electoral system must not only be transparent; it must also ensure that the wishes of the majority-as expressed through the number of votes cast-are reflected in the final result. In 'first-past-the-post systems' (e.g. in most current UK elections) a simple majority is sufficient to ensure victory; as a conse-quence some winning candidates may be elected with fewer than half of the votes cast. Where a system of 'proportional representation' operates (e.g. in many other European countries) a redistribution of votes occurs when there is no outright winner, resulting in a final decision which can be said to more closely represent the wishes of the whole electorate. While the intricacies of different electoral systems are beyond the scope of this book, it is worth observing that the voting system a country uses can have important ramifications for the government elected to office. On the whole, a 'plurality' or 'first-past-the-post system' of voting usually results in majority government, with a single party dominating the organs of decision making and able to pursue its legislative programme relatively free from constraint by the losing side(s). In contrast, where a proportional representation system is used the resulting government is often made up of a coalition of different parties, some of which may hold radically different views from the largest party within the coalition. In effect, coalition government is predominantly a matter of negotiation, accommodation and compromise, an exercise in consensus building and persuasion, as commonly found in most types of organisational setting, including the business world.

The Party System

While it is possible to have democratic government in a one-party state, democracy is normally taken to imply that citizens get to choose between alternative candi-dates when casting their vote at an election. Invariably such candidates tend to represent different political parties and to this extent a vote for a specific candidate can be said to equate to a vote for the party that he or she represents and which is ultimately hoping to form the government.

The existence of political parties, which compete for office at election time, is clearly a convenient-if sometimes questionable-means of organising a system of representative democracy; hence the universality of party systems in democratic states and the relative lack of candidates standing with no party tag at governmental elections at all spatial levels. Parties not only help to choose most of the candidates who compete in these elections, but usually also support and sustain them (e.g. financially) before, during and after the election campaign and help to organise a system of (largely unpaid) volunteers to work to get them elected, as well as providing candidates with a platform of policies on which to stand for office. Whereas some of these activities tend to be the responsibility of the party at national level, others are undertaken at a regional and/or local level, often in the constituency (i.e. geographi-cal area) that a candidate represents. Since questions of organisation, policy making and finance are central to the operation and success of a political party in modern democratic states, party structures have tended to become complex, bureaucratic, multi-layered and increasingly professionalised. As in other types of organisation framework, they also provide an arena in which a substantial degree of in-fighting occurs between individuals of different temperaments, views and ambitions who are seeking to push the party in a particular direction.

From the electors' point of view one of the primary benefits of the party system is that it provides a means of selecting political leaders and the kind of policies they are likely to pursue if the party achieves political office. Describing candidates by a party label (e.g. Democratic, Republican, Socialist, Conservative, Liberal, etc.) allows voters to choose those candidates whose views most closely represent their own, given that parties normally have an identifiable policy stance and produce some form of statement (or manifesto) outlining their policy preferences during an election campaign. Thus, while an individual elector is unlikely to agree with every single policy or proposed piece of legislation that a party puts forward in its attempts to gain office, he/she is at least able to express a preference between alter-native approaches to government at the ballot box. To that extent it can be argued that there is likely to be a degree of congruence between the legislative programme of the party democratically elected to form the government and the wishes of the people who elected it, albeit that in some cases the government may have received less than 50 per cent of the popular vote.

It is worth remembering that party labels are not always a good guide to the policy or legislative preferences of individual candidates, since someone described as a 'Democrat' or 'Liberal' in one part of a country may hold radically different views on a range of issues from others of the same title elected to constituencies in other areas. If anything, identifying election candidates in party political terms gives voters a broad indication of the underlying values and beliefs to which an individual subscribes: parties in practice are always destined to be (sometimes frag-ile) coalitions of groups and individuals representing a range of opinions and preferences under a party banner.

A Representative Assembly

As previously indicated, one of the key features of democratic government is the existence of a representative decision-making body; a group of individuals chosen by a country's citizens to help make important decisions on their behalf. In the same way that shareholders in a public company elect directors to guide the organi-sation and to represent their interest, voters at election time choose individuals they wish to represent them in government in the various organs of decision making and policy implementation. While not everyone chosen by the electorate becomes part of the small group of key decision makers (the government or political executive), all normally have some kind of role to play in the decision-making process and usually get an opportunity to scrutinise policy and legislative proposals put forward by the governing element and to vote upon them. The fact that the electorate periodically has the opportunity to express its opinion on the performance of the incumbent decision makers-and where necessary to replace them-provides for a degree of political accountability, a central tenet of a demo-cratic system of government.

As over two centuries of political theory have demonstrated, the concept of 'representation' can have at least two meanings: decision makers may represent the views of their constituents in the literal sense that they articulate them in or to government or they may simply represent them in so far as they have been elected by a majority (simple or otherwise) of voters to be the representative of a geographical area. In practice both these interpretations of representation can be seen to operate at different times, according to the predispositions of individual decision makers and the influences emanating from the prevailing political culture in a country, region or area. For example, in a system of government where national political parties are relatively weak and where an individual's success in elections depends very much on supporting policies which are consistent with those of significant elements in one's electorate (e.g. in the United States), repre-sentation tends to be seen in the more literal sense of supporting local views and preferences. In contrast, where there is a strong party system and where individu-als are held to be elected on the basis of party affiliation (e.g. the United Kingdom), elected representatives are generally expected to be loyal to the party in a policy sense, even if this results on occasions in a conflict with the views of the majority of one's constituents.

In modern democratic states the model of representative decision making usu-ally operates at all spatial levels. In Europe, for example, voters not only elect their own national governments but also choose decision makers at a local and/or regional level and many European citizens are also able to vote in elections for pan-European institutions (i.e. for the European Parliament-see Appendix 3.3). One of the consequences of this arrangement is that on occasions the party (or parties) elected to office at national level may be different from that (or those) in power locally, regionally and/or supranationally. Where this occurs, clashes between deci-sion makers representing different geographical areas tend to be inevitable and can give rise to problems of decision making and policy implementation, thus poten-tially disrupting the programme on which a government has been elected to office.

In this context a useful distinction can be drawn between 'federal' and 'unitary' systems of government. In the former, sovereignty (i.e. the legitimate power to make decisions) is divided between two levels of government (e.g. national and local/regional), each with independent powers that are usually laid down in a writ-ten constitution which is interpreted by the courts. Thus in the United States education is in the hands of the elected government at state (i.e. subnational) level, while defence and foreign affairs are federal (i.e. national) governmental responsi-bilities. In Germany, the federal government similarly has exclusive jurisdiction over foreign and defence policy and environmental protection, while the Länder (states) control such areas as education and the police.

In contrast, under a unitary system ultimate authority rests with the national government and any powers granted to subnational levels by the central sovereign authority can ultimately be rescinded, including the right of government at subna-tional level to exist. Under such an arrangement-particularly where it is written down in the form of a constitution-government at national level clearly holds the whip hand and would normally expect its view to prevail where a dispute over an issue or policy occurred between it and a subnational authority. That said, decision makers in democratic states at all levels and under different governmental systems have, on the whole, a tendency to settle such conflicts through negotiation, bar-gaining and compromise rather than by exerting their power and authority, although this might be used on occasions. This predisposition goes some way to explaining why in democratic systems of government, the policies and legislative programmes of elected governments are much more likely to be incremental than they are to be radical.

ACTION ON THE ENVIRONMENT

The failure of markets to take into account the external costs and benefits of economic behaviour is often put forward as a key justification for government intervention in the economy. Thus while governments on the whole prefer to allow the market to determine most economic choices, there are circumstances in which the state feels it appropriate to use means such as legislation, regulation and fiscal intervention to shape some of the day-to-day decisions made by individuals and organisations. The environment has increasingly become one such arena of government action.

Writing in the *Guardian* on 2 February 2002, Philip Willan reported that the President of Italy's Lombardy region was planning to ban the sale of new petrol-and diesel-powered cars as part of an ambitious plan to reduce the chronic levels of air pollution being experienced by local citizens in many of the region's large towns and cities. Despite weekend bans on cars in many Italian cities and other restrictions on their use on weekdays, atmospheric pollution in parts of Italy frequently reaches danger levels. In Lombardy, one of the industrial powerhouses of Europe, the problem has proved particularly acute; hence the response by the regional authorities.

In essence the President's plan is to challenge car manufacturers to design alternative 'green' vehicles for introduction from 2005 onwards. The initiative-said to be the first of its kind in Europe-aims to promote the sort of environmental awareness found in California, where the state authorities have promoted the development of cars running on hydrogen. Given the large measure of support for the proposal from local citizens and from the national government, Lombardy's president is confident the plan is feasible and will form a key part of a multifaceted strategy to tackle environmental pollution in the region. Early indications suggest that some of the major car manufacturers-including Fiat, BMW and Citroen-are responding positively to the proposed initiative.

A System for Articulating Sectional Interests

Elections and a party system provide one way in which the views of an individual can be represented in government; an alternative is via pressure group activity. Like competing political parties, the existence of pressure groups is usually regarded as an important indicator of a democratic system of government. For many citizens in democratic countries, joining such a group is seen as a much more effective way of influencing government than through the party system.

Whereas political parties seek influence by formally contesting political office, pressure groups seek to influence government in other ways, although this distinc-tion is increasingly becoming blurred. In essence pressure groups (or lobbies') are collections of like-minded people who have voluntarily joined together to try to influence government thinking and behaviour and to represent the interest of their members. As a sectional interest within society, pressure groups provide a vehicle through which a collective and non-party political view can be articulated in deci-sion-making circles;,as such they can be said to operate as kind of safety-valve within a democratic system of government.

Traditionally in pressure group literature, a distinction tends to be drawn between groups which represent 'somebody' and those which represent 'some-thing'. The former are usually referred to as 'interest groups' or 'protective groups' and would include groups representing a particular section of the community such as trade unions or professional associations. The latter tend to be known as 'cause groups' or 'issue groups', as exemplified by Greenpeace, Amnesty International and the various animal rights groups. In practice, of course, it is often difficult to make such a clear-cut distinction, given that some interest groups such as trade unions often associate themselves with particular causes and may campaign vigorously alongside other groups in support of or against the issue concerned.

Most large pressure groups have websites which contain useful information. Greenpeace, for example, can be accessed at *www.greenpeace.org*

From a governmental point of view the existence of structures for articulating sectional interests is seen as an aid to efficient and representative decision making. Pressure groups not only provide government with detailed information on specific areas of everyday activity without which rational decision making would be diffi-cult; they also fulfil a number of other important functions in a democratic system. These would include:

- helping to defend minority interests;
- assisting in the implementation of government policy and legislation;
- providing for continuity in communication and consultation between the gover-nors and the governed between elections.

The successful introduction of reforms in a country's health service, for example, is dependent upon support from the various arms of the medical profession and from organisations representing the different interests of health service workers. Similarly the effectiveness of government economic policies, and their subsequent impact on the business community, will be conditioned at least in part by the reac-tions of groups representing large employers, small and medium enterprises, workers, financial interests, etc., as well as by individual entrepreneurs and con-sumers.

This relative interdependence between government and pressure groups under a democratic system is exemplified by the practice of prior consultation; this is the arrangement whereby the elected government actively seeks the views of interested parties during the policy and/or legislative process. Such consultation may be 'formal' (e.g. where a group has representation on an advisory or executive body or where it is invited to offer its views on a proposal) or 'informal' (e.g. off-the-record meetings between representatives of the group and the government) or a mixture of the two; it may also involve a group in hiring the services of a professional lobbyist-often an ex-politician or bureaucrat familiar with the structure of decision making in govern-ment and with access to key decision makers.

Groups which are regularly consulted and whose opinion is readily sought by government may acquire 'insider status' and may even be incorporated into the formal decision-making process-prizes which are highly valued since they imply that the group has a legitimate right to be consulted by government prior to deciding on a particular course of action or inaction. In com parison, 'outsider groups' often find it difficult to make their voice heard in decision-making circles and for this reason may be forced to resort to different forms of direct action in order to publicise their views in the wider community in the hope of gaining influence through public sympathy and support.

As this discussion of 'insider' and 'outsider groups' illustrates, pressure groups can use a variety of methods to attract support for their cause or to protect and promote the interests of their members. These range from direct lobbying of government to marches, strikes, disruption and other forms of demonstrative action designed to attract media and hence public attention-although frequently such action can have an adverse effect.

In addition, some of the larger and better-resourced groups may employ experts to advise on policy issues and/or establish their own research facilities to provide information to strengthen their case (e.g. Greenpeace).

What method(s) a group employs and where it seeks to bring its influence to bear tends to vary from issue to issue and group to group, and generally reflects not only differences in group status and resources but also the structure of decision making within the policy community concerned. In the United States for instance, direct lobbying of Congressmen/women is a common tactic used by pressure groups, given the relative weakness of the party system and the tendency for an individual's electoral fortunes to be tied up with the views of key groups in the con-stituency In contrast in the United Kingdom, the pressures of party discipline, the domination of the executive branch of government and the influence of senior civil servants tend to make direct appeals to key actors in government a more effec-tive method of achieving political influence than operating at constituency level.

As a final comment it is worth recalling that decisions in a democracy may be made locally, nationally, supranationally or internationally and often require co-operation between different levels of government and/or between different agencies and arms of government at both the formulation and implementation stages. Accordingly, pressure groups are increasingly to be found operating at the interface between the institutions of government and across the whole range of spatial levels from the local to the global (see Mini case: Supranational lobbying). Given the large number of pressure points where vested interests can bring their influence to bear, it tends to be easier for a group to prevent or limit government action rather than to persuade decision makers to change the direction of policy. To this extent policy formulation and implementation in democratic states is perhaps best portrayed as the 'art of the possible' rather than the 'science of the desirable'.

THE THREE BRANCHES OR FUNCTIONS OF GOVERNMENT

In a broad sense the process of governing involves three major activities: making decisions, putting them into effect and adjudicating over them in the event of dis-pute or non-compliance. Each of these functions or branches of government, as they operate at a national level, is discussed in turn below. A similar form of analy-sis could, if necessary, be applied at other spatial levels.

The Legislative Function

Governing, as we have seen, is about making decisions which affect the lives of large numbers of people. Some of these decisions require new laws or changes to existing laws to bring them into effect so that the individuals and/or groups to whom they apply become aware of the government's wishes and requirements. In a democratic system of government this formal power to make the law (i.e. to legis-late) is vested in a legislative body (the legislature) which is elected either wholly or partly by the people. As indicated above, this process of choosing a representative decision-making body by popular election is a central feature of the democratic approach to government.

Leaving aside for one moment the relative power of the legislative and executive branches of government, it is possible to identify a number of common features which apply to legislatures and the legislative function in most, if not all, demo-cratic states. These include the following:

- *A bicameral legislature,* that is, a legislature with two chambers: an upper house and a lower house, each with specific powers and roles in the legislative process. In most countries each chamber comprises representatives chosen by a separate electoral process and hence may be dominated by the same party or different parties or by no single party, depending on the electoral outcome. For a legisla-tive proposal to be accepted, the consent of both chambers is normally required. This is one of the many checks and balances normally found in democratic sys-tems of government.
- *A multi-stage legislative process*-involving the drafting of a legislative proposal, its discussion and consideration, where necessary amendment, further debate and consideration and ultimate acceptance or rejection by either or both legisla-tive chambers. Debates on the general principles of a proposed piece of legislation would normally involve all members of each chamber, whereas detailed discussion tends to take place in smaller groups or committees.
- *An executive-led process,* that is, one in which most major legislative proposals emanate from the executive branch of government. In a presidential system of government (e.g. the USA) the chief executive (the President) is normally elected separately by the people and is not part of the legislature (in other words there

is a 'separation of powers'). In a parliamentary system (e.g. the UK) members of the executive may also be members of the legislative body and hence may be in a position to control the legislative process.

- *Opportunities for legislative initiatives by ordinary representatives,* that is, arrange-ments which permit ordinary members of the legislative assembly to propose new laws or changes to existing laws. In practice such opportunities tend to be limited and dependent to a large degree for their success on a positive response from the political executive.
- *Opportunities to criticise and censure the government and, in some cases, remove it from office* (e.g. through impeachment)-this is a vital function within a demo-cratic system of government in that it forces decision makers to defend their proposals, explain the logic of their actions and account for any mistakes they may have made. Opposition parties play an important role in this context within the legislative body and through media coverage can attack the government and articulate alternative views to the wider public. Specialist and Standing Committees for scrutinising legislation and the day-to-day work of the executive branch of government also usually exist in democratic regimes.
- *Control of the purse strings,* that is, the power to grant or deny government the money required to carry out its policies and legislative programme. In theory this is a formidable power, given that no government can operate without funds. In practice the power of the legislature to deny funding to a democratically elected government may be more apparent than real and, where necessary, compromise tends to occur between the executive and legislative branches of government.

As will be evident from the comments above, legislating is a complex and time-consuming process, offering numerous opportunities for individuals and groups both within and outside the legislative body (e.g. pressure groups) to delay and dis-rupt the passage of legislation. While no government can guarantee to achieve all its legislative aims, there is a cultural expectation in a democracy that, as far as pos-sible, promises made before an election will be put into effect at the earliest opportunity by the democratically elected government. Such an expectation usu-ally provides the incumbent administration with a powerful argument for legislative support on the occasions when it is confronted with intransigence within the legislative assembly or hostility from outside sectional interests.

SUPRANATIONAL LOBBYING

Lobbying government is a key and familiar feature of the political process in democratic states. In seeking to influence government decisions, pressure groups (or 'lobbies') tend to target their activities at those parts of government where they are likely to have the maximum impact on official thinking and action. Where decisions are taken on a supranational (or inter-governmental) basis, it is common to find many of the major vested interests establishing facilities to lobby decision makers at this level.

A good example of such activity is provided by the lobbying of EU governments by a number of groups representing European business organisations. Concerned that the process of structural reform and market liberalisation in the EU was faltering, the European Round Table of Industrialists (ERT), the Association of European Chambers of Commerce and Industry and the EU Banking Federation each produced reports in 2001 urging Member State governments to take more action to achieve the target-set at the Lisbon Summit in March 2000-of making the EU the world's most competitive economy by 2010. The ERT, representing the 45 leaders of very large European-based companies, called for clearer and more predictable decision making and for an improved democratic process within the EU, including greater use of qualified majority voting and greater policy co-ordination. In contrast the Banking Federation and Chambers of Commerce stressed the need for more flexible labour markets as part of a process of improving the EU's potential for growth and employment.

In a separate report (December 2001) on the functioning of the product and capital markets, the European Commission echoed business concerns about the speed of reform in the post-Lisbon period. The report complained that start-up costs for entrepreneurs were still too high and warned that the process of market integration was beginning to slow down, particularly in the service sector. According to the Commission, the elimination of barriers to cross-border trade in services alone could boost the EU's GDP by between about 1 and 4 per cent.

The Executive Function

Governing is not only about making decisions, it is also about ensuring that these decisions are put into effect in order to achieve the government's objectives. Implementing governmental decisions is the responsibility of the executive branch of government.

In modern states the term 'the executive' refers to that relatively small group of individuals chosen to decide on policy and to oversee its implementation; some of these individuals will hold political office, others will be career administrators and advisers, although some of the latter may also be political appointees. Together they are part of a complex political and administrative structure designed to carry out the essential work of government and to ensure that those responsible for policy making and implementation are ultimately accountable for their actions.

The policy-making aspect of the executive function is normally the responsibility of a small political executive chosen (wholly or in part) by popular election. Under a presidential system of government, the chief executive or President is usually chosen by separate election for a given period of office and becomes both the nom-inal and political head of state. He/she subsequently appoints individuals to head the various government departments/ministries/bureaux which are responsible for shaping and implementing government policy. Neither the President nor the heads of departments normally sit in the legislative assembly, although there are some-times exceptions to this rule (e.g. the Vice-President in the United States).

In contrast, in a parliamentary system the roles of head of state and head of gov-ernment are separated, with the former usually largely ceremonial and carried out by either a president (e.g. Germany, India) or a monarch (e.g. UK, Japan). The head of government (e.g. Prime Minister), while officially appointed by the head of state, is an elected politician, invariably the head of the party victorious in a general elec-tion or at least seen to be capable of forming a government, possibly in coalition with other parties. Once appointed, the head of government chooses other individ-uals to head the different government departments/ministries and to be part of a collective decision-making body (e.g. a Cabinet) which meets to sanction policy proposals put forward through a system of executive committees and subcommit-tees (e.g. Cabinet Committees). These individuals, along with the head of government, are not only part of the executive machinery of the state but also usu-ally members of the legislative assembly and both 'individually' and 'collectively' responsible to the legislature for the work of government.

The day-to-day administration of government policy is largely carried out by non-elected government officials (sometimes referred to as civil servants or bureau-crats) who work for the most part in complex, bureaucratic organisations within the state bureaucracy. Apart from their role in implementing public policy, govern-ment officials help to advise ministers on the different policy options and on the political and administrative aspects of particular courses of action. Needless to say, this gives them a potentially critical role in shaping government policy a role which has been substantially enhanced over the years by the practice of granting officials a significant degree of discretion in deciding on the details of particular policies and/or on how they should be administered.

Whereas politicians in the executive branch of government tend to be transitory figures-who come and go at the whim of the head of government or of the elec-torate-most, if not all, officials are permanent, professional appointees who may serve a variety of governments of different political complexions and preferences during a long career in public administration. Whatever government is in power, officials are generally expected to operate in a non-partisan (i.e. 'neutral') way when advising their political masters and when overseeing the implementation of government policy. Their loyalty in short is to the current administration in office, a principle which helps to ensure a smooth transition of government and to guar-antee that the upheaval caused by a general election does not prevent the business of the state from being carried out 'as usual'.

The Judicial Function

Governing is not just about making and implementing laws; it is also about ensur-ing that they are applied and enforced; the latter is essentially the role of the third arm of government, namely the judiciary and the system of courts. Like political institutions, legal structures and processes tend to a degree to be country specific and vary according to a number of influences including history, culture and poli-tics. For example, while some states have a relatively unified legal system, others organised on a federal basis usually have a system of parallel courts adjudicating on federal and state/provincial law, with a Supreme Court arbitrating in the event of a dispute. In some countries a proportion of the judges may be directly or indirectly elected by the public, in others they may be appointed by government and/or co-opted by fellow judges. Business students should make themselves familiar with the legal arrangements within their own country. In this section we look briefly at the judicial function as related to the concept of democracy.

Whereas in totalitarian systems of government the judiciary is essentially the ser-vant of the ruling élite (e.g. the 'party'), in a democracy it is an accepted principle that there should be a separation between the judicial function and the other two branches of government in order to protect the citizen from a too powerful state. This notion of an impartial and independent judiciary, free to challenge the gov-ernment and to review its decisions, is regarded as one of the hallmarks of a democratic system of government; a further manifestation of the doctrine of the separation of powers.

In practice of course, notions of judicial independence and role within the demo-cratic political process tend to be the subject of certain amount of debate, particularly in countries where senior appointments to the judiciary appear to be in the gift of politicians (e.g. Supreme Court judges in the United States are nominated by the President with the consent of the Senate) or where individuals with judicial powers also have an executive and/or legislative role (e.g. the Lord Chancellor and Home Secretary in Britain). Equally there are questions over the degree to which the courts should have the power to review the constitutionality of decisions made by a democratically elected government. In the United States, for example, the Supreme Court has a long-established right to declare a law void if it conflicts with its own interpretation of the American constitution. In contrast in Britain, the legal sover-eignty of Parliament and the absence of a codified written constitution push the judiciary towards trying to interpret the intentions of the framers of government legislation and any legal decision unwelcomed by the government can be reversed by further legislation. That said, it is interesting to note that in recent years there has been an increased willingness on the part of the British judiciary to review administrative decisions, particularly those made by ministers.

Other aspects, too, call into question how far in modern democratic states there is a total separation between the different arms of government (e.g. increasing use of administrative courts/tribunals) and whether it makes sense to rigidly distin-guish between rule making and rule adjudication. Certainly some of the past judgments by the United States Supreme Court (e.g. in the area of civil rights) demonstrate that the courts can be influential in shaping decisions on major issues of policy and suggest that the judiciary are susceptible to influences from their own values or to general societal pressures. In short it seems fair to suggest that under current legal arrangements, legal adjudication is not far removed from the world of politics; arguably we may like to perpetuate the myth of an entirely separate and independent judiciary since this is a necessary aspect of the stability of many exist-ing political systems.

CHECKS AND BALANCES IN DEMOCRACIES

As will be evident from the analysis above democracy implies the existence of a system of checks and balances, arrangements which serve to curb government action and restrict its influence on the day-to-day lives of its citizens. These restraints on the actions of the state at national level can be divided into two main types: political and social/ economic.

Political checks and balances emanate primarily from three main sources:

- *the separation of powers*-particularly the notion that the three arms of goven-ment are in separate hands and that decisions require the concurrence of all branches of government;
- *a bicameral legislature*-with legislation having to be accepted by both houses and subject to scrutiny and amendment by opposition parties;
- *the territorial division of powers*-whether under a federal arrangement or through the devolution of power to regional bodies and/ or local authorities. Supranationalism is a further development.

The point is not that these arrangements necessarily exist in their most complete form in democratic states, but that-however imperfect in practice-their existence helps to provide time for reflection and delay in the decision-making process and to encourage consultation, negotiation and consensus building: the essence of the democratic approach to conflict resolution. The notion of social and economic checks and balances refers to those counter-vailing pressures on the activities of the state and its agencies that derive from the existence of non-state structures and processes which affect the lives of individuals and which ultimately restrict the scope of government influence. These include pri-vate business organisations, professional associations, promotional bodies, churches and other groups which help to shape our economic, social and moral environment. As subsequent chapters will demonstrate, the bulk of economic deci-sions in democratic states are not taken by the government but by private individuals and organisations (i.e. firms) interacting through a market system. This acts as a kind of check and balance on the free activity of the public sector and is a fundamental characteristic of democratic government.

A MODEL OF THE POLICY PROCESS

It is appropriate to conclude this examination of the political environment with a brief discussion of the process of governmental decision making in democratic sys-tems. Here, the basic model of the organisation in its environment introduced in Chapter 1 serves as a useful analytical tool. Governments, like firms, are organisations which transform inputs into output and they do so in an environ-ment largely the same as that which confronts other types of enterprise. Like other organisations, government is a user of resources, especially land, labour, capital, finance and expertise, but in addition all governments face political demands and supports when considering their policy options.

As indicated above, political demands-including those directly or indirectly impinging on business activity-become translated into action through a variety of mechanisms, including the electoral system, party activity, pressure group influ-ence and political communication; hence a government is always keen to point out that electoral victory implies that it has a mandate for its policies. The supports of the political system are those customs, conventions, rules, assumptions and senti-ments which provide a basis for the existence of the political community and its constituent parts and thus give legitimacy to the actions and existence of the incumbent government. In democratic systems, the belief in democratic principles, and the doctrines and practices emanating from that belief, are seen as central to the activities of government and its agencies.

The outputs of the political system vary considerably and range from public goods and services (e.g. healthcare)-provided predominantly from money raised through taxation-to rules and regulations (e.g. legislation, administrative proce-dures, directives) and transfer payments (i.e. where the government acts as a reallocator of resources, as in the case of the provision of state benefits). Taken together, the nature, range and extent of government output not only tend to make government the single biggest 'business' in a state, they also influence the environment in which other businesses operate and increasingly in which other governments make decisions.

As far as governmental decision making is concerned, this is clearly a highly complex process which in practice does not replicate the simple sequence of events suggested by the model. Certainly governments require 'means' (inputs) to achieve 'ends' (output), but the outputs of the political system normally only emerge after a complex, varied and ongoing process involving a wide range of individuals, groups and agencies.

To add further confusion, those involved in the process tend to vary according to the decision under discussion as well as over time, making analysis fraught with difficulties. One possible solution may be to distinguish between the early development of a policy proposal ('initiation') and its subsequent 'formula-tion' and 'implementation', in the hope that a discernible 'policy community' can be identified at each stage. But even this approach involves a degree of guesswork and arbitrary decision making, not least because of the difficulty of distinguishing precisely between the different stages of policy making and of discerning the influ-ence of individuals and groups at each phase of the process.

Notwithstanding these difficulties, it is important for students of business and for businesses themselves to have some understanding of the structure of decision making and of the underlying values and beliefs which tend to shape governmen-tal action, if they are to appreciate (and possibly 'influence') the political environment in which they exist. In short, studies of political systems, institutions and processes help to provide insight into how and why government decisions are made, who is important in shaping those decisions and how influence can be brought to bear on the decision-making process. As an increasing number of indi-viduals and groups recognise, knowledge of this kind can prove a valuable organisational resource that on occasions is of no less significance than the other inputs into the productive process.

SYNOPSIS

Laws and policies which influence business activity are made by politicians and bureaucrats, operating at a variety of spatial levels. In the United Kingdom, the deci-sions of local and central government emanate from a complex process of discussion and negotiation involving a range of formal and informal institutions, including political parties and pressure groups, and frequently involving international and supranational bodies. This process is part of the democratic approach to decision making and pro-vides opportunities for individuals and groups to influence government thinking on both the formulation and implementation of policy and legislation. Students of business and managers need to have a broad understanding of this political environment in order to appreciate one of the key influences on a firm's operations.

SUMMARY OF KEY POINTS

- Politics is a universal activity which affects businesses of all types and sizes.
- It occurs at a variety of spatial levels from the local to the global.
- Political systems, structures and processes reflect underlying social values and philosophies and these influence the ways in which major decisions are taken.
- In any democratic system of government the key political institutions are likely to include an electoral system, a party system, a representative decision-making assembly and a system for articulating sectional interests.
- The three key functions of government are legislative, executive and judicial.
- While political institutions, practices and processes tend to vary between countries, democratic government is typified by a system of representative democracy and by political, social and economic checks and balances which act as a constraint on the actions of government.

- Such checks and balances in the system include the activities of pressure groups which seek to influence government through a variety of means and who often play a key role in policy formulation and implementation.
- Business organisations and the bodies which represent them are key pressure groups in democratic societies and an important part of the external environment in which government and its agencies operate.

A DEMOCRATIC POLITICAL SYSTEM IN ACTION: UK NATIONAL GOVERNMENT

Through a system of regular elections British citizens (the electorate) vote for candidates of competing political parties who are seeking to form the national gov-ernment (or to be members of the devolved assemblies inNorthern Ireland, Scotland or Wales). Successful candidates at the national elections become Members of Parliament (MPs) and the party with the largest number of MPs is invited by the monarch to form a government, with individuals within the govern-ment being allocated specific responsibilities for particular areas of work. The work of government is scrutinised by Parliament, which acts as the people's representative between elections, thereby providing for a measure of public accountability. Equally, between (or during) elections individuals are free to seek to influence government by joining pressure groups or other types of organisation (e.g. political parties) and by making their views known to their elected representa-tives. The media is free and therefore able to scrutinise the government's performance and to inform the public about political developments.

The Legislative Branch of Government at National Level

As indicated above, a directly elected legislature-representative of the people and responsible for making laws-is an important component of a democratic system of government. In the United Kingdom as a whole this function is carried out by Parliament, which currently comprises a non-elected upper chamber (the House of Lords) and an elected lower chamber (the House of Commons) whose members (cur-rently 646 MPs) are elected by universal suffrage by the majority of citizens aged 18 and over. While it is true to say that the Lords still retains some important powers, including the power to delay government legislation, the upper house is currently being reformed and in future is likely to contain an elected element. Whatever hap-pens it seems likely that the House of Commons will remain the most important part of the UK legislature, particularly since it contains key members of the political exec-utive, including the Prime Minister and most of the Cabinet.

As far as political representation and responsibility are concerned, this is achieved in a number of ways. For a start, Members of Parliament are directly elected by their constituents and one of the MP's main roles is to represent the con-stituency for the period between general elections. Apart from holding regular surgeries at which individuals (including businessmen and women) can discuss their problems and views with their representative, MPs also speak on constituency matters in Parliament, frequently raise questions which require answers from gov-ernment ministers, and generally scrutinise government proposals for any potential effects they may have on the constituency, including key groups within the local electorate (e.g. local businesses). Needless to say, there will be occasions on which the views of the elected member may differ from those of his or her constituents, particularly those who voted for candidates of an opposing political party; but this does not negate the idea of representation under the British system of parliamen-tary democracy. MPs represent their constituents first and foremost by having been elected *by them* and hence they provide a direct link between the electorate and the government of the day, which is essentially drawn from the senior members of the majority party in Parliament.

Parliament also provides opportunities for the people's representatives to scruti-nise and, where necessary, to criticise and challenge the decisions of government. In addition to such parliamentary mechanisms as question time and the adjourn-ment debate, Parliament provides for a system of Select Committees of backbench MPs whose primary role is to scrutinise the work of government departments and other state agencies. Such committees-chaired by both government and opposi-tion backbenchers-are able to question ministers and civil servants, call for departmental papers, cross-examine experts from outside government, and gener-ally investigate the work of the executive, prior to reporting to Parliament on their findings. In bringing their views before Parliament and the public generally (espe-cially through the media), Select Committees provide a check on government activity and hence form one of the strands by which governments remain answer-able to the electorate in the period between elections.

Another significant strand is provided by the Opposition who represent not only an alternative choice of government, but also a means of scrutinising and criticis-ing the work of the incumbent administration. Fundamental to this role is the ability of opposition MPs to publicise the decisions of government and to present alternative views to the public via party political broadcasts or promotional litera-ture or debates in parliament, or by general media coverage. Such free and open discussion of issues and policies is a necessary condition for democracy and is an important element in the political education of the nation. Even where governments have large majorities-as is currently the case-the role of opposition parties remains a vital component of democracy and helps to provide a curb on unlimited government action.

Turning to its role as a legislative body there is little doubt that the UK Parliament is largely a legitimising institution, giving formal authority to the wishes of the majority party. Through its control of the process of legislation, the parliamentary timetable, the flow of information and the votes of its members, the government is able to ensure that its legislative proposals not only come before Parliament, but also are almost invariably accepted, even if some delay occurs from time to time in enact-ing the government's programme. Opportunities for individual MPs to sponsor legislation (e.g. through private members' bills) are few and far between and the out-come of such proposals depends ultimately on government support (or reluctant acquiescence), if the legislation is to get through its various stages in Parliament. Not surprisingly, this effective stranglehold by the government on the legislative process has led some commentators to talk of an 'elective dictatorship' and to question the true extent of democratic decision making, particularly when modern governments are invariably elected by less than 50 per cent of the electorate.

The Executive Branch of Government

Putting laws and policies into effect is formally the work of the executive. In the UK this role is carried out by a wide variety of institutions and agencies that are part of the machinery of government. These include the Cabinet, government departments, local authorities, nationalised industries and a large number of other non-departmental public bodies or quasi-autonomous national government agen-cies, often referred to as 'quangos'. In the discussion below attention is focused initially on the key institutions at central level since these are fundamental to the process of decision making in Britain. Discussion of some of the other agencies can be found in subsequent sections of this chapter. Under the British system of government, the core of the executive is the Cabinet, headed by the Prime Minister, an office of crucial importance given the absence of an elected head of state with effective political powers. British Prime Ministers not only have a number of significant political roles-including leader of the governing party, head of the government and head of the Cabinet-but also have a formida-ble array of political powers, including the power to:

- choose members of the Cabinet;
- choose other non-Cabinet ministers;
- promote, demote or dismiss ministers;
- appoint individuals to chair Cabinet committees;
- appoint top civil servants;
- confer certain appointments and titles; and
- determine the date of the general election within the five-year term of office.

While the existence of such rights and responsibilities does not infer that Prime Ministers will inevitably be all-powerful, it is clear that holders of the office have a key role to play in the decision-making process and much will depend upon how an individual interprets that role, upon their personality, and upon the constraints they face (both 'real' and 'imagined') in carrying it out. As the Conservative Prime Minister Mrs Thatcher (1979-90) found to her cost, retaining the office of Prime Minister is dependent not only on the electorate, but also on maintaining the sup-port and confidence of parliamentary colleagues in the period between elections.

As indicated above, as head of the Cabinet the Prime Minister chairs the commit-tee of senior ministers that is the overall directing force-or board of management-within British central government. Comprising about 25 to 30 ministers who have been appointed by the Prime Minister to head the various government departments (or to fulfil some other important functions), the Cabinet is responsible for directing and co-ordinating the work of the whole executive machine. Its functions include:

- making decisions on the nature and direction of government policy, including public expenditure, economic policy, defence, foreign relations, industrial policy, and so on;
- overseeing and co-ordinating the administration of government;
- arbitrating in the event of disputes between ministers or departments;
- discussing, deciding and generally directing the government's legislative pro-gramme, including laws relating to business.

A large part of this work, of course, is carried out using a system of committees and subcommittees, which are comprised of individuals chosen by the Prime Minister (including the chairperson) and which are supported by a small but powerful secre-tariat, headed by the Cabinet Secretary (a civil servant). Apart from providing an opportunity for more detailed discussions of issues and policies prior to full consid-eration by the Cabinet, the committee system has the advantage of allowing non-members of the Cabinet (including non-Cabinet ministers and civil servants) to participate in discussions in which they may have an interest. In this way, the system helps to provide a mechanism for communication and co-ordination between government departments and serves as a training ground for junior minis-ters, many of whom will subsequently achieve full Cabinet responsibilities. A selected list of Cabinet committees for 2005 is shown in Table 3.1.

Table 3.1 : Selected Cabinet committees, 2005

Committee name	*Designation*
Ministerial Committee on Economic Affairs, Productivity and Competitiveness	EAPC
Ministerial Committee on Energy and the Environment	EE
Ministerial Committee on European Policy	EP
Ministerial Committee on the Legislative Programme	LP
Ministerial Group on Public Services and Public Expenditure	PSX
Ministerial Committee on Science and Innovation	SI
Ministerial Committee on Domestic Affairs	DA
Ministerial Committee on the Olympics	MISC25
Ministerial Sub-Committee on Electronic Service Delivery	PSX(E)

Source: Cabinet Office *(www.cabinetoffice.gov.uk/secretariats/committees)*.

Much of the day-to-day work of central government is carried out in vast and complex administrative structures called government departments-a selected list of which is shown in Table 3.2. Most government departments are headed by Cabinet ministers (usually called the Secretaries of State) and include other minis-ters outside the Cabinet (e.g. Ministers of State, Parliamentary Under Secretaries of State) who have been appointed by the Prime Minister. Together these ministers constitute the political executive. As the head of a department, the Secretary of State has ultimate responsibility for its work and is answerable to Parliament through the various mechanisms referred to above. In addition, he or she is expected to give overall direction to the work of the department-within the policy of the government as a whole-and to represent its interest in the Cabinet (e.g. over the size and use of its budget), in Parliament (e.g. in steering through legisla-tion) and in the outside world (e.g. in the media). Large areas of this work are delegated to the Ministers of State who assume responsibility for specific areas of departmental work and they in turn will tend to delegate some duties to the depart-ment's junior ministers. Such an arrangement not only ensures coverage of the different aspects of a department's responsibilities, but also provides invaluable experience and training for ambitious young MPs appointed to a ministerial post.

Table 3.2: Key government departments, 2005

Cabinet Office

HM Treasury

Foreign and Commonwealth Office

Home Office

Environment, Food and Rural Affairs

Education and Skills

Defence

Health

Work and Pensions

Trade and Industry

Culture, Media and Sport

Transport

Office of the Deputy Prime Minister

Ministers are assisted in their work by permanent officials, known as civil ser-vants, many of whom have spent a large part of their working lives in the government machine and hence are familiar with how it works and how to manip-ulate it in order to achieve particular objectives. Whereas ministers are politicians, civil servants are administrators vested formally with the task of carrying out the policies of the incumbent government, irrespective of their own political views and preferences. Perhaps not surprisingly, as key advisers to ministers on policy formu-lation and implementation, senior civil servants can exercise considerable influence over the nature and shape of government policy and legislation-a point amus-ingly emphasised in a popular British television programme *Yes, Minister.* For this reason, individuals or groups seeking to shape government thinking on an issue or piece of legislation frequently 'target' senior departmental officials in the hope of gaining influence in the policy process.

This potential for influence by senior civil servants is, of course, enhanced by the scope and complexities of modern government and by the fact that government ministers have a wide range of non-departmental as well as departmental responsi-bilities (e.g. as constituency MPs). Ministers consequently rely heavily on their officials for information and advice and civil servants are normally entrusted, under ministers, with the conduct of the whole gamut of government activities, including filling in the details of some legislation. Added to this, the need for policy co-ordination between departments requires regular meetings between senior officials, in groups which mirror the meetings of Cabinet subcommittees. Since these meetings of officials help to provide the groundwork and briefing papers for future discussions by ministers, they permit civil servants to influence the course of events, especially when a particular line or policy option is agreed by the senior officials in a number of departments.

Criticism of the influence of the senior civil service and of its secrecy and reluc-tance to change has led to a number of inquiries into how to improve its efficiency and *modus operandi.* For example, in 1979, the new Conservative government appointed Sir Derek Rayner of Marks & Spencer to introduce private-sector manage-ment methods into the service and this was continued by his successor, Sir Robin Ibbs of ICI, who produced a report called *The Next Steps* (1988). This report led to many civil service responsibilities being 'hived off to 'executive agencies', which operate semi-independently of government ministers, with their own budgets and performance targets and with a greater degree of independence over pay, financial and staffing matters, despite remaining formally part of the civil service. In the early 1990s the government under John Major introduced 'market testing', under which a proportion of the work of each department and agency had to be put out to competitive tender.

It is perhaps worth noting at this point that, however pervasive its influence, the civil service is not the only source of policy advice for governments. Apart from tra-ditional bureaucratic channels, ministers often turn to specially appointed bodies for help and guidance in making policy choices. Some of these sources are permanent (or relatively permanent) and would include the various advisory bodies set up by past and present governments to assist in the policy process in specific functional areas (e.g. the Arts Council). Others are temporary, having been specially constituted by government to consider a particular problem and to report on their findings prior to going out of existence (e.g. public inquiries, Royal Commissions). While the appointment of these advisory sources does not oblige the government to follow their advice, they can be regarded as useful sources of information, ideas and advice from outside the formal bureaucratic machine. Moreover the fact that they tend to have a membership representing a wide cross-section of interests (including repre-sentatives of particular pressure groups, industrialists, trade unionists, MPs, academics and others drawn from the list of 'the great and the good') helps to widen the scope of consultation and thus to enhance the democratic process.

The last generation has also seen governments turning increasingly to special advisers and policy planning units for help with policy development. Whereas advisers are individuals appointed by ministers (including the Prime Minister), usu-ally from outside the civil service, policy planning units and/or research units are groups of individuals generally recruited from and located within the government machine, with the aim of providing a range of policy and programme advice to both policy makers and administrators. Often comprised of young and highly qual-ified individuals seconded to a unit from a wide range of occupational categories and disciplines (including statisticians, social scientists, economists, and general administrators), policy units are a valuable source of information and advice, and their operation at both central and local government level provides policy makers with detailed research and analysis with which to support their policy judgements.

A further important development has been the increased use of 'focus groups', collections of individual citizens consulted by government on policy proposals prior to legislation and/or implementation. In canvassing the views of individuals affected by government policy, the current government hopes to improve the policy process in a wide range of areas, including the delivery of public services, where it has a programme to provide round-the-clock availability and (ultimately) complete electronic access. While some see citizens' panels or focus groups as noth-ing more than a gimmick, others regard their use as a move towards a more modern and democratic form of government with increased levels of public accountability and access to information.

The Judicial Branch of Government

The third arm of government, the judiciary-comprising the judges and the courts-is formally separate from and independent of Parliament and the government, despite the fact that the head of the judiciary, the Lord Chancellor, is both a member of the government and a member of the House of Lords, where he or she presides as Speaker. In essence the role of the judiciary is to put into effect the laws enacted by Parliament and to keep the government within the limits of its powers as laid down in statutes and in common law, as interpreted by the judiciary. Since 1973, it has also been responsible for interpreting European Union law. Given the complexities of the legal system and its relevance to the world of business, it is important to examine this aspect of government in more detail.

Postscript

In Britain as elsewhere, both 'change' and 'continuity' are features of the political system. Apart from the developments mentioned above (e.g. reform of the House of Lords, elections to the new Scottish Parliament, Welsh Assembly and Northern Ireland Assembly, proposed reforms of the civil service), there are proposals to intro-duce a new voting system (see, for example, the Jenkins Report 1998), to reform government policy-making and delivery systems and to consider regional assemblies in England, though the latter still appear relatively unpopular.

Various systems of proportional representation have been used for the elections to the new regional assemblies and for the European elections (in June 1999) and London elected a mayor in the year 2000 (see below). Developments such as these clearly have implications for the business environment.

SUBNATIONAL GOVERNMENT: UK LOCAL AUTHORITIES

Democratic government occurs at subnational as well as national level and takes a wide variety of forms. In addition to the local branches of central government departments and public utilities, many states have local agencies for the adminis-tration of justice, local special-purpose authorities (e.g. in the health service) and a system of regional and/or local government, whether under a federal or a unitary arrangement. Such decentralisation and deconcentration of political authority is generally seen as beneficial, since it brings the formulation and administration of policy 'nearer to the people' and is said to provide for decisions which are more sensitive to local needs and aspirations. Concomitantly, however, it can raise the question as to the degree of autonomy of local agencies within a centralised system of government and as recent history has demonstrated this is a controversial and perennial source of debate and dispute in many parts of the world.

Within the United Kingdom as a whole, political power is devolved at two main levels: regionally and locally. Scotland and Wales now have their own directly elected regional assemblies with differing levels of devolved authority. The Scottish Parliament, for example, essentially took over the role of the Scottish Office in 2000, with responsibilities including education, health and transport and the power to raise income tax in Scotland by up to 3p in the pound. The Welsh Assembly, in contrast, has no fiscal powers and is able to make secondary legisla-tion in areas where executive functions have been transferred to it. The Northern Ireland Assembly is currently suspended.

Local government-the focus of this section-has a considerable historical pedi-gree and remains a key element of the country's system of institutionalised democracy and a major actor in the national as well as the local economy. Given its impact in the business environment, it deserves special attention.

As one form of local administration, local government has a number of distinc-tive features. For a start it involves self-government by the people of the locality as well as for them, with local authorities exercising considerable discretion in the ways they apply national laws within their areas. In addition, local decision-makers (councillors) are elected to oversee multi-purpose authorities, financed by revenue raised predominantly from local sources-although the proportion from central government has risen in recent years. In short, each local authority constitutes a miniature political and administrative system: each has the institutions and processes of government-including an electoral system, a legislative body (the council), appointed officials (local government officers), party activity, and conflict between individuals and groups within the local community over the allocation of resources and the enforcement of values.

Figure 3.4 illustrates this parallel between the basic operation of government at central and local level. The electorate in each local constituency (e.g. district, county, metropolitan district) periodically choose between candidates who are mostly representing the same parties as those found at national level and the suc-cessful candidates in the election are elected to represent their constituency in the deliberating body (the council). Senior members of this body are chosen to serve on the various committees and subcommittees, with the leading party on the council having an in-built majority in the committee system, where most decisions have traditionally been made prior to being sanctioned (or not) by the full council. Since the passage of the Local Government Act (2000), councils have been allowed to adopt one of three broad categories of constitution which provide for a separate executive. These three categories are (1) a directly elected mayor with a cabinet selected by the mayor, (2) a cabinet either elected by the council or appointed by its leader, and (3) a directly elected mayor and council manager.

For the most part, senior councillors are the political heads of the various local authority departments and agencies (e.g. housing, social services, education, and so on) that are responsible for providing those services within the local community which national laws require or, in some cases (e.g. sports centres), do not forbid. Much of this work is carried out by local officials who are appointed by the local authority to administer local services and to advise councillors on policy matters. As the local equivalent of civil servants, local government officers exercise considerable influence over the formulation as well as the implementation of local deci-sions. For this reason, they too tend to be targeted by local pressure groups which operate at all levels and stages of the political process in their attempts to influence local decision making.

The current structure of local government in the United Kingdom is illustrated in Table 3.3. In England, outside the metropolitan areas, most 'shire' counties have a two-tier structure of county councils and district councils, with the former pro-viding the larger services (e.g. education and social services) while the latter have responsibility for a range of other services (such as housing, leisure, refuse collec-tion and local planning). Elsewhere (e.g. Avon, Cleveland, Humberside, Isle of Wight) new 'unitary authorities' either have taken over the functions of the former county and district councils or operate alongside them as all-purpose authorities (e.g. Leicester, York). In the metropolitan areas (including London) the single tier of district councils (or London borough councils) remains unchanged from previous years.

Table 3.3: The structure of UK local government, 2005

Types of local authority		
England	Wales and Scotland	N. Ireland
Non-metropolitan areas County councils District councils Unitary councils (plus joint arrangements)	*All mainland areas* Unitary councils (plus three island councils in Orkney, Shetland and the Western Isles)	For the purpose of local government Northern Ireland has 26 district councils with limited powers (e.g. collecting rubbish and providing leisure facilities)
Metropolitan areas Metropolitan district councils (plus joint boards)		
London London Borough Councils (plus Corporation of the City of London and joint boards)		

Following legislation in 1994, the two-tier structure in Wales and Scotland was abolished and was replaced (on 1 April 1996) with single-tier, all-purpose, unitary authorities which have inherited the majority of the functions of the previous councils. In Northern Ireland the system of single-tier district councils remains, although these authorities still have limited responsibility for service provision.

Like central government, UK local government has also faced pressures for reform, and a number of important developments have taken place in recent years.

- London elected its first executive mayor in 2000 and a streamlined assembly (25 members) to control its budget and appointments. The assembly of the Greater London Authority was elected by proportional representation and is responsible for major strategic issues such as transport, economic development, planning and the environment.
- Compulsory Competitive Tendering has been replaced by 'Best Value' in the delivery of local services.
- Councils have been asked to consider reform of the decision-making process and to consider alternative models. Some councils have implemented such changes.

As indicated previously, such changes in the political system have implications for the relationship between business and government.

SUPRANATIONAL GOVERNMENT: THE EUROPEAN UNION

Decisions and law affecting business activity are increasingly being made at supra-national as well as national and subnational levels. Nowhere is this more evident than in western Europe, where the influence of the European Union is profound. As a significant part of the political environment of the major world economies, the EU deserves special consideration, particularly since its decisions often have global as well as regional consequences-affecting not only firms within its member states, but also businesses and governments trading with these states both directly and indirectly.

In the following analysis, attention is focused on the politi-cal institutions of the European Union and their relative importance in the process of decision-making. The economic significance of the EU within the international marketplace.

The European Parliament

The European Parliament is a directly elected body currently of 732 members (MEPs), with each member state's representation being roughly equivalent to the size of its population. The United Kingdom, for example, has 78 MEPs, elected at five-yearly intervals by UK citizens using a regional list system of proportional representation introduced for the June 1999 European elections. Since voting under a proportional system enhances the prospects of representation by smaller political parties, the European Parliament contains members representing a diversity of political parties who sit in political groups with similar affiliations. Figure shows, for example, the number of MEPs by broad affiliation as they stood at June 2004.

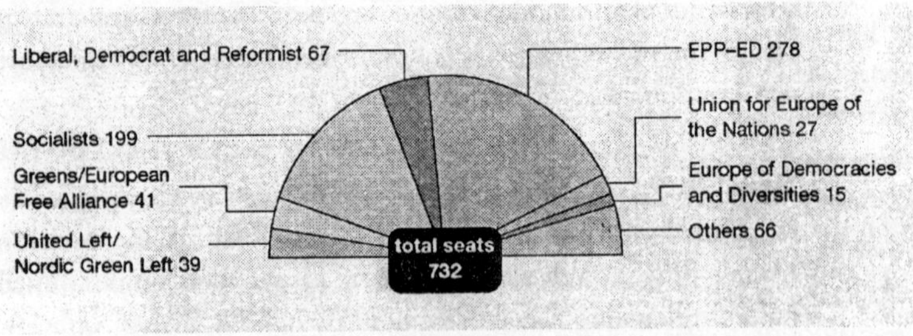

Figure : MEPs by party affiliation at June 2004

Source: Adapted from European Parliament data.

The importance of party affiliation is emphasised by the fact that Parliament's organisation is deliberately biased in favour of multinational groupings, with recog-nition of a political grouping entitling the group to offices, funding, representation on committees and influence in debates and legislation. In order to decide its atti-tude to an issue or policy proposal coming before the Parliament or one of its committees, a group would normally meet for several days in the week before each session and the issue would be discussed and an agreed line would be decided. As in the case of national parliaments, the attitudes of the political groups have a sig-nificant impact on the discussions and decisions within the European Parliament, both in committee and when the House is in full session. Given the number of party groups, however, and the fact that no single group tends to have an absolute majority-unlike in some national parliaments-there is often a need for a group to try to build a coalition of support if it is to achieve its objectives in Parliament. Understandably-and perhaps inevitably-decisions by the European Parliament thus tend to involve compromise between individuals and groups, with the final outcome frequently being a course of action which is 'acceptable' to a majority.

In terms of its role and methods of operation, the European Parliament essen-tially mirrors national parliaments. Much of its detailed work is handled by specialist committees, meeting mostly in Brussels, which report on and offer rec-ommendations to full sessions of the House which take place in Strasbourg. Membership of each committee is broadly representative of the strengths of the party groupings and the chairmen and women of the permanent committees tend to be influential figures in their own right. In addition to carrying out detailed examination and amendment of draft laws, the committees discuss issues (e.g. women's rights, consumer protection, employment), question officials, hold public hearings at which experts and representatives of specialist organisations give evi-dence, and generally offer their opinion and advice on issues of concern to the EU. As in the case of national parliaments, detailed discussion in committee prior to debate and decision by the full house provides Parliament with an effective means of carrying out its duties and serves as a mechanism for scrutinising the work of both the Council and the Commission.

With regard to its functions, these predominantly fall into four main areas:

1 *Legislation.* The Parliament's formal approval is required on most proposals before they can be adopted by the Council of Ministers.
2 *The budget.* Along with the Council of Ministers, the Parliament acts as the Community's 'budgetary authority' and can reject the Council's draft budget and may modify expenditure proposals on 'non-compulsory' items. It can question the Commission's management of the budget and call in the Court of Auditors.
3 *Supervision.* The Parliament supervises the Commission, which it has the power to dismiss by a vote of censure and whose work it scrutinises using a variety of mechanisms. Under the Maastricht Treaty (1992) it has the right to be consulted on the appointment of a new Commission and can veto its appointment. The power of democratic supervision has been

extended to other EU institutions including the Council of Ministers.

4 *Initiative.* This includes debates on important regional and international issues and demands for changes to existing policies and/or legislation. Parliament must also approve applications from countries wishing to join the EU.

In the legislative field, authority traditionally rested with the Council of Ministers and the Commission, and Parliament's role was largely to sanction proposals put before it. Changes under the Single European Act (1986), the Maastricht Treaty (1992) and the Amsterdam Treaty (1997) have, however, helped to strengthen Parliament's position by establishing new procedures for 'assent', 'co-operating' and 'co-decision'. Thus:

- In certain fields an absolute majority of the European Parliament must vote to approve laws before they are passed (e.g. foreign treaties, accession treaties, the Common Agricultural Policy).
- In specified areas Parliament now has a second reading of proposals and its rejec-tion of such proposals can only be overturned by a unanimous decision of the Council of Ministers (e.g. Single Market laws, trans-European networks).
- Parliament can also reject certain legislation by an absolute majority vote if, after the second reading of a proposal and subsequent conciliation, the Council and Parliament are unable to agree (e.g. education and training, health, consumer protection).

The Amsterdam Treaty extends the co-decision procedure to all areas covered by qualified majority voting.

The Council of The European Union (the Council of Ministers)

The Council of The European Union (the Council of Ministers)-the Union's ulti-mate decision-making body-comprises one minister from each of the 25 member states, with participants on the Council varying according to the issue under dis-cussion (e.g. agricultural issues are discussed by Ministers of Agriculture from each state). Meetings of the Council, which are mainly held in Brussels, are chaired by the minister from the country holding the presidency, which rotates on a six-monthly basis (e.g. Luxembourg and the UK held the presidency in 2005). Along with the meetings of ministers are regular meetings of officials (Council Working Groups), together with the work of the Committee of Permanent Representatives of the Member States (COREPER) whose task is to co-ordinate the groundwork for Union decisions undertaken by the numerous meetings of senior officials. In addi-tion, the Council is serviced by a general secretariat also based in Brussels.

In essence, the role of the Council of Ministers is to make major policy decisions and to respond to legislative proposals put forward mainly by the Commission. In general, major EU decisions require unanimity in the Council but, increasingly, many decisions (especially after the Amsterdam and Nice Treaties) are now being taken by a qualified majority vote (qmv). Member states have weighted votes in the Council that are roughly proportional to their relative population sizes, with the total number of votes now being 321. Since November 2004, a qualified majority will be reached if two conditions are met: (1) a majority of member states approve (in some cases a two-thirds majority is needed); (2) a minimum of 232 votes (i.e. 72.3 per cent) is cast in favour of the proposal. In addition, a member state can also ask for confirmation that the votes in favour represent at least 62 per cent of the total population of the EU. If not, the decision will not be adopted.

While the 'right of initiative' under the Treaties rests with the Commission, the ultimate power of decision essentially lies with the Council, which may adopt Commission proposals as drafted, amend them, reject them, or simply take no deci-sion, having consulted the European Parliament and normally a number of other bodies (see below). If adopted, Council of Ministers' decisions have the force of law and are described as regulations, directives, decisions, or recommendations and opinions. Regulations apply directly to all member states and do not have to be confirmed by national parliaments to have binding legal effect. Directives lay down compulsory objectives, but leave it to member states to translate them into national legislation. Decisions are binding on those states, companies or individu-als to whom they are addressed, while recommendations and opinions have no binding force, but merely state the view of the institution which issues them.

The Council's power to pass a law-even if the European Parliament disagrees with it-was reduced under the Maastricht Treaty. In specified policy areas, joint approval is now necessary and MEPs have an effective veto if the two sides cannot reach agreement following conciliation. Moreover, following Maastricht a Committee of the Regions has been established to advise the Commission and the Council on issues concerning the European regions-a development which should help to ensure a stronger regional voice at European level. That said, it is still the case that the Council remains responsible for setting general policy within the EU and relies on the Commission to take decisions on the detailed application of legis-lation or to adapt legislative details to meet changing circumstances. To this extent-and given the Commission's other responsibilities-the ultimate influence over EU decisions is, to say the very least, open to question, as is often the case at national level.

The European Council

The work of the 'specialist' Councils within the Council of Ministers (e.g. Agriculture, Economics and Finance, Employment and Social Affairs) is co-ordinated by the General Affairs Council, comprising the Foreign Ministers of the 25 member states.

This Council is also responsible for preparing for the meetings of the European Council which occur two or three times each year. The European Council is attended by the Heads of Government/State of each member state along with their Foreign Ministers and the President of the Commission, and its work invariably attracts sub-stantial media coverage. Under the chairmanship of the country holding the presidency the European Council's role is to discuss important policy issues affecting the EU and to propose policy to the Council of Ministers. As the meeting at Maastricht in December 1991 indicated, these 'summits' of Heads of Governments can have a profound effect on the development of the Union and its institutions.

The European Commission

The Commission, which has its headquarters in Brussels and Luxembourg, is the EU's bureaucratic arm, currently comprising 25 Commissioners (one from each member state) nominated by their respective governments and a staff of about 16 000 permanent civil servants drawn from all member states. Headed by a presi-dent, and organised into Directorates-General, each with a Commissioner responsible for its work, the European Commission's role is essentially that of ini-tiator, supervisor and executive. More specifically its tasks are:

1 To act as guardian of the Treaties so as to ensure that EU rules and principles are respected.
2 To propose policies and legislation for the Council of Ministers to discuss and, if appropriate, adopt or amend.
3 To implement EU policies and supervise the day-to-day running of these policies, including managing the funds which account for most of the EU budget (e.g. EAGGF, ERDF, ECSC).

In carrying out these duties, the Commissioners are required to act in the interest of the EU as a whole and may not receive instructions from any national govern-ment or from any other body (Article 157 of the Treaty of Rome). Moreover, while each Commissioner is responsible for formulating proposals within his or her area of responsibility, the final decision is taken on a collegiate basis and the work is subject to the supervision of the European Parliament. As mentioned above, Parliament is the only body which can force the Commission to resign collectively; interestingly, it has no authority over individual Commissioners, although its endorsement is needed when the President of the Commission and the other Commissioners are appointed.

Much of the undoubted power and influence of the Commission stems from its central involvement in the legislative process. Proposals for consideration by the Council and the Parliament are initially drafted by the Commission, usually follow-ing consultation with the Economic and Social Committee (representing the interests of employers, trade unions, farmers, consumers, etc.) and other advisory bodies as appropriate. Moreover EU Treaties specifically give the Commission the power to make regulations, issue directives, take decisions, make recommendations and deliver opinions, as well as to implement policies based on either Council deci-sions or Treaty provisions. Thus, while legislative power in the EU in general rests with the Council of Ministers, the Commission is also able to legislate in order to implement earlier Council regulations, particularly where technical or routine mat-ters are concerned-a situation which has parallels in the operation of government at national level.

Further powers with regard to specific sectors (e.g. coal and steel) or particular aspects of EU work (e.g. the budget, international agreements) serve to enhance the Commission's influence and to confirm its position as the 'driving force' of the Union. Perhaps understandably, pressure groups seeking to influence the policy process within the European Union regard the Commission as an important insti-tution to target, together with Parliament and the Council of Ministers. Recent and proposed changes in the relationship between these three institutions will undoubtedly have an effect not only on the legislative process, but also on the practice of lobbying within the EU context.

The European Court of Justice

The European Court of Justice, which sits in Luxembourg, comprises 25 judges who are appointed for a six-year period by consent of the member states and eight advocates-general. The Court's role is:

1 To pass judgment, at the request of a national court, on the interpretation or validity of points of EU law.

2 To quash, at the request of an EU institution, government or individual, any measures adopted by the Commission, the Council or national governments which are judged to be incompatible with the existing treaties.

The Court can also be invited to offer an opinion, which then becomes binding, on agreements the EU proposes to undertake with third countries. Three aspects of its work are particularly worthy of note:

1 Individuals as well as member states can bring cases to the Court, and its judg-ments and interpretations apply to all (i.e. EU institutions, member states, national courts and private citizens) and are backed by a system of penalties for non-compliance.

2 Its rulings on matters of European law, which has primacy over national law, are final and its decisions are binding on member countries.

3 The Court has tended to follow the principle that EU Treaties should be inter-preted with a degree of flexibility so as to take account of changing conditions and circumstances. This has permitted the Community to legislate in areas where there are no specific Treaty provisions, such as the fight against pollution.

Current Developments

With the decision to enlarge the EU, steps have been taken to establish a Constitution for Europe which is designed to replace the exisiting treaties and to streamline the EU's decision-making process. The draft Constitution was ratified by Heads of Government/State in October 2005 and has subsequently been subject to referendums in a number of member states. Rejection of the constitution by voters in Holland and France in 2005 has left the future unclear.

LEFT OUT IN THE COLD—CASE STUDY

We saw in the Mini case ('Action on the environment') how governments at subna-tional level sometimes act to tackle problems of 'market failure'.

The same is true at national, supranational and international levels, particularly over cross-border issues such as environmental pollution and degradation which invariably have no simple cause or solution. When governmental proposals in areas such as this are being formulated, then thought needs to be given by the relevant authori-ties to how any new policies or laws will be implemented and the implications that such changes may bring for affected groups and individuals. Failure to consider the different dimensions of the implementation process can prove problematic (and fre-quently embarrassing) for government and/or for its citizens.

The problem of the United Kingdom's 'fridge mountain' illustrates this issue very clearly. As a member of the European Union, the UK helped to shape a new EU reg-ulation which outlawed the traditional method of dumping CFC foam from fridges and freezers into landfill sites because of the danger of it escaping into the atmos-phere and causing further damage to the ozone layer. From 1 January 2002 when the new regulation came into effect, it became illegal to send unwanted fridges and freezers to giant metal crushers which prepared them prior to going to landfill. Instead they now have to be crushed in special closed units which capture the CFCs in liquid form so they can be burned and destroyed.

Believing that the new regulation applied only to industrial fridges and freezers, the Department of the Environment was slow to establish a system for dealing with the looming problem of discarded equipment.

In particular the government's failure to ensure that the special closed recycling units were in place when the regulation came into force meant that thousands of redundant fridges and freezers began to pile up in warehouses and hangars across the country (or were dumped illegally by the roadside) with no means of disposal. UK stores and suppliers of equipment had stopped taking away old models for free from November 2001 and consequently local authorities have had to be funded by central government to deal with the growing problem of storage until proper means of disposal can be arranged.

While this misreading of the regulations is by no means unique to the UK (e.g. only Germany, Holland and Sweden had new closed units in place by 1 January 2002), it has proved something of a *cause célèbre* in UK political circles and a task force has been set up to tackle the immediate problem of the country's fridge mountain. Ultimately the plan is to send the discarded equipment to new recycling units which will be run by licensed entrepreneurs who are currently collecting and storing fridges from all over the country ready for when the new equipment arrives. Given the commercial opportunities arising from the new regulations, some observers feel that the supply side of the market for this service might ultimately become over-subscribed by the new breed of licensed operators, as has evidently happened in Holland. At the time of writing this is less of a concern for the govern-ment than the embarrassment of having no facilities in place to tackle the problem-a situation which might easily be repeated over the issue of scrap cars and waste electrical and electronic equipment when new recycling regulations come into force (see e.g. *Guardian*, 2 February 2002).

4

The Macroeconomic Environment

INTRODUCTION

In September 1992, following a period of sustained turbulence on the foreign exchanges, the British government decided to withdraw sterling from what was then known as the Exchange Rate Mechanism (ERM) of the European Monetary System (EMS). As a result, the value of the pound continued to fall against a number of curren-cies, particularly the Deutschmark (DM) and large-scale speculation against sterling forced its value down to a level well below its previously agreed 'floor' in the ERM. Freed from the constraints of the ERM, the British government announced a series of cuts in interest rates in an effort to boost the British economy, which at the time was in the midst of a substantial recession. These cuts in interest rates-together with the more favourable exporting conditions resulting from a weaker pound-were welcomed by most British businesses, which were struggling to find customers. At the same time, a number of influential commentators from both the academic and the business world warned of the likelihood of increased inflation in the future as a result of dearer import prices and of the uncertainties caused by a free floating currency. Business leaders, in particular, called for a statement of government intentions and for a clear guide to future government economic policy with regard to inflation, recession and membership of the ERM. Over a decade later, Britain still retains a measure of independence in cur-rency matters, having declined to commit itself to adopting the 'Euro' in the first wave of monetary union within the EU.

What this simple example is designed to demonstrate is the intimate relationship between business activity and the wider economic context in which it takes place, and a glance at any quality newspaper will provide a range of similar illustrations of this interface between business and economics. What is important at this point is not to understand the complexities of exchange rate systems or their effect on businesses, but to appreciate in broad terms the importance of the macroeconomic environment for business organisations and, in particular, the degree of compatibility between the preoccupations of the entrepreneur and those of the economist.

To the economist, for example, a recession is generally marked by falling demand, rising unemployment, a slowing down in economic growth and a fall in investment. To the firm, it usually implies a loss of orders, a likely reduction in the work-force, a decline in output (or a growth in stocks) and a general reluctance to invest in capital equipment and/or new projects.

Much of the detailed discussion of the economic aspects of business can be found in Parts Three and Four. In this chapter the focus is on the broader question of the eco-nomic structure and processes of a market-based economy and on the macroeconomic influences affecting and being affected by business activity in this type of economic system. As suggested in the previous chapter, an understanding of the overall economic context within which businesses operate and its core values and principles is central to any meaningful analysis of the business environment.

Three further points are worth highlighting at this juncture. First, business activity not only is shaped by the economic context in which it takes place, but helps to shape that context; consequently the success or otherwise of government economic policy depends to some degree on the reactions of both the firms and markets (e.g. the stock market) which are affected by government decisions. Second, economic influences operate at a variety of spatial levels-as illustrated by the plight of the pound-and governments can find that circumstances largely or totally beyond their control can affect businesses either favourably or adversely. Third, the economic (and for that matter, political) influence of industry and commerce can be considerable and this ensures that business organisations-both individually and collectively-usually consti-tute one of the chief pressure groups in democratic states. This political and economic relationship between government and business.

ECONOMIC SYSTEMS

The Concept of Economic Scarcity

Like 'politics', the term 'economic' tends to be used in a variety of ways and con-texts to describe certain aspects of human behaviour, ranging from activities such as producing, distributing and consuming, to the idea of frugality in the use of a resource (e.g. being 'economical' with the truth). Modern definitions stress how such behaviour, and the institutions in which it takes place (e.g. households, firms, governments, banks), are concerned with the satisfaction of human needs and wants through the transformation of resources into goods and services which are consumed by society. These processes are said to take place under conditions of 'economic scarcity'.

The economist's idea of 'scarcity' centres around the relationship between a society's needs and wants and the resources available to satisfy them. In essence, economists argue that whereas needs and wants tend to be unlimited, the resources which can be used to meet those needs and wants are finite and accordingly no society at any time has the capacity to provide for all its actual or potential requirements. The assumption here is that both individual and collective needs and wants consistently outstrip the means available to satisfy them, as exemplified, for instance, by the inability of govern-ments to provide instant health care, the best roads, education, defence, railways, and so on, at a time and place and of a quality convenient to the user. This being the case, 'choices' have to be made by both individuals and society concerning priorities in the use of resources, and every choice inevitably involves a 'sacrifice' (i.e. forgoing an alter-native). Economists describe this sacrifice as the 'opportunity cost' or 'real cost' of the decision that is taken (e.g. every pound spent on the health service is a pound not spent on some other public service) and it is one which is faced by individuals, organi-sations (including firms), governments and society alike.

From a societal point of view the existence of economic scarcity poses three seri-ous problems concerning the use of resources:

1 What to use the available resources for? That is, what goods and services should be produced (or not produced) with the resources (sometimes described as the 'guns v. butter' argument)?

2 How best to use those resources? For example, in what combinations, using what techniques and what methods?

3 How best to distribute the goods and services produced with them? That is, who gets what, how much and on what basis?

In practice, of course, these problems tend to be solved in a variety of ways, includ-ing barter (voluntary, bilateral exchange), price signals and the market, queuing and rationing, government instruction and corruption (e.g. resources allocated in exchange for personal favours), and examples of each of these solutions can be found in most, if not all, societies, at all times. Normally, however, one or other main approach to resource allocation tends to predominate and this allows analyti-cal distinctions to be made between different types of economic system. One important distinction is between those economies which are centrally planned and those which operate predominantly through market forces, with prices forming the integrating mechanism. Understanding this distinction is fundamental to an exam-ination of the way in which business is conducted and represents the foundation on which much of the subsequent analysis is built.

The Centrally Planned Economy

In this type of economic system-associated with the post-Second World War socialist economies of eastern Europe, China, Cuba and elsewhere-most of the key decisions on production are taken by a central planning authority, normally the state and its agencies. Under this arrangement, the state typically:

- owns and/or controls the main economic resources;
- establishes priorities in the use of those resources;
- sets output targets for businesses which are largely under state ownership and/or control;
- directs resources in an effort to achieve these predetermined targets; and
- seeks to co-ordinate production in such a way as to ensure consistency between output and input demands.

The fact that an economy is centrally planned does not necessarily imply that all eco-nomic decisions are taken at central level; in many cases decision making may be devolved to subordinate agencies, including local committees and enterprises. Ultimately however, these agencies are responsible to the centre and it is the latter which retains overall control of the economy and directs the use of scarce productive resources.

The problem of co-ordinating inputs and output in a modern planned economy is, of course, a daunting task and one which invariably involves an array of state planners and a central plan or blueprint normally covering a number of years (e.g. a five-year plan). Under such a plan, the state planners would establish annual output targets for each sector of the economy and for each enterprise within the sector and would identify the inputs of materials, labour and capital needed to achieve the set targets and would allocate resources accordingly. Given that the outputs of some industries (e.g. agricultural machinery) are the inputs of others (e.g. collective farms), it is not difficult to see how the overall effectiveness of the plan would depend in part on a high degree of co-operation and co-ordination between sectors and enterprises, as well as on good judgement, good decisions and a considerable element of good luck. The available evidence from planned economies suggests that none of these can be taken for granted and each is often in short supply.

Even in the most centralised of economies, state planning does not normally extend to telling individuals what they must buy in shops or how to use their labour, although an element of state direction at times may exist (e.g. conscription of the armed forces). Instead, it tends to condition *what* is available for purchase and the *prices* at which exchange takes place, and both of these are essentially the outcome of political choices, rather than a reflection of consumer demands. All too often consumers tend to be faced by queues and 'black markets' for some consumer products and overproduction of others, as state enterprises strive to meet targets frequently unrelated to the needs and wants of consumers. By the same token, businesses which make losses do not have to close down, as the state would nor-mally make additional funds available to cover any difference between sales revenue and costs. This being the case, the emphasis at firm level tends to be more on meeting targets than on achieving efficiency in the use of resources and hence a considerable degree of duplication and wastage tends to occur.

In such an environment, the traditional entrepreneurial skills of efficient resource management, price setting and risk taking have little, if any, scope for development and managers behave essentially as technicians and bureaucrats, administering decisions largely made elsewhere. Firms, in effect, are mainly ser-vants of the state and their activities are conditioned by social and political considerations, rather than by the needs of the market-although some market activity normally occurs in planned economies (especially in agriculture and a number of private services). Accordingly, businesses and their employees are not fully sensitised to the needs of the consumer and as a result quality and choice (where it exists) may suffer, particularly where incentives to improved efficiency and performance are negligible. Equally, the system tends to encourage bribery and corruption and the development of a substantial black market, with differences in income, status and political influence being an important determinant of individ-ual consumption and of living standards.

The Free-market Economy

The free-market (or capitalist) economy stands in direct contrast to the centrally planned system. Whereas in the latter the state controls most economic decisions, in the former the key economic agencies are private individuals (sometimes called 'households') and firms, and these interact in free markets, through a system of prices, to determine the allocation of resources.

The key features of this type of economic system are as follows:

- Resources are in private ownership and the individuals owning them are free to use them as they wish.
- Firms, also in private ownership, are equally able to make decisions on produc-tion, free from state interference.
- No blueprint (or master plan) exists to direct production and consumption.
- Decisions on resource allocation are the result of a decentralised system of mar-kets and prices, in which the decisions of millions of consumers and hundreds of thousands of firms are automatically co-ordinated.
- The consumer is sovereign, i.e. dictates the pattern of supply and hence the pat-tern of resource allocation.

In short, the three problems of what to produce, how to produce and how to distribute are solved by market forces.

The basic operation of a market economy. In essence individuals are owners of resources (e.g. labour) and consumers of products; firms are users of resources and producers of products. What products are produced-and hence how resources are used-depends on consumers, who indicate their demands by purchasing (i.e. paying the price) or not purchasing, and this acts as a signal to producers to acquire the resources necessary (i.e. pay the price) to meet the preferences of consumers. If consumer demands change, for whatever reason, this will cause an automatic reallocation of resources, as firms respond to the new market condi-tions. Equally, competition between producers seeking to gain or retain customers is said to guarantee that resources are used efficiently and to ensure that the most appro-priate production methods (i.e. how to produce) are employed in the pursuit of profits.

The distribution of output is also determined by market forces, in this case oper-ating in the markets for productive services. Individuals supplying a resource (e.g. labour) receive an income (i.e. a price) from the firms using that resource and this allows them to purchase goods and services in the markets for products, which in turn provides an income for firms that can be spent on the purchase of further resources. Should the demand for a particular type of productive resource increase-say, as a result of an increase in the demand for the product pro-duced by that resource-the price paid to the provider of the resource will tend to rise and hence, other things being equal, allow more output to be purchased. Concomitantly it is also likely to result in a shift of resources from uses which are relatively less lucrative to those which are relatively more rewarding.

This matching of supply and demand through prices in markets and the analysis can also be applied to the market for foreign currencies. In practice, of course, no economy operates entirely in the manner suggested above; firms after all are influenced by costs and supply decisions as well as by demand and generally seek to shape that demand, as well as simply responding to it. Nor for that matter is a market-based economy devoid of government involvement in the process of resource allocation, as evidenced by the existence of a public sector responsible for substantial levels of consumption and output and for helping to shape the conditions under which the private sector operates.

In short, any study of the market economy needs to incorporate the role of government and to examine, in par-ticular, its influence on the activities of both firms and households. Such an analysis can be found below in the later sections of this chapter.

EASTERN EUROPE: ECONOMIES IN TRANSITION

The political and economic disintegration of eastern Europe in the late 1980s pro-vides an excellent historical example of the difficulties faced by states moving from one form of economic system to another.

Prior to the collapse of the old order, the communist states of eastern Europe had systems of centralised state planning basically of the type described above, although some countries, especially Hungary, were experimenting with various forms of free enterprise. Growing dissatisfaction with the command system, and in particular with its failure to deliver living standards equivalent to those being enjoyed at the time by most citizens in the market economies of western Europe, gave rise to demands for reform, and these were translated into political action with the elec-tion of Mikhail Gorbachev to the post of Soviet leader in the mid-1980s. Gorbachev's programme of economic reconstruction *(perestroika)* signalled the start of a move towards a more market-based economic system and this was bolstered by his commit-ment to greater openness *(glasnost)* and democratic reform. By the late 1980s and early 1990s, the old Soviet empire had effectively ceased to exist and the newly inde-pendent states, almost without exception, had committed themselves to radical economic change of a kind unthinkable just a few years before.

Table 4.1: Comparative economic indicators, 1988

	Population (million)	*GDP ($ billion)*	*GDP per capita ($)*
East Germany	17	156	9360
Czechoslovakia	16	118	7600
Hungary	11	69	6500
Bulgaria	9	51	5630
Poland	37	207	5540
Romania	23	94	4120
European Union	325	4745	14609
West Germany	61	1202	19575

Source: *The Amex Bank Review,* November 1989.

For states anxious to move from an entrenched system of state planning to a market-based economic system, the obstacles have proved formidable and have helped to slow down the progress of economic (and political) reform in some coun-tries. Among the problems faced by eastern European countries in the transitionary phase have been:

- The need to create a legal and commercial framework to support the change to a market economy (e.g. company laws, laws on property rights, competition, external trade, the development of an appropriate accounting system).
- The need to establish different forms of free enterprise and to develop financial institutions capable of providing risk and venture capital, at commercial rates of return.
- The need to develop truly competitive markets, free from state control and pro-tection.
- The need to liberalise labour markets and to develop entrepreneurial skills in a workforce traditionally demotivated by the old bureaucratic system.
- The need to allow prices to move to levels determined by market forces, rather than by political decision.
- The need to achieve macroeconomic stability as markets become more open both internally and externally.
- The need to reduce the burden of international debt.
- The need to attract substantial overseas investment to assist in the rebuilding of the collapsed old socialist economies.

Meeting these requirements has not been made any easier by economic collapse and the perceived need on the part of some reformers to bring about rapid eco-nomic change whatever the consequences. In Russia, in particular, widespread bribery, corruption and criminal activity have helped to undermine an economy struggling with economic and political instability that appears endemic.

Evidence suggests that, given these and other requirements, the process of sys-temic change is destined to be long and painful and will be subject to political as well as economic developments, many of which are as yet unpredictable. Central to this process will be the attitude of western countries towards such issues as debt relief, financial assistance, investment and other forms of help, and perhaps under-standably the approach thus far has been relatively cautious, particularly given the relative uncertainty that comes from dealing with countries historically perceived to be adversaries. For example, a contemporary analysis by the accountants Ernst & Young in 1992 suggested that the uncertainty was at its greatest in countries such as Russia, Ukraine and Albania and at its least in Hungary, the then Czechoslovakia and Poland, where reforms were often further down the road (see Table 4.2). Hungary's high notional score, for instance, was justified by its relative degree of political and economic stability and its favourable attitude to foreign investment, backed by a legal framework to encourage it. In contrast, in Albania-one of the most rigid of the old communist regimes-political and economic instability, lim-ited business opportunities and a reluctance to change were seen as considerable obstacles to involvement on the part of western companies and governments.

Table 4.2 : Eastern Europe: A comparative risk analysis

	Business opportunities	*Political risk*	*Credit rating*	*Status of economy*	*Stability of local economy*	*Business infrastructure*	*Total*
Hungary	2	1	2	3	2	2	12
Czechoslovakia	2	3	2	3	2	2	14
Poland	2	3	3	3	3	2	16
Baltic States	4	3	3	4	3	3	20
Bulgaria	4	3	4	4	3	3	21
Romania	4	4	4	4	4	3	23
Russia and Ukraine 1	4	5	5	4	4	23	
Albania	5	4	4	5	5	4	27

Note: Countries are rated on a scale 1 to 5, where low scores are best and high scores worst. Source: Adapted from the *Daily Telegraph*, 13 May 1992.

With regard to western corporate involvement, in practice this has taken a variety of forms including direct acquisition, joint ventures (which tend to carry tax advan-tages) and the development of local distribution networks, and much of it has been undertaken by multinational companies seeking to establish market share and to gain low-cost production sites. Coca-Cola, Pepsico, Levi Strauss, Philip Morris, BAT, Mars, Unilever, McDonald's, Procter & Gamble and General Electric are just some of the organisations that have sought to take advantage of the growing demand for western consumer goods, and Hungary, Poland and the former Czechoslovakia have proved the most favourable locations for much of the investment.

How this interest in eastern Europe will develop in the future is still open to question, given the political developments in the Balkans and in the former Soviet Union and because of the severe economic problems arising from the move to a market-based system (e.g. hyperinflation). Some observers believe that in the cir-cumstances a policy of 'wait-and-see' is the best option for western companies looking for market expansion at a time of lower growth in their traditional markets. Others have argued that the risks involved are far outweighed by the potential ben-efits and that businesses willing to take a long-term view and commitment will come to dominate some of the fastest growing markets of the future, at the expense of competitors who are more cautious or conservative. The case for the optimists has undoubtedly been strengthened by the recent process of enlargement within the EU.

POLITICO-ECONOMIC SYNTHESIS

The economic problem of resource allocation, described above, clearly has a politi-cal dimension, given its focus on the ownership, control and use of wealth-producing assets within society. This allows links to be made between a country's chosen economic system and its political regime. A useful way of repre-senting possible relationships, political systems can be characterised as ranging from democratic to authoritarian, depending on the degree of public involvement in decision-making processes. Similarly, economic systems can be seen to range from free market to planned, according to the level of state intervention in the process of resource allocation. This two-dimensional model thus provides for four major combinations of politico-economic systems, ranging from democratic-free-market on the one hand (quadrant 1) to authoritarian-planned on the other (quadrant 3).

In applying this model to specific cases, it is clear that free-market approaches to resource allocation are predominantly associated with democratic states. Such a link is not surprising. Democracy, after all, includes the notion of individuals being able to express their preferences through the ballot box and having the opportunity to replace one government with another at periodic intervals. In free markets simi-lar processes are at work, with individuals effectively 'voting' for goods and services through the price system and their expressed preferences being reflected in the pat-tern of resource allocation.

A link between authoritarian regimes and planned economic systems can equally be rationalised, in that government control over the political system is considerably facilitated if it also directs the economy through the ownership and/or control of the means of production, distribution and exchange. In effect, the relative absence of democratic mechanisms, such as free elections and choice between alternative forms of government, is echoed in the economic sphere by the inability of individ-uals to exercise any real influence over resource allocation. At the extreme, this could involve a government ban on any forms of free enterprise and total govern-ment control of the pattern of output and consumption in an economy which is devoid of effective consumer sovereignty.

In practice, of course, the picture is much more complicated than suggested by this simple dichotomy. Some authoritarian states, for instance, have predominantly capitalist economic systems (quadrant 4), while some democratic countries have a substantial degree of government intervention (i.e. moving them towards quadrant 2), either by choice or from necessity (e.g. wartime). Added to this, even in states where the political or economic system appears to be the same, considerable differ-ences can occur at an operational and/or institutional level and this gives each country a degree of uniqueness not adequately portrayed by the model. That said, it is still the case that the basic congruity between democracy and free-market sys-tems represents a powerful and pervasive influence in the business environment of the world's principal democratic states. The process of economic reform-as in east-ern Europe-accordingly tends to be accompanied by corresponding pressures for political change and these are often resisted by regimes not prepared to give up their political and economic powers and their élite status.

THE MACROECONOMY

Levels of Analysis

As indicated above, economics is concerned with the study of how society deals with the problem of scarcity and the resultant problems of what to produce, how to produce and how to distribute. Within this broad framework the economist typi-cally distinguishes between two types of analysis:

1 Microeconomic analysis, which is concerned with the study of economic deci-sion taking by both individuals and firms.

2 Macroeconomic analysis, which is concerned with interactions in the economy as a whole (i.e. with economic aggregates).

The microeconomic approach is exemplified by the analysis of markets and prices undertaken, for example, how individual consumers in the market for beer might be affected by a price change. This analysis could be extended to an investigation of how the total market might respond to a move-ment in the price, or how a firm's (or market's) decisions on supply are affected by changes in wage rates or production techniques or some other factor. Note that in these examples, the focus of attention is on decision taking by individuals and firms in a single industry, while interactions between this industry and the rest of the economy are ignored: in short, this is what economists call a 'partial analysis'.

In reality, of course, all sectors of the economy are interrelated to some degree. A pay award, for example, in the beer industry (or in a single firm) may set a new pay norm that workers in other industries take up and these pay increases may subse-quently influence employment, production and consumer demand in the economy as a whole, which could also have repercussions on the demand for beer. Sometimes such repercussions may be relatively minor and so effectively can be ignored. In such situations the basic microeconomic approach remains valid.

In contrast, macroeconomics recognises the interdependent nature of markets and studies the interaction in the economy as a whole, dealing with such questions as the overall level of employment, the rate of inflation, the percentage growth of output in the economy and many other economy-wide aggregates-exemplified, for instance, by the analysis of international trade in Chapter 14 and by the macro-economic model discussed below. It should be pointed out, however, that while the distinction between the micro and macro approaches remains useful for analytical purposes, in many instances the two become intertwined. UK Chancellor Nigel Lawson's decision (in 1988) to cut the top rate of income tax from 60 per cent to 40 per cent was presented at the time as a means of boosting the economy by provid-ing incentives for entrepreneurs-clearly a macroeconomic proposition. However, to investigate the validity of the Chancellor's view, it is necessary to lean heavily on microeconomic analysis to see how lower taxation might influence, say, an individ-ual's preference for work over leisure. Given that macroeconomic phenomena are the result of aggregating the behaviour of individual firms and consumers, this is obviously a common situation and one which is useful to bear in mind in any study of either the firm or the economy as a whole.

The 'Flows' of Economic Activity

Economic activity can be portrayed as a flow of economic resources into firms (i.e. productive organisations), which are used to produce output for consumption, and a corresponding flow of payments from firms to the providers of those resources, who use them primarily to purchase the goods and services produced. These flows of resources, production, income and expenditure accordingly represent the fundamen-tal activities of an economy at work. The flow of resources and of goods and services in the economy-what economists describe as 'real flows'.

In effect, firms use economic resources to produce goods and services, which are consumed by private individuals (private domestic consumption) or government (government consumption) or by overseas purchasers (foreign consumption) or by other firms (capital formation). This consumption gives rise to a flow of expendi-tures that represents an income for firms, which they use to purchase further resources in order to produce further output for consumption.

The interrelationship between income flows and real flows can be seen by combin-ing the two diagrams into one, which for the sake of simplification assumes only two groups operate in the economy: firms as producers and users of resources, and private individuals as consumers and providers of those resources. Real flows are shown by the arrows moving in an anti-clockwise direction; income flows by the arrows flowing in a clockwise direction.

Despite a degree of over-simplification, the model of the economy illustrated in Figure 4.5 is a useful analytical tool which highlights some vitally important aspects of economic activity which are of direct relevance to the study of business. The model shows, for example, that:

1 Income flows around the economy, passing from households to firms and back to households and on to firms, and so on, and these income flows have corre-sponding real flows of resources, goods and services.

2 What constitutes an income to one group (e.g. firms) represents an expenditure to another (e.g. households), indicating that

income generation in the economy is related to spending on consumption of goods and services and on resources (e.g. the use of labour).

3 The output of firms must be related to expenditure by households on goods and services, which in turn is related to the income the latter receive from supplying resources.

4 The use of resources (including the number of jobs created in the economy) must also be related to expenditure by households on consumption, given that resources are used to produce output for sale to households.

5 Levels of income, output, expenditure and employment in the economy are, in effect, interrelated.

From the point of view of firms, it is clear from the model that their fortunes are intimately connected with the spending decisions of households and any changes in the level of spending can have repercussions for business activity at the micro as well as the macro level. In the late 1980s, for instance, the British economy went into recession, largely as a result of a reduction in the level of consumption that was brought about by a combination of high interest rates, a growing burden of debt from previous bouts of consumer spending, and a decline in demand from some overseas markets also suffering from recession. While many businesses man-aged to survive the recession, either by drawing from their reserves or slimming down their operations, large numbers of firms went out of business, as orders fell and costs began to exceed revenue. As a result, output in the economy fell, unem-ployment grew, investment by firms declined, and house prices fell to a point where some houseowners owed more on their mortgage than the value of their property (known as 'negative equity'). The combined effect of these outcomes was to further depress demand, as individuals became either unwilling or unable to increase spending and as firms continued to shed labour and to hold back on investment. By late 1992, few real signs of growth in the economy could be detected, unemployment stood at almost 3 million, and business confidence remained persistently low.

The gradual recovery of the British economy from mid-1993-brought about by a return in consumer confidence in the wake of a cut in interest rates-further emphasises the key link between consumption and entrepreneurial activity high-lighted in the model. Equally, it shows, as did the discussion on the recession, that a variety of factors can affect spending (e.g. government policy on interest rates) and that spending by households is only one type of consumption in the real econ-omy. In order to gain a clearer view of how the economy works and why changes occur over time, it is necessary to refine the basic model by incorporating a number of other key variables influencing economic activity. These variables-which include savings, investment spending, government spending, taxation and overseas trade-are discussed below.

Changes in Economic Activity

The level of spending by consumers on goods and services produced by indigenous firms is influenced by a variety of factors. For a start, most households pay tax on income earned, which has the effect of reducing the level of income available for consumption. Added to this, some consumers prefer to save (i.e. not spend) a pro-portion of their income or to spend it on imported products, both of which mean that the income of domestic firms is less than it would have been had the income been spent with them. Circumstances such as these represent what economists call a 'leakage' (or 'withdrawal') from the circular flow of income and help to explain why the revenue of businesses can fluctuate over time.

At the same time as such 'leakages' are occurring, additional forms of spending in the economy are helping to boost the potential income of domestic firms. Savings by some consumers are often borrowed by firms to spend on investment in capital equipment or plant or premises (known as investment spending) and this generates income for firms producing capital goods. Similarly, governments use tax-ation to spend on the provision of public goods and services (public or government expenditure) and overseas buyers purchase products produced by indigenous firms (export spending). Together, these additional forms of spending represent an 'injec-tion' of income into the circular flow.

While the revised model of the economy illustrated in Figure 4.7 is still highly simplified (e.g. consumers also borrow savings to spend on consumption or imports; firms also save and buy imports; governments also invest in capital proj-ects), it demonstrates quite clearly that fluctuations in the level of economic activity are the result of changes in a number of variables, many of which are out-side the control of firms or governments. Some of these changes are autonomous (i.e. spontaneous), as in the case of an increased demand for imports, while others may be deliberate or overt, as when the government decides to increase its own spending or to reduce taxation in order to stimulate demand. Equally, from time to time an economy may be subject to 'external shocks', such as the onset of recession among its principal trading partners or a significant price rise in a key commodity (e.g. the oil price rise in the 1970s), which can have an important effect on internal income flows. Taken together, these and other changes help to explain why demand for goods and services constantly fluctuates and why changes occur not only in an economy's capacity to produce output, but also in its structure and per-formance over time.

It is important to recognise that where changes in spending do occur, these invariably have consequences for the economy that go beyond the initial 'injec-tion' or 'withdrawal' of income. For example, a decision by government to increase spending on infrastructure would benefit the firms involved in the various projects.

GLOBAL ECONOMIC CRISIS

Throughout the 1980s and early 1990s the Asian Tiger economies-Indonesia, Hong Kong, Malaysia, Singapore, South Korea, Taiwan and Thailand-were widely regarded as an unqualified success story with their rapid rates of growth and booming stock markets. As exemplars of free-market capitalism, these economies had an enviable reputation in the west and attracted considerable funds from foreign investors. This miracle began to unravel in 1997 with the onset of an economic crisis in the Far East which sent shock waves throughout the world financial system.

The roots of the crisis appear to lie in unregulated investment decisions which ultimately resulted in the inability of the Tiger economies to protect their currencies which at the time were pegged against the US dollar. Following the collapse of a number of Thai property companies which had overextended themselves in the boom times and the subsequent withdrawal of loans by an increasing number of foreign investors, the Thai government was forced to let the currency (the baht) float. As the speculators gathered, other currencies came under pressure and were ultimately forced to give up the dollar peg. As currency values collapsed and forced up the size of multibillion-dollar loans, foreign investors rapidly withdrew their funds, resulting in a collapse on Asian stock markets which spread to London, New York and elsewhere, provoking fears of a worldwide recession.

The Asian crisis was followed in 1998 by the collapse of the Russian rouble which also came under speculative attack. The subsequent announcement by the Russian government that it was to devalue the currency and to suspend repaying its foreign debts simply convinced investors that emerging markets were too risky an investment and other countries' currencies came under pressure, particularly Brazil. Understandably the American stock market reacted very unfavourably to the problem in Latin America and share prices plummeted, sparking off similar falls on other stock exchanges across the globe.

Fears that the global economic crisis could plunge the whole world into recession gradually subsided, but we should not underestimate the human cost of the problems in the countries affected by economic collapse, particularly widespread job loss and growing poverty. Nor should we forget that our own economy and its business felt the effect, whether from deferred investment by Far Eastern companies, lost trade, bad debts or reduced overseas earnings for UK multinationals. As economies across the globe become increasingly interlinked, economic collapse in one country or region spreads to other parts of the world. Arguably this makes the role of international institutions such as the IMF and the World Bank more rather than less relevant in the twenty-first century. and some of the additional income they receive would undoubtedly be spent on hiring labour. The additional workers employed would have more income to spend on consumption and this would boost the income for firms producing consumer goods, which in turn may hire more staff, generating further consumption and so on. In short, the initial increase in spending by government will have additional effects on income and spending in the economy, as the extra spending circulates from households to firms and back again. Economists refer to this as the 'multiplier effect' to emphasise the reverberative consequences of any increase or decrease in spending by consumers, firms, governments or overseas buyers.

Multiple increases in income and consumption can also give rise to an 'accelera-tor effect', which is the term used to describe a change in investment spending by firms as a result of a change in consumer spending. In the example above it is pos-sible that the increase in consumption caused by the increase in government spending may persuade some firms to invest in more stock and capital equipment to meet increased consumer demands. Demand for capital goods will therefore rise, and this could cause further increases in the demand for industrial products (e.g. components, machinery) and also for consumer goods, as firms seek to increase their output to meet the changing market conditions. Should consumer spending fall, a reverse accelerator may occur and the same would apply to the multiplier as the reduction in consumption reverberates through the economy and causes fur-ther cuts in both consumption and investment. As Peter Donaldson has suggested, everything in the economy affects everything else; the economy is dynamic, inter-active and mobile and is far more complex than implied by the model used in the analysis above.

GOVERNMENT AND THE MACROECONOMY: OBJECTIVES

Notwithstanding the complexities of the real economy, the link between business activity and spending is clear to see. This spending, as indicated above, comes from consumers, firms, governments and external sources and collectively can be said to represent total demand in the economy for goods and services. Economists fre-quently indicate this with the following notation:

Aggregate Monetary Demand = Consumer spending + Investment spending + Government spending + Export spending-Import spending

or AMD = C + I + G + X-M

Within this equation, consumer spending (C) is regarded as by far the most impor-tant factor in determining the level of total demand.

While economists might disagree about what are the most significant influences on the component elements of AMD, it is widely accepted that governments have a crucial role to play in shaping demand, not only in their own sector but also on the market side of the economy. Government policies on spending and taxation or on interest rates clearly have both direct and indirect influences on the behaviour of individuals and firms, which can affect both the demand and supply side of the economy in a variety of ways. Underlying these policies are a number of key objec-tives which are pursued by government as a prerequisite to a healthy economy and which help to guide the choice of policy options. Understanding the broad choice of policies available to government, and the objectives associated with them, is of prime importance to students of the business environment.

Most governments appear to have a number of key economic objectives, the most important of which are normally the control of inflation, the pursuit of eco-nomic growth, a reduction in unemployment, the achievement of an acceptable balance of payments situation, controlling public (i.e. government) borrowing, and a relatively stable exchange rate.

Controlling Inflation

Inflation is usually defined as an upward and persistent movement in the general level of prices over a given period of time; it can also be characterised as a fall in the value of money. For governments of all political complexions reducing such movements to a minimum is seen as a primary economic objective (e.g. the current UK government's target for 'underlying inflation' was 2.5 per cent. Under the new Consumer Prices Index the target is now 2 per cent).

Monitoring trends in periodic price movements tends to take a number of forms; in the UK these include:

1 The use of a Retail Price Index (RPI), which measures how an average family's spending on goods and services is affected by price changes. The RPI has tradi-tionally been the measure used for 'headline inflation' in the UK and includes mortgage interest payments.

2 An examination of the 'underlying rate of inflation', which excludes the effects of mortgage payments (known as RPIX in the UK).

3 Measuring 'factory gate prices', to indicate likely future changes in consumer prices.

4 Comparing domestic inflation rates with those of the United Kingdom's chief overseas competitors, as an indication of the international competitiveness of UK firms.

With regard to the latter, the UK has recently introduced a new measure of infla-tion known as the Consumer Prices Index (CPI) to allow for a more direct comparison of the inflation rate in the UK with that of the rest of Europe. The CPI excludes a number of items that have historically been part of the RPIX, especially items relating to housing costs (e.g. mortgage interest payments and council tax).

In addition, changes in monetary aggregates, which measure the amount of money (and therefore potential spending power) in circulation in the economy, and movements of exchange rates are also seen as a guide to possible future price increases, as their effects work through the economy.

Explanations as to why prices tend to rise over time vary considerably, but broadly speaking fall into two main categories. First, supply-siders tend to focus on rising pro-duction costs-particularly wages, energy and imported materials-as a major reason for inflation, with firms passing on increased costs to the consumer in the form of higher wholesale and/or retail prices. Second, demand-siders, in contrast, tend to emphasise the importance of excessive demand in the economy, brought about, for example, by tax cuts, cheaper borrowing or excessive government spending, which encourages firms to take advantage of the consumer's willingness to spend money by increasing their prices. Where indigenous firms are unable to satisfy all the additional demand, the tendency is for imports to increase. This not only may cause further price rises, particularly if imported goods are more expensive or if exchange rate movements become unfavourable, but also can herald a deteriorating balance of pay-ments situation and difficult trading conditions for domestic businesses.

Government concern with inflation-which crosses both party and state bound-aries-reflects the fact that rising price levels can have serious consequences for the economy in general and for businesses in particular, especially if a country's domestic inflation rates are significantly higher than those of its main competitors. In markets where price is an important determinant of demand, rising prices may result in some businesses losing sales, and this can affect turnover and may ultimately affect employ-ment if firms reduce their labour force in order to reduce their costs. Added to this, the uncertainty caused by a difficult trading environment may make some businesses unwilling to invest in new plant and equipment, particularly if interest rates are high and if inflation looks unlikely to fall for some time. Such a response, while under-standable, is unlikely to improve a firm's future competitiveness or its ability to exploit any possible increases in demand as market conditions change. Rising prices may also affect businesses by encouraging employees to seek higher wages in order to maintain or increase their living standards. Where firms agree to such wage increases, the temptation, of course, is to pass this on to the consumer in the form of a price rise, especially if demand looks unlikely to be affected to any great extent. Should this process occur generally in the economy, the result may be a wages/prices inflationary spiral, in which wage increases push up prices which push up wage increases which further push up prices and so on. From an interna-tional competitive point of view, such an occurrence, if allowed to continue unchecked, could be disastrous for both firms and the economy.

Economic Growth

Growth is an objective shared by governments and organisations alike. For govern-ments, the aim is usually to achieve steady and sustained levels of non-inflationary growth, preferably led by exports (i.e. export-led growth). Such growth is normally indi-cated by annual increases in real national income or gross domestic product (where 'real' = allowing for inflation, and 'gross domestic product (GDP)' = the economy's annual output of goods and services measured in monetary terms). To compensate for changes in the size of the population, growth rates tend to be expressed in terms of real national income per capita (i.e. real GDP divided by population).

Exactly what constitutes desirable levels of growth is difficult to say, except in very broad terms. If given a choice, governments would basically prefer:

- steady levels of real growth (e.g. 3-4 per cent p.a.), rather than annual increases in output which vary widely over the business cycle;
- growth rates higher than those of one's chief competitors; and
- growth based on investment in technology and on increased export sales, rather than on excessive government spending or current consumption.

It is worth remembering that, when measured on a monthly or quarterly basis, increases in output can occur at a declining rate and GDP growth can become nega-tive. In the United Kingdom, for example, a recession is said to exist following two consecutive quarters of negative GDP.

From a business point of view, the fact that increases in output are related to increases in consumption suggests that economic growth is good for business prospects and hence for investment and employment, and by and large this is the case. The rising living standards normally associated with such growth may, how-ever, encourage increased consumption of imported goods and services at the expense of indigenous producers, to a point where some domestic firms are forced out of business and the economy's manufacturing base becomes significantly reduced (often called deindustrialisation) Equally, if increased consumption is based largely on excessive state spending, the potential gains for businesses may be offset by the need to increase interest rates to fund that spending (where govern-ment borrowing is involved) and by the tendency of government demands for funding to 'crowd out' the private sector's search for investment capital. In such cases, the short-term benefits from government-induced consumption may be more than offset by the medium-and long-term problems for the economy that are likely to arise.

Where growth prospects for the economy look good, business confidence tends to increase, and this is often reflected in increased levels of investment and stock holding and ultimately in levels of employment. In Britain, for example, the monthly and quarterly surveys by the Confederation of British Industry (CBI) pro-vide a good indication of how output, investment and stock levels change at different points of the business cycle and these are generally seen as a good indica-tion of future business trends, as interpreted by entrepreneurs. Other indicators-including the state of the housing market and construction generally-help to pro-vide a guide to the current and future state of the economy, including its prospects for growth in the short and medium term.

Reducing Unemployment

In most democratic states the goal of 'full employment' is no longer part of the politi-cal agenda; instead government pronouncements on employment tend to focus on job creation and maintenance and on developing the skills appropriate to future demands. The consensus seems to be that in technologically advanced market-based economies some unemployment is inevitable and that the basic aim should be to reduce unemployment to a level which is both politically and socially acceptable. As with growth and inflation, unemployment levels tend to be measured at regu-lar intervals (e.g. monthly, quarterly, annually) and the figures are often adjusted to take into account seasonal influences (e.g. school-leavers entering the job market). In addition, the statistics usually provide information on trends in long-term unemployment, areas of skill shortage and on international comparisons, as well as sectoral changes within the economy. All of these indicators provide clues to the current state of the economy and to the prospects for businesses in the coming months and years, but need to be used with care. Unemployment, for example, tends to continue rising for a time even when a recession is over; equally, it is not uncommon for government definitions of unemployment to change or for interna-tional unemployment data to be based on different criteria.

The broader social and economic consequences of high levels of unemployment are well documented: it is a waste of resources, it puts pressure on the public serv-ices and on the Exchequer (e.g. by reducing tax yields and increasing public expenditure on welfare provision), and it is frequently linked with growing social and health problems. Its implication for businesses, however, tends to be less clear-cut. On the one hand, a high level of unemployment implies a pool of labour available for firms seeking workers (though not necessarily with the right skills), generally at wage levels lower than when a shortage of labour occurs. On the other hand, it can also give rise to a fall in overall demand for goods and services which could exacerbate any existing deflationary forces in the economy, causing further unemployment and with it further reductions in demand. Where this occurs, econ-omists tend to describe it as cyclical unemployment (i.e. caused by a general deficiency in demand) in order to differentiate it from unemployment caused by a deficiency in demand for the goods produced by a particular industry (structural unemployment) or by the introduction of new technology which replaces labour (technological unemployment).

A Favourable Balance of Payments

A country's balance of payments is essentially the net balance of credits (earnings) and debits (payments) arising from its international trade over a given period of time. Where credits exceed debits a balance of payments surplus exists; the opposite is described as a deficit. Understandably governments tend to prefer either equilibrium in the balance of payments or surpluses, rather than deficits. However, it would be fair to say that for some governments facing persist-ent balance of payments deficits, a sustained reduction in the size of the deficit may be regarded as signifying a 'favourable' balance of payments situation.

Like other economic indicators, the balance of payments statistics come in a variety of forms and at different levels of disaggregation, allowing useful compar-isons to be made not only on a country's comparative trading performance, but also on the international competitiveness of particular industries and commodity groups or on the development or decline of specific external markets. Particular emphasis tends to be given to the balance of payments on current account, which measures imports and exports of goods and services and is thus seen as an indicator of the competitiveness of an economy's firms and industries. Sustained current account surpluses tend to suggest favourable trading conditions, which can help to boost growth, increase employment and investment and create a general feeling of confidence amongst the business community. They may also give rise to surpluses which domestic firms can use to finance overseas lending and investment, thus helping to generate higher levels of corporate foreign earnings in future years.

While it does not follow that a sustained current account deficit is inevitably bad for the country concerned, it often implies structural problems in particular sectors of its economy or possibly an exchange rate which favours importers rather than exporters. Many observers believe, for instance, that the progressive decline of Britain's visible trading position after 1983 was an indication of the growing uncompetitiveness of its firms, particularly those producing finished manufactured goods for consumer markets at home and abroad. By the same token, Japan's cur-rent account trade surplus of around $120 billion in late 1995 was portrayed as a sign of the cut-throat competition of Japanese firms, particularly those involved in producing cars, electrical and electronic products, and photographic equipment.

Controlling Public Borrowing

Governments raise large amounts of revenue annually, mainly through taxation, and use this income to spend on a wide variety of public goods and services. Where annual revenue exceeds government spending, a budget surplus occurs and the excess is often used to repay past debt (formerly known in the United Kingdom as the 'public sector debt repayment' or PSDR). The accumulated debt of past and present governments represents a country's National Debt.

In practice, most governments often face annual budget deficits rather than budget surpluses and hence have a 'public sector borrowing requirement' or PSBR (now known in the UK as 'public sector net borrowing' or PSNB). While such deficits are not inevitably a problem, in the same way that a small personal over-draft is not necessarily critical for an individual, large scale and persistent deficits are generally seen as a sign of an economy facing current and future difficulties which require urgent government action. The overriding concern over high levels of public borrowing tends to be focused on:

1 Its impact on interest rates, given that higher interest rates tend to be needed to attract funds from private sector uses to public sector uses.

2 The impact of high interest rates on consumption and investment and hence on the prospects of businesses.

3 The danger of the public sector 'crowding out' the private sector's search for funds for investment.

4 The opportunity cost of debt interest, especially in terms of other forms of public spending.

5 The general lack of confidence in the markets about the government's ability to control the economy and the likely effect this might have on inflation, growth and the balance of payments.

6 The need to meet the 'convergence criteria' laid down at Maastricht for entry to the single currency (e.g. central government debt no higher than 3 per cent of GDP).

The consensus seems to be that controlling public borrowing is best tackled by restraining the rate of growth of public spending rather than by increasing revenue through changes in taxation, since the latter could depress demand.

A Stable Exchange Rate

A country's currency has two values: an internal value and an external value. Internally, its value is expressed in terms of the goods and services it can buy and hence it is affected by changes in domestic prices. Externally, its value is expressed as an 'exchange rate' which governs how much of another country's currency it can purchase (e.g. £1 = $1.50 or £1 = €1.63). Since foreign trade normally involves an exchange of currencies, fluctuations in the external value of a currency will influence the price of imports and exports and hence can affect the trading prospects for business, as well as a country's balance of payments and its rate of inflation.

On the whole, governments and businesses involved in international trade tend to prefer exchange rates to remain relatively stable, because of the greater degree of certainty this brings to the trading environment; it also tends to make overseas investors more confident that their funds are likely to hold their value. To this extent, schemes which seek to fix exchange rates within predetermined levels (e.g. the ERM), or which encourage the use of a common currency (e.g. the 'euro'), tend to have the support of the business community, which prefers predictability to uncertainty where trading conditions are concerned.

INDICATORS OF SUCCESS

Government success in managing the macroeconomy tends to be measured in terms of certain key economic indicators: most notably 'inflation', 'growth', 'unemployment' and 'international trade'. In mid-1996, for example, the Paris-based Organisation for Economic Co-operation and Development (OECD) reported that the prospects for the British economy in the short to medium term were very bright, thanks to an anticipated combination of the low inflation, falling unemployment and robust growth. Much of the UK's 'success' was attributed to the policy of labour market deregulation pursued by successive Conservative administrations. According to the OECD, labour market reforms had been responsible for creating a more conducive environment for employment than in many continental European countries and this was felt to be responsible for helping the UK to become more competitive in international markets.

Broader measures of performance can often paint a different picture. One such measure-produced by the International Institute for Management Development (IMD)-has examined the relative competitiveness of the leading world economies, using a wide range of indicators to assess an economy's strengths and weaknesses. Apart from standard measures such as GDP growth and export performance, the IMD survey took into account aspects as varied as investment in training, retaining and technology, management quality and public trust in bankers. Using these and other criteria, the 1996 IMD survey ranked the UK as 19th on the international scoreboard, compared to 15th in 1995 and 11th in 1989. By these measures Britain was becoming relatively less competitive and was clearly trailing the Asian 'Tiger' economies and many of its main European rivals (e.g. in 1996 Singapore was ranked 2nd; Hong Kong 3rd; Japan 4th; Denmark 5th; Luxembourg 8th; Germany 10th; Sweden 14th; Austria 16th; Belgium 17th; Taiwan 18th).

At the time the IMD defined competitiveness as being concerned with 'the ability of a country to create added value and... increase national wealth by managing assets and processes, attractiveness and aggressiveness, globality and proximity, and by integrating these relationships into an economic and social model'. A much simpler definition suggested by the World Economic Forum (WEF) related competitiveness to a country's ability to achieve sustained high rates of growth in GDP per capita. Under the WEF approach, countries were ranked according to around 150 criteria which were selected for their reliability and correlation with growth rates (e.g. tax levels, savings rates, human capital), with the different factors being weighted in relation to their perceived contribution to GDP growth. Thus the Forum's 1996 index* ranked the UK as 15th, well behind Singapore (1st), Hong Kong (2nd), Malaysia (10th) and the 'rising star' New Zealand (3rd). Interestingly, under the WEF index countries such as Germany (22nd) and Japan (13th) fared less well than under the IMD survey. In Germany's case, this seems to have reflected the additional weighting given by the Forum to relative labour market inflexibility and the impact on growth of a substantial welfare state. It probably also helps to explain why under the Forum's index the UK was rated higher relative to the rest of the EU than under the IMD report.

More recently the IMD and WEF measures of competitiveness have become more finely tuned. WEF, for instance, has enlisted staff from Harvard University-including Professor Michael Porter-to produce enhanced measures of global competitiveness based on two indices: one for 'current competitiveness' and one for 'growth competitiveness'. The former examines what underpins high current productivity and economic performance. The latter looks at the factors that contribute to the future growth of an economy, measured as the rate of change of GDP per person.

*WEF and IMD were originally partners in producing their annual world competitiveness report. They are now competitors!

GOVERNMENT AND THE MACROECONOMY: POLICIES

Governments throughout Europe and beyond play various key roles in their respec-tive economies. These include the following functions:

- consumer of resources (e.g. employer, landowner);
- supplier of resources (e.g. infrastructure, information);
- consumer of goods and services (e.g. government spending);
- supplier of goods and services (e.g. nationalised industries);
- regulator of business activity (e.g. employment laws, consumer laws);
- regulator of the economy (e.g. fiscal and monetary policies); and
- redistributor of income and wealth (e.g. taxation system).

The extent of these roles, and their impact on the economy in general and on busi-ness in particular, varies from country to country as well as over time.

Despite the economic significance of these roles, in most market-based economies democratically elected governments prefer levels and patterns of pro-duction and consumption to be determined largely by market forces, with a minimum of government interference. This approach is exemplified by the philo-sophical stance of the UK and US governments in the 1980s, that became colloquially known as 'Thatcherism' (UK) and 'Reaganomics' (USA). At the same time, the recognition that market forces alone are unable to guarantee that an economy will automatically achieve the objectives established by governments has meant that state intervention-to curb inflation, encourage growth, reduce unem-ployment, correct a balance of payments or budgetary problem or restore currency stability-invariably occurs to some degree in all countries. In broad terms, this intervention usually takes three main forms, described as fiscal policy, monetary policy and direct controls. These policy instruments-or 'instrumental variables' and their effects on the business community are discussed below.

Fiscal Policy

As indicated above, each year governments raise and spend huge amounts of money. The UK government's estimates for 2005/6, for example, suggest that gov-ernment spending will be about £519 billion and is to be allocated in the manner illustrated in Figure 4.8. This spending will be funded mainly from taxation (direct and indirect), and national insurance contributions. The PSNB is estimated at £32 billion.

Fiscal policy involves the use of changes in government spending and taxation to influence the level and composition of aggregrate demand in the economy and, given the amounts involved, this clearly has important implications for business. Elementary circular flow analysis suggests, for instance, that reductions in taxation and/or increases in government spending will inject additional income into the economy and will, via the multiplier effect, increase the demand for goods and services, with favourable con-sequences for business. Reductions in government spending and/or increases in taxation will have the opposite effect, depressing business prospects and probably dis-couraging investment and causing a rise in unemployment.

Apart from their overall impact on aggregate demand, fiscal changes can be used to achieve specific objectives, some of which will be of direct or indirect benefit to the business community. Reductions in taxes on company profits and/or increases in tax allowances for investment in capital equipment can be used to encourage business to increase investment spending, hence boosting the income of firms pro-ducing industrial products and causing some additional spending on consumption. Similarly, increased government spending targeted at firms involved in exporting, or at the creation of new business, will encourage increased business activity and additionally may lead to more output and employment in the economy.

In considering the use of fiscal policy to achieve their objectives, governments tend to be faced with a large number of practical problems that generally limit their room for manoeuvre. Boosting the economy through increases in spending or reductions in taxation could cause inflationary pressures, as well as encouraging an inflow of imports and increasing the public sector deficit, none of which would be particularly welcomed by entrepreneurs or by the financial markets. By the same token, fiscal attempts to restrain demand in order to reduce inflation will generally depress the economy, causing a fall in output and employment and encouraging firms to abandon or defer investment projects until business prospects improve.

Added to this, it should not be forgotten that government decision makers are politicians who need to consider the political as well as the economic implications of their chosen courses of action. Thus while cuts in taxation may receive public approval, increases may not, and, if implemented, the latter may encourage higher wage demands. Similarly, the redistribution of government spending from one pro-gramme area to another is likely to give rise to widespread protests from those on the receiving end of any cuts; so much so that governments tend to be restricted for the most part to changes at the margin, rather than undertaking a radical reallo-cation of resources and may be tempted to fix budgetary allocations for a number of years ahead (e.g. the Comprehensive Spending Review in the UK).

Other factors too-including changes in economic thinking, self-imposed fiscal rules, external constraints on borrowing and international agreements-can also play their part in restraining the use of fiscal policy as an instrument of demand management, whatever a government's preferred course of action may be. Simple prescriptions to boost the economy through large-scale cuts in taxation or increases in government spending often fail to take into account the political and economic realities of the situation faced by most governments.

Monetary Policy

Monetary policy seeks to influence monetary variables such as the money supply or rates of interest in order to regulate the economy. While the supply of money and interest rates (i.e. the cost of borrowing) are interrelated, it is convenient to con-sider them separately.

As far as changes in interest rates are concerned, these clearly have implications for business activity, as circular flow analysis demonstrates. Lower interest rates not only encourage firms to invest as the cost of borrowing falls, but also encourage consumption as disposable incomes rise (predominantly through the mortgage effect) and as the cost of loans and overdrafts decreases. Such increased consump-tion tends to be an added spur to investment, particularly if inflation rates (and, therefore 'real' interest rates) are low and this can help to boost the economy in the short term, as well as improving the supply side in the longer term. Raising interest rates tends to have the opposite effect-causing a fall in con-sumption as mortgages and other prices rise, and deferring investment because of the additional cost of borrowing and the decline in business confidence as con-sumer spending falls. If interest rates remain persistently high, the encouragement given to savers and the discouragement given to borrowers and spenders may help to generate a recession, characterised by falling output, income, spending and employment and by increasing business failure.

Changes in the money stock (especially credit) affect the capacity of individuals and firms to borrow and, therefore, to spend. Increases in money supply are gener-ally related to increases in spending and this tends to be good for business prospects, particularly if interest rates are falling as the money supply rises. Restrictions on monetary growth normally work in the opposite direction, espe-cially if such restrictions help to generate increases in interest rates which feed through to both consumption and investment, both of which will tend to decline.

As in the case of fiscal policy, government is usually able to manipulate mone-tary variables in a variety of ways, including taking action in the money markets to influence interest rates and controlling its own spending to influence monetary growth. Once again, however, circumstances tend to dictate how far and in what way government is free to operate. Attempting to boost the economy by allowing the money supply to grow substantially, for instance, threatens to cause inflation-ary pressures and to increase spending on imports, both of which run counter to government objectives and do little to assist domestic firms. Similarly, policies to boost consumption and investment through lower interest rates, while welcomed generally by industry, offer no guarantee that any additional spending will be on domestically produced goods and services, and also tend to make the financial mar-kets nervous about government commitments to control inflation in the longer term.

This nervousness among market dealers reflects the fact that in modern market economies a government's policies on interest rates and monetary growth cannot be taken in isolation from those of its major trading partners and this operates as an important constraint on government action. The fact is that a reduction in interest rates to boost output and growth in an economy also tends to be reflected in the exchange rate; this usually falls as foreign exchange dealers move funds into those currencies which yield a better return and which also appear a safer invest-ment if the market believes a government is abandoning its counterinflationary policy. As the UK government found in the early 1990s, persistently high rates of interest in Germany severely restricted its room for manoeuvre on interest rates for fear of the consequences for sterling if relative interest rates got too far out of line.

Dircct Controls

Fiscal and monetary policies currently represent the chief policy instruments used in modern market economies and hence they have been discussed in some detail. Governments, however, also use a number of other weapons from time to time in their attempts to achieve their macroeconomic objectives. Such weapons, which are designed essentially to achieve a specific objective-such as limiting imports or controlling wage increases-tend to be known as direct controls. Examples of such policies include:

- *Incomes policies,* which seek to control inflationary pressures by influencing the rate at which wages and salaries rise.
- *Import controls,* which attempt to improve a country's balance of payments situa-tion, by reducing either the supply of, or the demand for, imported goods and services.
- *Regional and urban policies,* which are aimed at alleviating urban and regional problems, particularly differences in income, output, employment, and local and regional decline.

A brief discussion of some of these policy instruments is found at various points in the text below. Students wishing to study these in more detail are recommended to consult the books referred to at the end of this chapter.

The Role of Financial Institutions

Interactions in the macroeconomy between governments, businesses and consumers take place within an institutional environment that includes a large number of financial intermediaries. These range from banks and building societies to pension funds, insurance companies, investment trusts and issuing houses, all of which pro-vide a number of services of both direct and indirect benefit to businesses. As part of the financial system within a market-based economy, these institutions fulfil a vital role in channelling funds from those able and willing to lend, to those individuals and organisations wishing to borrow in order to consume or invest. It is appropriate to consider briefly this role of financial intermediation and the supervision exercised over the financial system by the central bank, before concluding the chapter with a review of important international economic institutions.

Elements of the Financial System

A financial system tends to have three main elements:

1. *Lenders and borrowers*-these may be individuals, organisations or governments.
2. *Financial institutions,* of various kinds, which act as intermediaries between lenders and borrowers and which manage their own asset portfolios in the inter-est of their shareholders and/or depositors.
3. *Financial markets,* in which lending and borrowing takes place through the transfer of money and/or other types of asset, including paper assets such as shares and stock.

Financial institutions, as indicated above, comprise a wide variety of organisations, many of which are public companies with shareholders. Markets include the mar-kets for short-term funds of various types (usually termed 'money markets') and those for long-term finance for both the private and public sectors (usually called the 'capital market'). Stock exchanges normally lie at the centre of the latter, and constitute an important market for existing securities issued by both companies and government.

The vital role played by financial intermediaries in the operation of the financial system is illustrated in Figure 4.10 and reflects the various benefits which derive from using an intermediary rather than lending direct to a borrower (e.g. creating a large pool of savings; spreading risk; transferring short-term lending into longer-term borrowing; providing various types of funds transfer services). Lenders on the whole prefer low risk, high returns, flexibility and liquidity; while borrowers prefer to minimise the cost of borrowing and to use the funds in a way that is best suited to their needs. Companies, for example, may borrow to finance stock or work-in-progress or to meet short-term debts and such borrowing may need to be as flexible as possible.

Alternatively, they may wish to borrow in order to replace plant and equipment or to buy new premises-borrowing which needs to be over a much longer term and which hopefully will yield a rate of return which makes the use of the funds and the cost of borrowing worthwhile.

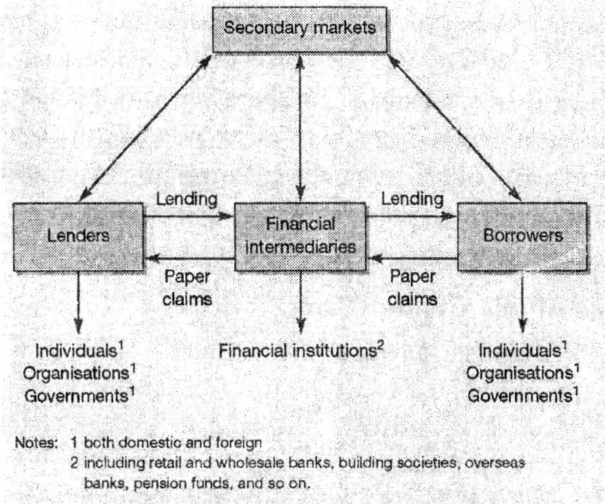

Figure : The role of financial intermediaries

The process of channelling funds from lenders to borrowers often gives rise to paper claims, which are generated either by the financial intermediary issuing a claim to the lender (e.g. when a bank borrows by issuing a certificate of deposit) or by the borrower issuing a claim to the financial intermediary (e.g. when government sells stock to a financial institution). These paper claims represent a liability to the issuer and an asset to the holder and can be traded on a secondary market (i.e. a market for existing securities), according to the needs of the individual or organisation holding the paper claim. At any point, financial intermediaries tend to hold a wide range of such assets (claims on borrowers), which they buy or sell ('manage') in order to yield a profit and/or improve their liquidity position. Decisions of this kind, taken on a daily basis, invariably affect the position of investors (e.g. shareholders) and cus-tomers (e.g. depositors) and can, under certain circumstances, have serious consequences for the financial intermediary and its stakeholders (e.g. the bad debts faced by western banks in the late 1980s and early 1990s).

Given the element of risk, it is perhaps not surprising that some financial institu-tions tend to be conservative in their attitude towards lending on funds deposited with them, especially in view of their responsibilities to their various stakeholders. UK retail banks, for instance, have a long-standing preference for financing industry's working capital rather than investment spending, and hence the latter has tended to be financed largely by internally generated funds (e.g. retained profits) or by share issues. In comparison, banks in Germany, France, the United States and Japan tend to be more ready to meet industry's medium-and longer-term needs and are often directly involved in regular discussions with their clients concerning corporate strategy, in con-trast to the arm's length approach favoured by many of their UK counterparts.

The Role of the Central Bank

A critical element in a country's financial system is its central or state bank; in the United Kingdom this is the Bank of England. Like most of its overseas counterparts, the Bank of England exercises overall supervision over the banking sector with the aim of maintaining a stable and efficient financial framework as part of its contri-bution to a healthy economy. Its activities have a significant influence in the financial markets (especially the foreign exchange market, the gilts market and the sterling money market). These activities include the following roles:

- banker to the government;
- banker to the clearing banks;
- manager of the country's foreign reserves;
- manager of the national debt;
- manager of the issue of notes and coins;
- supervisor of the monetary sector; and
- implementer of the government's monetary policy.

In the last case, the Bank's powers were significantly enhanced following the decision by the incoming Labour government (1997) to grant it 'operational independence' to set interest rates and to conduct other aspects of monetary policy free from Treasury interference. This historic decision has given the Bank the kind of independence experienced by the US Federal Reserve and the Deutsche Bundesbank and has been designed to ensure that monetary policy is conducted according to the needs of the economy overall, particularly the need to control inflation.

INTERNATIONAL ECONOMIC INSTITUTIONS AND ORGANISATIONS

Given that external factors constrain the ability of governments to regulate their economy, it is appropriate to conclude this analysis of the macroeconomic context of business with a brief review of a number of important international economic institutions and organisations which affect the trading environment. Foremost among these is the European Union, which is examined at length. In the discussions below, attention is focused on the International Monetary Fund (IMF), the Organisation for Economic Co-operation and Development (OECD), the European Bank for Reconstruction and Development (EBRD), the World Trade Organisation (WTO) and the World Bank (IBRD).

The International Monetary Fund (IMF)

The IMF is an international organisation currently of 184 member countries. It came into being in 1946 following discussions at Bretton Woods in the USA which sought to agree a world financial order for the post-Second World War period that would avoid the problems associated with the worldwide depression in the inter-war years. In essence, the original role of the institution-which today incorporates most countries in the world-was to provide a pool of foreign currencies from its member states that would be used to smooth out trade imbalances between coun-tries, thereby promoting a structured growth in world trade and encouraging exchange rate stability. In this way, the architects of the Fund believed that the danger of international protectionism would be reduced and that all countries would consequently benefit from the boost given to world trade and the greater stability of the international trading environment.

While this role as international 'lender of last resort' still exists, the IMF's focus in recent years has tended to switch towards international surveillance and to helping the developing economies with their mounting debt problems and assist-ing eastern Europe with reconstruction, following the break-up of the Soviet empire. It has also been recently involved in trying to restore international stabil-ity following the global economic turmoil in Asia and elsewhere. To some extent its role as an international decision-making body has been diminished by the tendency of the world's leading economic coun-tries to deal with global economic problems outside the IMF's institutional framework. The United States,

Japan, Germany, France, Italy, Canada, Britain and Russia now meet regularly as the 'Group of Eight' (G8) leading industrial economies to discuss issues of mutual interest (e.g. the environment, eastern Europe). These world economic summits, as they are frequently called, have tended to supersede discussions in the IMF and as a result normally attract greater media attention.

The Organisation for Economic Co-operation and Development (OECD)

The OECD came into being in 1961, but its roots go back to 1948 when the Organisation for European Economic Co-operation (OEEC) was established to co-ordinate the distribution of Marshall Aid to the war-torn economies of western Europe.

Today it comprises 30 members, drawn from the rich industrial countries and including the G7 nations, Australia, New Zealand and most other European states. Collectively, these countries account for less than 20 per cent of the world's population, but produce around two-thirds of its output-hence the tendency of commentators to refer to the OECD as the 'rich man's club'.

In essence the OECD is the main forum in which the governments of the world's leading industrial economies meet to discuss economic matters, particularly ques-tions concerned with promoting stable growth and freer trade and with supporting development in poorer non-member countries.

Through its council and commit-tees, and backed by an independent secretariat, the organisation is able to take decisions which set out an agreed view and/or course of action on important social and economic issues of common concern. While it does not have the authority to impose ideas, its influence lies in its capacity for intellectual persuasion, particu-larly its ability through discussion to promote convergent thinking on international economic problems.

To assist in the task, the OECD provides a wide variety of economic data on member countries, using standardised measures for national accounting, unemployment and purchasing-power parities. It is for these data-and especially its economic forecasts and surveys-that the organisation is perhaps best known.

The European Bank for Reconstruction and Development (EBRD)

The aims of the EBRD, which was inaugurated in April 1991, are to facilitate the transformation of the states of central and eastern Europe from centrally planned to free-market economies and to promote political and economic democracy, respect for human rights and respect for the environment. It is particularly involved with the privatisation process, technical assistance, training and investment in upgrading of the infrastructure and in facilitating economic, legal and financial restructuring. It works in co-operation with its members, private companies and organisations such as the IMF, OECD, the World Bank and the United Nations.

The World Trade Organisation (WTO)

The World Trade Organisation, which came into being on 1 January 1995, super-seded the General Agreement on Tariffs and Trade (the GATT), which dated back to 1947. Like the IMF and the International Bank for Reconstruction and Development, which were established at the same time, the GATT was part of an attempt to reconstruct the international politico-economic environment in the period after the end of the Second World War. Its replacement by the WTO can be said to mark an attempt to put the question of liberalising world trade higher up the international political agenda.

With a membership of around 150 states, and which now includes China, the WTO is a permanent international organisation charged with the task of liberalis-ing world trade within an agreed legal and institutional framework. In addition it administers and implements a number of multilateral agreements in fields such as agriculture, textiles and services and is responsible for dealing with disputes arising from the Uruguay Round Final Act. It also provides a forum for the debate, negotia-tion and adjudication of trade problems and in the latter context is said to have a much stronger and quicker trade compliance and enforcement mechanism than existed under the GATT.

The World Bank (IBRD)

Established in 1945, the World Bank (more formally known as the International Bank for Reconstruction and Development or IBRD) is a specialised agency of the United Nations, set up to encourage economic growth in developing countries through the provision of loans and technical assistance. The IBRD currently has over 180 members.

The European Investment Bank (EIB)

The European Investment Bank was created in 1958 under the Treaty of Rome and is the financing institution of the European Union. Its main task is to contribute to the integration, balanced development and the economic and social cohesion of EU Member States. Using funds raised on the markets, it finances capital projects which support EU objectives within the European Union and elsewhere.

SYNOPSIS

Business and economics are inextricably linked. Economics is concerned with the problem of allocating scarce productive resources to alternative uses-a fundamental aspect of business activity. In market-based economies, this problem of resource allo-cation is largely solved through the operation of free markets, in which price is a vital ingredient. The existence of such markets tends to be associated primarily, though not exclusively, with democratic political regimes. In all democratic states, government is a key component of the market economy and exercises considerable influence over the level and pattern of business activity-a point illustrated by the use of elementary circular flow analysis. A government's aims for the economy help to shape the policies it uses and these policies have both direct and indirect consequences for business organisations of all kinds. In examining the economic context in which firms exist, due attention needs to be paid to the influence of a wide range of institutions and organisations, some of which operate at international level. Equally, as markets become more open and business becomes more global, the fortunes of firms in trading economies become increasingly connected and hence subject to fluctuations that go beyond the boundaries of any individual state.

SUMMARY OF KEY POINTS

- Business activity exists in and is affected by the broader macroeconomic environ-ment; it also helps to shape that environment.
- Economics is concerned with how societies allocate scarce economic resources to alternative uses and the 'real costs' of the choices that are made.

- Broadly speaking two main approaches to the problem of resource allocation exist: state planning and the market.
- Most economies in the world are market-based economies which operate through a price mechanism. Within such economies the state also plays a key role in some allocative decisions.
- In market economies economic activity essentially involves 'real flows' and corre-sponding flows of income and expenditure between producers and consumers.
- Combining these flows into a simple model of the macroeconomy illustrates that income basically flows round the economy in a circular motion.
- Levels of income in the economy are related to levels of output, expenditure and employment.
- Changes in the level of economic activity can be explained by examining changes in one or more of the key economic variables such as consumer spending, saving, government decisions on state spending/taxation and external trade.
- Within the macroeconomy governments often play a key role in influencing both the levels and patterns of demand in pursuit of their macroeconomic objectives.
- Key government objectives usually include controlling inflation, promoting economic growth, reducing unemployment, and creating a stable macroeconomic environ-ment.
- To pursue these objectives governments use a range of policies, most notably fiscal and monetary policies.
- Government policy decisions take place within a broader economic and financial framework which includes the influence of financial institutions and markets and the requirements which accrue from membership of different supranational and interna-tional organisations.

CASE STUDY : TOYATA UK

Toyota's origins can be traced back to the early twentieth century when the inven-tor of Japan's first automatic loom, Sakidu Toyoda, established a spinning and weaving company. By the 1930s, using funds from selling patent rights to a British machine maker, the company had begun to invest in automotive technology research and soon produced its first prototype passenger vehicle. In August 1937, Kiichiro Toyoda, the son of the original owner, established the Toyota Motor Company, beginning mass production at its Koromo plant in 1938, just before the outbreak of the Second World War.

Despite experiencing considerable difficulties in the post-war period, Toyota recommenced production and began to build up a sales network to market its vehi-cles. In 1950, the company was split into two parts-production and sales-with the Toyota Motor Company the manufacturing arm of the organisation. Using techniques which have subsequently been emulated by other large companies (e.g. total quality control, just-in-time), Toyota began to increase its output and sales and was beginning to make significant inroads into overseas markets by the mid-1960s. By 1982, when the sales and manufacturing arms of the organisation merged to form the Toyota Motor Corporation, export sales of vehicles had exceeded domestic registrations and Toyota had grown into a large multinational corporation with a range of interests in various parts of the world.

For much of the early post-war period, Toyota focused its attention on the American market and established sales facilities in California in 1957, to be followed by a design base in 1973 and a joint production venture with General Motors in 1984. Less than two years later, the Corporation established its first wholly owned production plant at Georgetown in Kentucky, from which the first of many US-built Toyotas emerged in 1988. Toyota's development in post-war Europe proceeded along broadly similar lines, with the company establishing local sales and distribution networks, followed by design and production facilities. Initially, production took place under licence (e.g. in Portugal in 1968) or through joint ventures (e.g. with Volkswagen in 1989) and was restricted to commercial vehicles and fork-lift trucks. By the late 1980s, however, the company had signalled its intention of establishing a passenger vehicle manufac-turing facility in Europe, as part of its programme of overseas market development. This plant was opened in mid-1992 at Burnaston near Derby and was followed by the opening of an engine plant at Deeside, North Wales, some months later.

Toyota's decision to establish production facilities in Europe is best understood against the political and economic realities of the period.

Japan's post-war success in export markets had, by the 1980s, given rise to a huge Japanese balance of pay-ments surplus that was bitterly resented by US and European governments and became the focus of attention in numerous meetings of the G7 countries. As part of this success, the Japanese car industry was under pressure from US and European car manufacturers and their governments to restrain exports, and this ultimately culminated in a system of agreed voluntary restraints (known as VERs) by Japanese car producers, for fear of more draconian measures. Since these restraints did not apply to vehicles produced by Japanese factories overseas ('transplants'), establish-ing a manufacturing presence outside Japan made sound commercial and political sense. This was particularly true in western Europe, where the EU's Common External Tariff made cars imported from Japan more expensive to consumers and hence relatively less competitive than locally produced vehicles.

The EU's decision to establish a 'single market' within the Union added a further impetus to the decision by Japanese car manufacturers (and others) to seek a European presence. The fact that the United Kingdom was a favoured location for Toyota-and for many other Japanese companies-is not difficult to explain. Apart from providing direct access to the largest single market for motor vehicles in the world, the United Kingdom had a substantial market in its own right and a devel-oped vehicle manufacturing industry with a significant parts and component sector. Added to this, the favourable response given to direct foreign investment by United Kingdom national and local government-including the use of financial and other inducements-made the United Kingdom an attractive proposition and a location of minimal risk for investing multinational corporations.

As far as the choice of Burnaston was concerned, this seems to have been dic-tated by economic and commercial rather than political factors, although Derbyshire County Council actively lobbied the parent company and offered it a number of inducements to locate in the Midlands. Being centrally placed in Britain and close to the M1, Burnaston offered direct access to all parts of the country and a relatively quick route to the Continent, via the ports and the Channel Tunnel. It also boasted a highly skilled local workforce, a developed infrastructure and a large site with room for further expansion.

There is no doubt that the multi-million Toyota development in Derbyshire has had a considerable impact on the local economy. Apart from the jobs created in building and operating the car plant, further employment has been created directly among local component suppliers and indirectly amongst those involved in provid-ing services and materials and from the extra spending resulting from the growth of jobs. The area has also benefited from the prestige of having attracted a famous company to invest and this is expected to encourage investment by other overseas organisations. How far these gains will ultimately be at the expense of the other car-producing areas of Britain still remains to be seen, but economic analysis sug-gests they may prove significant.

5

The Demographic, Social and Cultural Context of Business

INTRODUCTION

As previous chapters have demonstrated, human beings are a critical element of busi-ness activity both in their role as producers (e.g. workers, managers, entrepreneurs) and as consumers of outputs provided by the private, public and voluntary sectors. Put simply, business activity ultimately takes place because of and for people, a point well illustrated by the concept of the circular flow of income (CFI) and by the systems model introduced in Chapter 1. In order to more fully understand the environ-ment in which business organisations exist and operate, it is important to consider how broader 'social' influences affect business organisations by examining how they can impact upon both the demand and supply side of the economy.

In this chapter we look at three such influences: demography, social aspects and the idea of 'culture' and illustrate how these can affect both the amount and types of goods and services consumed within an economy and different aspects of the production process. In the next chapter, on the resource context, we examine 'people' as a key factor of production and look at a number of areas associated with the concept of the 'workforce'.

As the CFI model clearly shows, both the demand and supply side of the economy are interrelated (e.g. consider the notion of 'derived demand') and the same is often true for demographic, social and cultural influences. For example, in some countries, changing attitudes to female participation in the workforce (a socio-cultural factor) have helped to influence family sizes (a demographic factor) and this in turn has had implica-tions for both the markets for goods and services and for human resources. To simplify the analysis, however, we have chosen to examine the different social influences and their impact on the economy separately but would encourage you to think of the vari-ous ways in which the different factors can be interconnected, both in themselves and with other macroenvironmental variables (e.g. the political environment).

The examples provided below are by no means exhaustive and you might like to think of others based on your own interest and/or experience (e.g. public administration students should consider the impact of a changing demographic and socio-cultural environment on the supply of and demand for public sector services such as educa-tion, pensions and healthcare). Moreover, the analysis can also be applied across different countries and cultures and ideally should seek to demonstrate the impact of socio-cultural and demographic change on business activity.

THE DEMOGRAPHIC ENVIRONMENT OF BUSINESS

Demography is the study of populations both in terms of their overall size and their structural characteristics. From a business point of view the key areas of inter-est include the age structure of a given population, its gender balance, its geographical distribution and the tendency for both the size and structure of the population to change over time. As noted above, demographic change can have important implications for both the demand and supply side of the economy and hence for organisations of all types.

The Size of the Population

A country's population normally increases over time and will vary according to such factors as changes in the birth and death rates and in the rate of net migration. For example, the UK population in 1971 was just under 56 million, by 2001 this had risen to 59.1 million. Estimates suggest that by 2021 the UK will have a population of just under 64 million and that this could peak at almost 67 million by 2050 before it starts to fall back again. In comparison, Russia's current popula-tion of around 145 million is projected to fall to about 100 million by 2050 as a result of a declining birth rate and a rising death rate in the wake of the country's economic collapse. If this occurs the world's biggest country will have fewer people than countries such as Uganda and Egypt.

Table 5.1 indicates the wide variations that can occur in the size of national pop-ulations by examining a range of countries across the globe. Within the EU we can see that major member countries such as France, Germany, Italy and the UK all had populations over 50 million in 2003, while the majority of the new member states had populations below 10 million. These figures are dwarfed, however, by India and China, which had populations of around 1 billion and 1.3 billion respectively. Such differences in overall population size have important economic implications in areas such as potential market size, workforce availability, public expenditure, economic growth and international trade.

Population size in selected countries, 2003

Country	*Population (millions)*
Germany	82.5
France	59.6
UK	59.6
Italy	57.3
Netherlands	16.2
Greece	11.0
Poland	38.2
Hungary	10.1
Slovakia	5.4
Malta	0.4
USA	290.8
India	1049.7
China	1287.0

Source: Various (including Eurostat)

The age and sex distribution of the population

In addition to examining the overall size of a country's population, demographers are also interested in its structural characteristics, including the balance between males and females and the numbers of people in different age categories. Table 5.2 provides illustrative data for the UK population by age and gender for selected age groups and intervals over the period 1971-2021. As can be seen from the figures in the right-hand column, women outnumber men in the UK population despite the fact that the annual number of male births slightly exceeds that of female births.

Moreover, the data clearly point to an ageing population, with an increasing per-centage of the population in the over 65 group and a decreasing percentage in the under 16 category. Projections suggest that by 2013 the number of over 65s in the UK population will exceed the number who are under 16, a trend which is some-times described as 'the demographic time-bomb' and which has important implications for both the private and public sectors, not least in terms of the over-all demand for goods and services including 'public goods' such as education, healthcare, social services, state pensions and social security arrangements.

Distribution of UK population by age and gender, 1971-2021, at selected intervals

	Under 16 (%)	*35-44 (%)*	*55–64 (%)*	*Over 65 (%)*	*All ages (millions)*
Males					
1971	27	12	11	10	27.2
2001	21	15	11	14	28.8
2021[1]	18	13	13	18	31.4
Females					
1971	24	11	12	16	28.8
2001	19	15	11	18	30.2
2021[1]	17	12	13	22	32.4

Note: [1] Projections.

Source: Adapted from *Social Trends* (2005)

It is worth noting that the UK's ageing population is a characteristic shared by many other countries, including those in the European Union. Data produced by Eurostat indicate similar trends in both the original EU-15 and in the new accession countries (Table 5.3). In comparison, both India and China have a much smaller percentage of the population in the over 65 category, the figures being 4.8 per cent and 7.4 per cent respectively for 2003.

Table 5.3: Percentage of EU populations aged 65 and over for selected EU countries, 1970-2003

Country	*1970*	*1991*	*2003*
Germany	13	15	17
Belgium	13	15	17
Spain	9	14	17
Finland	9	13	15
Denmark	12	16	15
Estonia	12	12	16
Lithuania	10	11	15
Czech Republic	12	13	14
Slovakia	9	10	12
EU-25 average	12	14	16

Source: Adapted from Eurostat

Other Structural Characteristics

Populations can also be examined in a number of other ways including their eth-nicity and geographical distribution. For instance, in the 2001 population census in the UK, around 8 per cent of people surveyed described themselves as belonging to a minority ethnic group, with the largest grouping being Indian, accounting for almost 2 per cent of the total population and nearly 23 per cent of those in the ethnic minority category.

The census data show that, in general, minority ethnic groups in the UK have a younger age structure than those in the 'White Group' and tend to be highly concentrated in large urban centres, particularly London.

For the UK population as a whole, the majority of people live in England, with significant concentrations in regions such as the south-east, the Midlands, the north-west and the north-east, a fact which has important economic, political and social ramifica-tions. Moreover, inter-regional movements of population, together with other factors such as international migration and differential birth and death rates, can result in significant local and regional variations in population over time with a knock-on effect for both the public and private sectors (for example, demand for housing and school places).

Population Change

As the previous analysis indicates, populations can change in either size and/or structure, with important consequences for economic activity both within and between countries. The size and structure of a country's population depend on a number of variables, the most important of which are the birth rate, the death rate and the net migration rate.

The Birth Rate

Birth rates tend to be expressed as the number of live births per thousand of the population in a given year. In many countries this figure has been falling steadily over a long period of time for a number of reasons. These include:

- A trend towards smaller families as people become better off and health improves and death rates fall.
- The increased availability of contraception.
- The trend towards later marriages and later childbearing.
- Declining fertility rates
- Changing attitudes towards women and work.

In some countries governments have offered financial and other incentives to mar-ried couples to try to reduce the birth rate (e.g. China) as a means of controlling population growth. In other countries incentives have been offered to try to reverse the actual or potential decline in the birth rate because of its economic conse-quences (e.g. France, Singapore). It is worth remembering that declining birth rates are an important contributor to an ageing population.

The Death Rate

Like birth rates, death rates are usually measured per thousand of the population in a given year. For developed economies such as the UK this figure has tended to fall over time before reaching a plateau. Among the main contributors to this trend have been:

- Rising living standards, including better housing, sanitation and nutrition.
- Developments in medical technology and practice.
- Better education. Improved working conditions.

The difference between the birth rate and the death rate represents the 'natural change' in the population (i.e. increase or decrease).

Net Migration

Apart from the movement of population within a country (internal migration), people may move from one country to another for a variety of reasons. The balance between those leaving (emigrants) and those entering (immigrants) a country over a given period of time represents the rate of net migration. Along with changes in the birth and/or death rate, this can be a significant factor in population change and can have important consequences for the economy (e.g. the gain or loss of cer-tain skills) and for the political system.

Influences on the rate of net migration include:

- Legal barriers (e.g. immigration laws).
- Economic migrancy.
- The numbers fleeing persecution.
- Government policy.

Demographic Change and Business

Changes in the size and/or structure of a country's population can have important consequences for enterprises in the public, private and voluntary sectors both in the short and long term. Given increased globalisation and international trade, the impact of demographic change has an international as well as a national dimen-sion for a growing number of trading organisations.

The following examples provide illustrations of how a changing demography can influence both the level and pattern of demand within an economy and in turn help to explain why changes can occur in a country's economic and industrial structure and why some countries engage in international trade. Demographic change can also have important effects on the supply side of the economy.

You should try to think of other examples.

- As populations grow in size the demand for many types of goods and services also tends to grow (e.g. energy, consumer durables, food). A growing population also provides a larger workforce, other things being equal.
- An 'ageing population' increases the demand for a range of public, private and voluntary sector goods and services (e.g. healthcare, pensions, specialist holi-days, sheltered housing). It also creates an increasingly 'dependent population'.

- A declining birth rate influences the demand for education, children's products, childcare, certain TV programmes, comics, toys, etc. It can also reduce the num-bers of young people available to enter the workforce to replace those who retire.
- Changes in the ethnic make-up of the population can affect the demand for par-ticular food products, clothing and media services and can place increased demands on public authorities (e.g. documents printed in different languages). Some researchers also argue that a more diverse workforce can improve an organ-isation's performance.
- The regional redistribution of the population will affect the consumption of a range of goods and services including housing, education, healthcare, transport, energy and many day-to-day products. It can also affect prices (e.g. in the hous-ing market) and the make-up of the local labour market.

On a more general level, it is also worth noting that demographic change can impact on a country's social as well as its economic structure and that this can result in increased (or reduced) demands on a range of organisations, particularly those in the public sector. For example, the growing imbalance being experienced in many countries between an increasing and dependent elderly population and a diminishing population of working age touches on many areas of public policy, from healthcare and social provision on the one hand to pensions and fiscal policy on the other. Governmental responses to the consequences of demographic change can have both direct and indirect consequences for a wide variety of organisations across the economy.

THE SOCIAL CONTEXT

Since organisations exist and operate in society, they are subject to a variety of soci-etal influences that operate at both a general and specific level. In this section we consider some of the key factors within an organisation's social environment, start-ing with the concept of 'social class'. The notion that organisations also have responsibilities to society.

Social Class

Throughout history, all societies have normally exhibited a certain degree of social and economic inequality that has given rise to the tendency to classify individuals into different social categories. For example, in India the 'caste system' has been an important source of social differentiation and one which has exerted a key influence over the life and opportunities available to members of the different castes. In other countries, including the United Kingdom, the categorisation of individuals has often been based around notions of 'social class', the idea of grouping people together who share a similar social status which is related to certain common features such as educational background, income and occupation. Whereas in some types of social system, movement between groups is either very difficult or impossible (e.g. the caste system), in others 'social mobility' is frequently observed, with some individu-als able to move relatively quickly between the different social strata (e.g. upper class, middle class, working class) as their personal circumstances change.

The ABC1 system of social grading

Social grading	Social status	Occupation
A	Upper middle class	Higher managerial, administrative and professional
B	Middle class	Intermediate managerial, administrative and professional
C1	Lower middle class	Supervisory or clerical, junior managerial, administrative and professional
C2	Skilled working class	Skilled manual workers
D	Working class	Semi and unskilled manual workers
E	Lowest subsistence level	State pensioners or widows, casual workers, lowest grade workers

In practice, the process of allocating individuals to a particular class category has generally been based on socio-economic criteria such as income, wealth and occu-pational status. Advertisers and market researchers-including the Institute of Practitioners in Advertising-have tended to favour a scheme known as 'ABC1' which uses an individual's occupation as a basis for allocation, the assumption being that a person's job is closely linked to key aspects of her/his atti-tudes and behaviour, including their choice of car, clothes, home furnishings, holidays, reading material and so on. There is even evidence to suggest that class might be influential in an individual's choice of retail outlets (e.g. different UK super-market chains appear to attract customers from different socio-economic groups).

Similar systems of classification have also been/are used for official purposes (e.g. the UK 10-year census of population). In the 1990s in the UK, government statistics used what was called the Registrar General's Social Scale-subsequently renamed 'Social Class based on Occupation'-to group the UK population into seven differ-ent categories according to their occupation (e.g. Group I was professional; Group II was managerial and technical; Group V was unskilled occupations). This system has now been replaced by NS-SEC (the National Statistics Socio-Economic Classifications) which again focuses on occupation as the key criterion for class allocation. NS-SEC is shown in Table 5.5. The figures in the right-hand column rep-resent the socio-economic classification of the UK population of working age in the summer of 2003.

While it would be unwise to assume that a factor such as a person's social class will invariably affect their choice of goods and services, empirical evidence reveals some interesting variations in the levels of expenditure on particular products among different groups in the UK population, a fact not lost on marketing organi-sations which often use socio-economic criteria as one way to segment a market . According to data produced in the annual survey of 'Social Trends' in the UK, total expenditure was highest among the managerial and professional group and was almost double that of people in the never worked/ unemployed category. Within this overall pattern of expenditure some interesting data emerges, particularly with regards to priorities, as indicated by expenditure on different items by the different social groupings. For instance, expenditure on housing, fuel and power was highest among the never worked/long-term unemployed group while spending on health was highest among the managerial group. Note that some of the high levels of spending among the former group, in areas such as education and communication, are probably largely to do with the fact that this category also contains students.

Lifestyles

Another factor that can clearly affect people's attitudes and behaviour is the lifestyle that they choose to adopt. Lifestyles are basically concerned with the way in which people live and how they spend their money, decisions which are not necessarily always linked to their socio-economic position. Two individuals with the same occupation-and nominally in the same social class-may have entirely different lifestyles, a point well illustrated by examining two university lecturers. My own lifestyle is highly sophisticated, environmentally sensitive, artistic and cos-mopolitan; that of a colleague-who happens to teach marketing-is narrow, parochial, philistine and consumption-driven. Then, what would one expect?!

Joking apart, lifestyle analysis provides another way of seeking to categorise and explain human behaviour, based on factors such as an individual's interests, activi-ties and opinions as well as on their demographic characteristics. In essence, the proposition is that by examining distinctive patterns of consumer response, a mar-keting organisation can build up a clearer picture of an individual's habits, preferences and behaviour and by doing so can design more effective and appealing products, marketing programmes and/or communications that can be aimed at spe-cific lifestyle groups.

While we should be cautious of over-generalising, the evidence suggests that in many countries the way in which people spend their time and money has changed considerably in recent decades as a result of changes in demography, working pat-terns, technology, income and a range of other factors. Once again we can illustrate this by looking at longitudinal data collected through the annual survey of social trends in the UK. These data show, for example, that:

- Cinema attendance in 2004 was the second highest figure in 30 years.
- In 2002/3 around 45 per cent of homes in the UK could access the Internet; this was four times the number in 1998/9.
- UK residents took over 41 million holidays abroad in 2003, six times the number in 1971.
- Household spending on communications (including mobile phones) trebled in value between 1991 and 2003.
- In 1993 80 per cent of men and 73 per cent of women held at least one plastic card (e.g. credit/debit/store card); by 2003 this had risen to 91 per cent and 90 per cent respectively.
- The number of licensed cars on Britain's roads more than doubled in the period 1971-2003.

- The number of households with two or more cars almost quadrupled-from 8 per cent to 29 per cent over the same period.
- In 1996/7 16 per cent of households had a mobile phone; by 2002/3 the figure was 70 per cent.
- About 60 per cent of homes had a CD player in 1996/7; by 2002/3 this had topped 80 per cent. During the same period sales of home computers grew from under 30 per cent to more than 50 per cent.
- Since 1974 UK consumers have halved their consumption of red meat and sales of butter, margarine and cooking fats have also fallen.
- During the period 1997-2003 the amount of household waste collected for recy-cling more than doubled while the amount of land dedicated to organic food production grew more than sevenfold.

If we take changing expenditure patterns in the UK as an indication of changes in lifestyles then there has been a discernible shift in emphasis from essential products such as food, housing, water and fuel to the less essential items such as communi-cations, foreign travel, recreation and culture. For example, after allowing for inflation, UK household expenditure on food and drink rose by only 41 per cent between 1971 and 2003 whereas spending on communication rose by over eight times. Interestingly spending on alcohol and tobacco actually fell over the same period while spending on healthcare doubled, suggesting a shift in public concern towards a healthier lifestyle.

Table : Volume of household expenditure on selected items, 1971-2003, expressed as index numbers (base year 1971)

Category of spending	1971	1991	2003
Food and non-alcoholic drink	100	117	141
Alcohol and tobacco	100	92	91
Housing, water, fuel	100	138	156
Health	100	182	205
Communication	100	306	846
Recreation and leisure	100	283	610
Household expenditure abroad	100	298	712

Source: Adapted from ONS

In light of the discussion on inflation in Chapter 4, it is worth noting that such changes in spending patterns over time are reflected in changes in the official 'basket of goods and services' used to calculate the Retail Prices Index in the UK. The 1980s saw CDs, CD players and condoms added to the basket, with computers, camcorders and mobile phone charges added in the next decade. More recently (2004 and 2005) dishwater tablets have replaced dishwasher powder, wooden garden furniture sets have replaced plastic sets and leather sofas have replaced ordi-nary ones. More bizarrely, hamsters and popcorn bought in cinemas have been added to the index while baguettes, corned beef and writing paper have been dropped. What does this tell us about the changing spending habits and lifestyles of UK citizens in the new millennium?

MINI CASE: FIT FOR PURPOSE?

One of the important social trends in recent years has been the move towards healthier lifestyles, a development which has been spurred on by concerns over the increased incidence of obesity, diabetes, heart disease and cancer-problems often associated with rising levels of affluence. Along with this trend has come numerous business opportunities including the growth in the number of fitness clubs, health farms and activity holidays and a general rise in the sale of products such as vitamin supplements, fruit juices, blood pressure monitors and books promoting healthier diets. Grocery retailers too have not been slow to exploit the new situation, offering a range of chilled, ready made 'healthier option' meals, often endorsed by a well-known personality (e.g. the UK grocery retailing chain Sainsbury's has used Jamie Oliver, the TV chef, to promote its products; Oliver has also begun a well-publicised campaign to improve the nutritional value of school meals in the UK).

As with any change of this kind there tend to be losers as well as winners. For example, according to research by Mintel, sales of the UK's favourite snack, the potato crisp, are in decline as consumers switch to products generally held to be healthier such as dried fruit, cereal bars and nuts. A particular concern for many consumers has been the high fat and high salt content of products such as crisps and this has driven some companies to produce low salt and/or low fat brands and to change the types of fat being used in the product in an effort to boost sales (e.g. the UK-based Walker's Snack Products has a variety cooked in olive oil). For other organisations, problems such as these may be more structural than cosmetic. According to a report in the *Guardian* (17 September 2005, p. 20), Unilever is considering selling or closing some of its struggling frozen food plants in western Europe as supermarket shoppers increasingly favour chilled rather than frozen meals.

A concerted effort by the Anglo-Dutch consumer group to promote its brands across Europe (e.g. BirdsEye in the UK; Iglo in Germany; Findus in Italy) has evidently had disappointing results and overall sales of frozen food have fallen. A Unilever spokesman has claimed that the main problem is that consumers have been switching to chilled foods because they are generally perceived to be a healthier option; efforts to promote the health benefits of frozen foods have failed to stem the tide.

Many of the trends referred to above are, of course, mirrored in consumer aspira-tions and behaviour in other countries, particularly in respect of issues such as healthier lifestyles, increased foreign travel, greater access to communications tech-nology and more environmentally friendly products (though not necessarily rodent purchases!). As the following examples illustrate, changes in consumer lifestyles can represent both an opportunity and a threat to trading organisations and can have important implications for businesses and countries alike.

- Coca-Cola has seen a decline in profits as consumers have switched to bottled water, fruit juice and other non-fizzy drinks as part of a healthier diet.
- GlaxoSmithkline has targeted the Italian market with its non-smoking products in the wake of the ban by the Italian government on smoking in public places.
- Beer consumption in Germany has dropped dramatically as young Germans reject a product that they evidently regard as 'uncool' and less healthy than some alternatives.
- China has overtaken the USA in sales of televisions and mobile phones and Chinese consumers are increasingly buying a wide range of western consumer goods from luxury confectionery and designer clothes to expensive cars and for-eign beers.
- With a rapidly expanding economy and growing liberalisation in many areas of private life, the sex industry in China is

booming. The country now provides 70 per cent of the world's sex toys and there is growing (sic) domestic market.

- Sales of organic food are growing significantly across Europe and beyond. The global market for organic food in 2005 was worth about £15 billion, with Europe responsible for just under half.
- With the immense popularity of the iPod and iTunes (its online record store), Apple has become the world's fastest-growing brand.
- Other brands in the technology/lifestyle field that are increasing in value include BlackBerry Google, Amazon, Yahoo and eBay.

Other Social Influences

While it is important to consider the influence of broad social factors such as class and lifestyles, it is also worth remembering that consumers are individuals and that they are subject to influences that operate at a personal level. Such influences include the wide variety of individuals and groups with whom we come into con-tact during our lifetime and who may influence our attitudes, values, opinions and/or behaviour. Primary among these are our interactions within the family, with friends or work colleagues and through our involvement with sports and social clubs, religious organisations, trade unions and so on. Such groups are sometimes referred to as 'reference groups'.

Groups that have a regular or direct (i.e. face-to-face) influence on us are known as 'primary reference groups' while those whose influence tends to be more indi-rect and formal are known as 'secondary reference groups'. The former, in particular, can be very influential in shaping our attitudes and behaviour including our decisions on consumption.

The importance of reference groups, especially family and friends, is recognised by both economists and marketers. Economists, for example, use the notion of 'households' to indicate that the consumption of goods and serv-ices often takes place within a collective family framework, as in the case of groceries, holidays, vehicles and many other everyday products. Marketers use con-cepts such as the 'family life cycle' to show changing patterns of consumption as the individual moves from being a child in a family to being a parent with different needs and responsibilities.

While it is difficult to be precise about when and how far an individual's demand is shaped by the family and other reference groups, it is not difficult to think of particu-lar examples when this is likely to be the case. For many services such as builders, restaurants, hotels, hairdressers and car repairs, consumers often rely on the advice of a trusted friend or colleague and many firms can gain new business through such word-of-mouth recommendations. Equally, through membership and/or support of a particular group or club, individuals may be tempted to purchase particular goods and/or services (e.g. football kit, trainers, a CD, tickets), especially those with a desir-able 'brand name' and endorsed by a well-known personality (e.g. sportsperson, musician, singer, film star). In such cases, the demand for the product is often less price sensitive since it is a 'must have' product.

THE CULTURAL ENVIRONMENT

The term 'culture' generally refers to a complex set of values, norms, beliefs, atti-tudes, customs, systems and artefacts which are handed down from generation to generation through the process of socialisation and which influence how individu-als see the world and how they behave in it. Defined in this way culture can be seen to have at least three important features:

- it comprises both material (e.g. human artefacts such as buildings, literature, art, music) and abstract elements (e.g. rituals, symbols, values);
- it is socially learned and transmitted over time; and
- it influences human behaviour.

As a concept, 'culture' is often applied in a variety of circumstances at both the macro and micro level: terms such as 'western culture', 'Asian culture', 'European culture', 'New York City culture', 'youth culture', 'pop culture', 'entrepreneurial cul-ture' and 'research culture' are just some of the examples of its usage in the modern world. What they have in common is that they imply certain shared aspects of human belief, understanding and behaviour that link individuals together into some form of definable group and/or range of activities.

In a business context, it can be easy to underestimate the degree to which a person's perceptions, attitudes and behaviour can be shaped by cultural influences, some of which may be relatively enduring (e.g.

certain 'core' values and beliefs) while others may be more open to change (i.e. secondary beliefs and values). In the United States, for example, American citizens believe in the right of individuals to bear arms and this is enshrined in the US Constitution. The buying and selling of handguns and rifles is thus acceptable within American society, despite the fact that they are frequently used in violent crimes including robbery and murder. In other countries, trade in such weapons tends to be seen as highly questionable by most people and is usually heavily regulated by the government to certain types of weapons for use in acceptable pursuits such as hunting or rifle shooting. Cultural differences such as this can, of course, apply not only to the kinds of goods and services that are consumed (e.g. eating horsemeat in France is acceptable but not in the UK) but also to other aspects of both the production and consumption process and this can have important implications for an organisation's behaviour.

Examples include:

- Who decides what is bought, how it is bought or where it is bought (e.g. in some cultures women have predominantly been the purchasers of household products).
- What colours are acceptable (e.g. the colour associated with bereavement varies across cultures).
- How far harmonisation of products and marketing activities is feasible (e.g. the EUs perennial debates over what constitutes an acceptable definition of certain products such as sausages, Feta cheese, chocolate).
- What factors can enhance the prospect of a sale (e.g. bribes are acceptable in some cultures).
- How business is conducted (e.g. the length of negotiations, the meaning of a handshake).
- The method of communicating with the target audience (e.g. in the UK a single shared language allows organisations to use national media).
- How customer enquiries/complaints are dealt with (e.g. UK businesses using call centres in India often give their operators British names and train them to talk about everyday British preoccupations such as the weather and sport).

In effect, culture not only influences an individual's response to products and the nature of the buying and selling process, but it also exercises a significant influence on the structure of consumption within a given society. For companies which can gain acceptability on a global scale, despite cultural differences between countries, the potential benefits are huge (e.g. global brands such as Coca-Cola, McDonald's, Nike).

While the so-called 'Americanisation' of consumption is not to everyone's taste, other forms of cultural exportation are often more acceptable and can prove highly lucrative for the country concerned. In the UK, for example, overseas earnings from culture and arts-related tourism make a significant contribution to the country's 'invisi-ble earnings' and many other countries benefit in similar ways.

MINI CASE: NATIONAL CULTURES

Recognising and responding to cultural differences between countries can have an important impact on how successful organisations are in international trade. But is it possible to generalise about a country's culture?

One academic who has made a significant contribution in this area is Professor Geert Hofstede, who has developed a theory of culture which allows comparisons to be made between the main cultural characteristics in different countries. Hofstede's research is based on data collected from IBM employees across the world while he was working at the company as a psychologist. On the basis of his research Hofstede identified four cultural dimensions; later he added a fifth. These dimensions can be used to compare value systems at different levels, from the family through to the state.

The five cultural dimensions are as follows:

1 *Power distance*-this is concerned with the degree to which the members of a society accept an unequal or hierarchical power structure. In societies where the power distance is large there is a perception that inequality exists and subordinates tend to be more dependent on their superiors. This can result in an autocratic or paternalistic style of management or governance (e.g. in some African countries) which can evoke either positive or negative reactions. Where the power distance is small, individuals tend to see themselves more as equals and

management/governance styles tend to be more consultative and less hierarchical (e.g. in northern European countries).

2 *Uncertainty avoidance*-this focuses on how members of society cope with uncertainty in their lives. Where levels of anxiety are generally high, this results in high uncertainty avoidance and people in these cultures are deemed to be more expressive and emotional (e.g. Latin American countries) than in low uncertainty avoidance countries (e.g. many Asian countries).

3 *Individualism*-refers to the extent to which individuals in society see themselves as independent and autonomous human beings or as part of a collectivity. High individualist countries tend to be countries such as the United States, the UK, Canada and Australia; low individualism is said to be prevalent in Asian and Latin American countries.

4 *Masculinity*-is concerned with how far a society is predisposed to aggressive and materialistic behaviour and is linked to gender role. Hofstede associates masculinity with toughness, assertiveness and materialism and with a predisposition to conflict and competition. Femininity, in contrast, is characterised as caring, sensitive and concerned with the quality of life; the result is a more accommodating style based on negotiation and compromise. Hofstede's analysis suggests the more masculine countries include Austria and Japan, while Scandinavian countries tend to be the most feminine.

5 *Long-term orientation*-relates to the degree to which a society embraces a long-term view and respect for tradition. In societies with a short-term orientation people tend to stress the 'here and now', typified by western countries. Eastern cultures, by comparison, are generally held to have a longer-term orientation that emphasises concern for the future and for tradition as well as the present.

One of the benefits of Hofstede's research is that it reminds us that cultural differences can and do occur between states and, as a result there is no 'one-size-fits-all' style of management or governance that would be suitable across all countries. For companies which are multinational organisations, management styles and approaches in the country of origin may not necessarily be suitable in other parts of the organisation for cultural reasons. Vive la difference!

Sub-culture

A society is rarely, if ever, culturally homogeneous. Within every culture sub-cultures usually exist, comprising groups of individuals with shared value systems based on common experiences, origins and/or situations. These identifiable sub-groups may be distinguished by nationality, race, ethnicity, religion, age, class, geographical location or some other factor and their attitudes, behaviour, customs, language and artefacts often reflect sub-cultural differences. At times such differ-ences can be relatively easily accommodated and ultimately may become institutionalised through the legal and/or political process. At other times sub-cultural differences can be the source of a considerable degree of conflict between various sub-groups, result-ing in serious divisions within a society and even in war and genocide.

The UK provides a good example of the notion of cultural diversity and can be used to illustrate how this can influence the demand for goods and services. In addition to nationality groups such as the Irish, Scots and Welsh, the country has pro-vided a home for successive generations of immigrants from around the globe and this has created a rich mix of ethnic and other sub-groups, often concentrated in par-ticular parts of the country and having their own language, traditions and lifestyles. In Leicester, for example, where a significant proportion of the population is of Asian origin, there is a substantial Asian business community, part of which has developed to cater specifically for the local ethnic population (e.g. halal butchers, saree shops), as well as attracting custom from the wider community (e.g. Indian restaurants). Many Asian businesses in Leicester are small, family owned enterprises, employing members of the extended family in keeping with cultural traditions. Aspects such as the organisation and financing of the business, its network of relationships and the working conditions for staff are also frequently influenced by cultural values, tradi-tions and norms, although changes in these areas are becoming more apparent, especially among second and third generation Asian-owned enterprises.

APPLICATION: MARKET SEGMENTATION

Marketers have long recognised the importance of demographic, social and cultural factors in shaping people's demand for goods and services. This is exemplified by the concept of market segmentation.

In essence, market segmentation refers to the practice of dividing a market into distinct groups of buyers who share the same or similar attitudes and patterns of behaviour and who might require separate products or marketing to meet their par-ticular needs. By segmenting a market into its broad component parts, businesses should be able to focus their marketing efforts more effectively and efficiently, for example by developing product offerings and marketing programmes which meet the requirements of the different market segments.

Markets can be segmented in a variety of ways and this tends to differ between consumer markets and those which involve business to business transactions. Table 5.8 below outlines some of the major variables used in segmenting consumer mar-kets. As the table indicates, demographic, social and cultural factors provide a basis for identifying distinct market segments within the markets for consumer goods and services. In practice, of course, marketers may use either one (e.g. demography) or a combination (e.g. age, location and social class) of different variables to seg-ment a market they are seeking to target.

A good example of combining the different variables is provided by the notion of geo-demographic segmentation which focuses on the relationship between an indi vidual's geographical location and her/his demographic characteristics, given that close links frequently exist between a person's place and type of residence and factors such as income, family size and attitudes. One well-known scheme of this type is ACORN (A Classification Of Residential Neighbourhoods) which uses 40 variables from population census data to differentiate residential areas. Another is MOSAIC, developed by Experian, which draws on a variety of data sources (e.g. census data, financial data, property characteristics, demographic information) and uses a range of sophisticated analytical techniques to produce household profiles at full postcode level. Under the MOSAIC scheme, UK households are currently divided into 11 groups with names such as 'Symbols of Success', 'Suburban Comfort' and 'Grey Perspectives' and these are then further sub-divided into 61 types, again with interest-ing and evocative names including 'Golden Empty Nesters', 'Sprawling Subtopia' and 'Childfree Serenity'. For a fuller description of MOSAIC and Experian's other products (e.g. commercial MOSAIC) and methodology you should access the company's web-site at *http://www.experian.co.uk* and follow the links.

With regard to factors such as social class and lifestyles, these tend to be grouped under the notion of psychographic segmentation, an approach which has attracted considerable attention in recent years given the reciprocal link between lifestyles and consumption indicated above.

Lifestyle segments can be developed either as 'off-the-shelf products by marketing agencies/management consultancies or can be customised for/by individual companies, although the latter often tend to be both complex and expensive to design. One established and popular example of the former is VALS (Values And Lifestyles) developed by SRI International.

Under this model, individuals are allocated to different categories on the basis of a combi-nation of demographic and lifestyle factors such as age, education, income and levels of self-confidence and then these categories are grouped into a number of broader segments which reflect a category's predominant orientations.

Thus, under VALS 2, the three broad groups identified were (1) people who were *principle-orientated* (i.e. guided by their views of how the world should be); (2) people who were *status-orientated* (i.e. guided by the opinions and actions of others); (3) people who were *action-orientated* (i.e. guided by the desire for social and physical activity, variety in life and risk taking). Again you can gain further information on this scheme by visiting the SRI website at *www.future.sri.com/vals.*

SYNOPSIS

All organisations are an integral part of the society in which they exist and carry out their activities and as a result they are affected by a range of influences emanating from the demographic, social and cultural environment. These influences can change over time and help to shape both the demand and supply side of business activity. Businesses and other organisations need to be aware of and respond to the process of societal change and to the opportunities and threats that such change can engender.

SUMMARY OF KEY POINTS

- Organisations exist and operate within society and are subject to a variety of demo-graphic and socio-cultural influences.

- Demography is concerned with population variables, including population size, structure and distribution.
- Changes in demography are primarily related to changes in birth and/or death and/or net migration rates.
- Demographic change can affect both the demand and supply side of the economy.
- The social context of business includes factors such as social class, lifestyles and reference group influences. The consumption of goods and services in an economy can be linked to such factors.
- The cultural environment of business comprises those institutions and other forces which help to shape society's basic attitudes, values, perceptions, preferences and behaviour.
- Societies usually also contain sub-cultures which can influence a person's beliefs, attitudes and actions.
- Like demography and social factors, cultural influences can change over time and can affect organisations. Businesses need to be sensitive to such change.
- The importance of demographic, social and cultural factors in business can be illus-trated by the concept of market segmentation.

CASE STUDY: THE EFFECTS OF AN AGEING POPULATION

There is no doubt that the world's population is ageing. In 2000 there were 69 million people in the world over the age of 80 years and this is the fastest growing segment of the population. By 2050 it is estimated that this figure will have risen to 379 million, which represents 4 per cent of the world's population. In 2000 many countries already had higher percentages of over 80s' including Sweden (5.1 per cent), Norway and Britain (both 4 per cent). In Japan (the fastest ageing country in the 1990s) it is predicted that by 2015 over 25 per cent of the population will be over 65 years of age.

Table 5.9 shows that in all parts of the world the fastest growing segments are the older ones, for the more developed countries reductions in the size of the 0 to 59 age groups are predicted. The predictions are made on the assumption that pres-ent trends in life expectancy and fertility rates will continue.

Why is the World Population Ageing?

There are two main causes-increased life expectancy and lower fertility rates. Fertility rates have fallen dramatically in all parts of the world between 1950 and 2000 and this trend is expected to continue into the future. Conversely life expectancy has risen in all parts of the world and is also expected to continue to do so. Putting these two trends together means that the average age of the world pop-ulation is increasing. (The factors behind these changes have already been discussed in this chapter.) There are of course wide differences between countries but the general picture is one of convergence.

What are the Implications of the Ageing Population for Business?

Production: Demand patterns vary a great deal with age and if the grey population is increasing in size businesses will have to respond to the changing demands. If the American experience is repeated in the rest of the world the grey population will spend more on education and leisure services. Many retirees take the opportunity to return to education to pursue their interests.

Projected growth rates between 2000 and 2050, percentages

	0-14	*15-59*	*60+*	*80+*
World	0.15	0.79	2.35	3.40
More developed countries	-0.34	-0.42	1.07	2.23
Less developed countries	0.21	1.01	2.87	4.22
Least developed countries	1.26	2.38	3.37	4.07

Sources: *World Population Prospects,* United Nations, 2000

The weekly expenditure on selected products in the UK in 2002. It can be seen that the older age groups spend less on beer and cider, cigarettes and visiting the cinema or theatre but more on holidays in the UK and medical insur-ance than the younger age groups.

As businesses respond to these changes there will be a shift of resources towards the service sector and this will bring about further change in industrial structure.

Marketing

Demographic change has long been recognised as an important part of the market-ing environment and one that needs continual monitoring. This is especially the case in the USA where the trends now evident in Europe started earlier and where the older population is large, affluent and with a great deal of market power. Older consumers have been dubbed 'woofs' by marketeers-well off older folk-and are accepted as an important part of the market.

Those currently in their 40s have been dubbed the 'third agers'. As they reach the 50-75 year age group they will have more free time, have better health, more money and higher expectations than their predecessors. The third agers in the USA have much higher demand than their predecessors for education and leisure serv-ices-they make heavy use of sports centres, cinemas and evening classes.

Demography is also important to marketers in the segmentation of markets and there are numerous examples of where age is the segregating factor. In recognition of the different needs and wants of the different age groups in the holiday market there is the 18-30 holiday company which caters for young people while Saga Holidays cater for the over 50s. Interestingly given the comments already made, Saga Holidays is now offering the kind of holidays often associated with younger travellers-like elephant riding in Nepal for example.

Table : Expenditure on selected products by age of head of household, UK, 2002, £ per week

	Under 30	*30 to 49*	*50 to 64*	*65+*
Eating out at restaurant	9.30	11.60	11.50	11.40
Take away meals	4.90	4.80	2.90	2.20
Beer and cider	9.90	10.60	10.80	5.10
Cigarettes	5.60	6.80	6.10	4.80
Visit cinema/theatre	1.30	1.50	1.30	1.20
Holiday in the UK	1.50	2.30	2.70	5.80
Holiday abroad	5.50	12.50	14.50	11.20
Medical insurance	0.40	0.80	1.70	3.20

Source: Adapted from *www.statistics.gov.uk/CC1/SearchRes.asp?tem=household+expenditure+age*

HRM

A greying population has implications for HR strategies within organisations, espe-cially in those industries which have traditionally employed young people. There will be fewer young people entering the labour market for two reasons: first there are fewer of them and second a higher percentage is now staying on at school. Other sources of labour will need to be found to meet the demand. At the same time people are continuing to retire early; in the USA only a half of men between the ages of 60 and 65 are still working and in some European countries the percent-age is much lower. Policies implemented in the 1980s and 1990s by organisations downsizing have created a 'retire early' culture among many, and some pension rules which penalise individuals who wish to work beyond retirement age have worked to exacerbate this. The combination of fewer younger people coming into the workforce and more people leaving early means that employers in many coun-tries are facing a contracting market.

One possibility is the increased participation of older people in the labour force. This means that ageist HRM practices will have to change. Employers often view older workers as more expensive, less flexible and lacking in the required skills, but statistics show that the over-40s age group receives less training than other groups. Many studies in this area have shown that age makes no difference to the ability to acquire new skills with training. It is often the case that older workers are more reli-able, are more experienced and have less absenteeism than younger workers. Many employers all around the world are recognising this and are implementing policies which positively encourage older workers.

The employment of older people will call for changes in recruitment practices. The retention of labour will become more important for organisations and there-fore training and development will take on greater significance. Work will need to be made more attractive, with more part-time or temporary contracts. This might also overcome the cost implication of having older employees who are higher up incremental pay scales.

From 2006 age discrimination will be banned in the EU under an EU directive but market forces are already making some companies adopt a different approach to older workers.

Financial

There are financial implications of an ageing population. The Potential Support Ratio (PSR) shows the number of persons aged 15 to 64 years per one person of 65 years and over. It gives an indication of the dependency burden of an ageing popu-lation on the working population. This fell from 12:1 to 9:1 between 1950 and 2002 and is forecast to fall further to 4:1 by the year 2050.

Again Table below shows a similar pattern all over the world-there will be an increasing financial burden on people of working age as a result of ageing popula-tions. Within the overall figures there are marked differences. In Japan for instance, the ratio is forecast to fall from 4:1 in 2002 to 1:1 in 2050. In the USA, where immi-gration is generally higher (and therefore ageing is less pronounced), the ratio is forecast to fall from 5:1 to 3:1.

Table : Projected Potential Support Ratio, 2002 and 2050

	2002	*2050*
World	9:1	4:1
More developed countries	5:1	2:1
Less developed countries	12:1	5:1
Least developed countries	17:1	10:1

Source: United Nations, 2002

This means that a higher proportion of the population will depend upon a smaller proportion of the population for support-in terms of resources for health care and the payment of pensions. Many countries are looking at their pension pro-visions to try to reduce the cost of dependency. In the UK for example there has been a shift in the burden of pension provision from the state to individuals and many companies have ended their 'final salary' pension schemes. Nevertheless, it is still estimated that to meet the demand for pensions of the ageing population by 2030 the UK needs a 5 per cent annual growth rate in GDP. This is much higher than growth rates have been. In the past in the UK, state pensions have been paid out of current taxation but this is likely to change so that state pensions will be funded from investments. It is also possible that the retirement age will be increased to reduce the cost of dependency.

In addition to the cost of pensions, an increase in the average age of a popula-tion has implications for health care and the cost of health care. Although this case study makes the point that the greying population is fitter and healthier than ever before, there are of course implications for the demand for health care. For exam-ple, the percentage of 65-year-olds in the UK with Altzheimers disease is 5 per cent, and this rises to 20 per cent in the over-80s. Therefore there is a need for greater provision for health care, whether this is done by the state or by individuals.

As well as these major changes the ageing populations will mean changes in:

- popular culture, which for some time has been dominated by youth
- crime rates-as most crime is carried out by younger people, crime rates should fall
- family relationships, with falling birth rates and longer life expectancy the 'bean-pole' family structure will become the norm.

It is clear from this discussion that the ageing population being experienced by much of the world has big implications for business in many diverse areas.

6

Legal Environment

INTRODUCTION

It is almost universally accepted that for a socieţy to exist and function in an ordered way a set of rules is required to regulate human behaviour. Irrespective of whether these rules are laid down in custom or practice or in statute, they constitute a means of regulating and controlling the activities of individuals and groups, and of enforcing mini-mum standards of conduct-even though they may be ignored or flouted on occasions.

This framework of rules and the institutions through which they are formu-lated and enforced represent what is normally understood as the 'law', which invariably evolves over time in response to changing social, economic and political circumstances (e.g. the influence of pressure groups). As one of the constraining (and enabling) influ-ences on business organisations, this legal environment is an important area of study for students of business, hence the tendency for courses in business-related subjects to have specialist modules or units on different aspects of business law (e.g. contract, agency, property and so on).

The aim of this chapter is not to examine business law in detail or to provide a defini-tive insight into particular areas of the law as it relates to business organisations. Rather it is to raise the reader's awareness of the legal context within which businesses func-tion and to comment briefly on those aspects of law which regularly impinge on a firm's operations. Students wishing to examine business law in more detail should consult the many specialist texts which have been written in this field, some of which are listed at the end of this chapter.

CLASSIFICATION OF LAW

Laws relating to both individuals and organisations can be classified in a number of ways: international and national, public and private, criminal and civil. In practice there are no hard and fast rules to classification and some categories may overlap (e.g. where a person's behaviour is deemed to infringe different areas of law). Nevertheless, distinguishing laws in these terms serves as an aid to explanation and commentary, as well as helping to explain differences in liabilities and in legal remedies in England and Wales (e.g. a child under the age of 10 cannot be held criminally liable).

Public and Private Law

Put simply, public law is the law which concerns the state, whether in international agreements or disputes or in the relationship between the state and the individual. Thus public law consists of international treaties and conventions, constitutional law, administrative law and criminal law. In contrast, private law is law governing the relationships between individuals and comprises laws in respect of contract, tort, property, trusts and the family.

Criminal Law

Criminal laws relate to a legal wrong (criminal offence)-a breach of a public duty, punishable by the state on behalf of society. Decisions on whether or not to bring a prosecution in a particular instance are taken by the Crown Prosecution Service (in England and Wales) and the matter may or may not involve trial by jury according to the seriousness of the alleged offence and the plea of the defendant(s). In some cases, the consent of both magistrates and defendants is required for a case to remain in the magistrates' court although this may change in the very near future. Moreover, while the criminal process may also arise from a private prosecution, such prosecutions are rare and, in these cases, the Attorney-General (the govern-ment's senior law officer) has the right to intervene if he or she sees fit.

Tort

A tort is a civil wrong other than a breach of contract or a breach of trust and is a duty fixed by law on all persons (e.g. road users have a duty in law not to act negli-gently). The law of tort, therefore, is concerned with those situations where the conduct of one party threatens or causes harm to the interests of another party and the aim of the law is to compensate for this harm. The most common torts are neg-ligence, nuisance, defamation and trespass.

Trusts

A trust is generally defined as an 'equitable obligation imposing on one or more persons a duty of dealing with property, over which they have control, for the ben-efit of other persons who may enforce the obligation'. This property may be in the form of money or stocks and shares or in other types of asset, particularly land, where trusts have become a very common way of permitting persons who are for-bidden to own legal estates in land to enjoy the equitable benefits of ownership. Partnerships, for example, cannot hold property as legal owners, so often several partners will act as trustees for all the partners. Similarly, minors may not hold legal estates, so their interests must be protected by a trust, administered by an individual or an institution.

Banks have duties as well as rights when dealing with the day-to-day affairs of their customers. Failure to discharge these duties, in some circumstances, may be deemed negligent behaviour.

In September 1995 the High Court ruled that Lloyds Bank had been negligent in lending money to two of its customers for use on a speculative property deal which had failed to come off because of a collapse in the property market in the late 1980s. In essence the customers had claimed that the bank owed them a duty of care in advising them on the merits of a loan to invest in property speculation and that it had been in breach of its duty when agreeing to proceed with the loan. In effect the claimants were arguing that they had been badly advised and that this had resulted in a loss which was not only suffered but also reasonably foreseeable.

In finding for the claimants-who were suing Lloyds under the tort of negligence-the judge ruled that the bank manager was in breach of his duty of care in advising them to proceed and that the couple had relied on his advice, including claims made in the bank's promotional literature. While a ruling of this kind sent shock waves through the financial community, it is, as yet, uncertain whether it set a legal precedent. Certainly, this is likely to prove a far more significant question to Lloyds (and other financial institutions) than the £77000 compensation awarded to the claimants by the High Court.

SOURCES OF LAW

Laws invariably derive from a number of sources including custom, judicial prece-dent, legislation and international and supranational bodies (e.g. the EU). All of these so-called legal sources of the law can be illustrated by reference to English law, which applies in England and Wales. Where laws made by Parliament are to apply only to Scotland or Northern Ireland the legislation will state this. Similarly, any Act which is to apply to all four home countries will contain a statement to this effect.

Custom

Early societies developed particular forms of behaviour (or 'customs') which came to be accepted as social norms to be followed by the members of the community to which they applied. In England many of these customary rules ultimately became incorporated into a body of legal principles known as the common law. Today cus-toms would be regarded as usage recognised by law, whether by judicial precedent (case law) or through statutory intervention and hence they are largely of histori-cal interest. Occasionally, however, they are recognised by the courts as being of local significance and may be enforced accordingly as exceptions to the general law (e.g. concerning land usage).

Judicial Precedent

Much of English law is derived from judicial precedent (previous decisions of the courts). The present system of binding precedent, however, is of fairly recent origin, dating from the latter part of the nineteenth century, when advances in recording legal judgments and a reorganisation of the court structure facilitated its general acceptance.

In essence, judicial precedent is based on the rule that the previous decisions of a higher court must be followed by the lower courts-hence the significance of the court structure. In any judgment will be found a number of reasons, arguments, explanations and cases cited and these must all be considered carefully by judges to determine whether there are material differences in the case before the court and the earlier deci-sion. To reach a decision, the court must find what is termed the *ratio decidendi* of the previous case. Put very simply, the *ratio* of a case are the essential steps in the legal rea-soning which led the court to make that particular decision. Anything which cannot be regarded as a *rationes* is termed *obiter dicta* or 'things said by the way'. The whole of a dissenting judgment in a case is regarded as *obiter. Obiter dicta* are not binding but may be regarded as persuasive arguments if the facts of the case permit.

Clearly there are times when, perhaps because of the position of a court in the hierarchy, decisions are not to be regarded as binding precedent. However, if the judgment has been delivered by a jurisdiction which has a common law system (e.g. Canada, Australia) or, most importantly, by the Judicial Committee of the Privy Council, then those decisions will be regarded as being of persuasive prece-dent, and may be used to help the court reach its own decision.

Legislation

A substantial proportion of current law-including laws governing the operations of business organisations-derives from legislation or statute, enacted by the Queen (or King) in Parliament. As Chapter 3 indicated, the initiative in this sphere lies effectively with the government of the day which can virtually guarantee a bill will become law, if it has a working majority in the House of Commons.

Apart from a limited number of bills proposed by backbench MPs (private mem-bers' bills), the vast majority of legislation emanates from government and takes the form of Acts of Parliament or delegated legislation. Acts of Parliament are those bills which have formally been enacted by Parliament and have received the Royal Assent and, except where overridden by EU law, they represent the supreme law of the land. In addition to creating new laws (e.g. to protect the consumer), statutes may also be used to change or repeal existing laws. In some instances they may be designed to draw together all existing law (a consolidating Act) or to codify it or to grant author-ity to individuals or institutions to make regulations for specific purposes (an enabling Act). Under the Consumer Credit Act 1974, for instance, the Secretary of State for Trade and Industry is permitted to make regulations governing the form and content of credit agreements under delegated authority from Parliament.

As its name suggests, delegated legislation is law made by a body or person to which Parliament has given limited powers of law-making-as illustrated by the example above. More often than not, authority will be delegated to a Minister of the Crown, but it may also be conferred on local authorities or other public under-takings, either through the use of a statutory instrument or by some other means of delegation. Since Parliament remains sovereign, such legislation is required to receive parliamentary approval and scrutiny, but time tends to prevent anything other than a cursory glance at a limited proportion of the legislation of this kind. It does, however, remain subject to judicial control, in so far as the body granted authority may be challenged in the courts for exceeding its powers *(ultra vires)*.

In addition to these two principal forms of domestic legislation, developments in the law also emanate from Britain's membership of the European Union. Under the Union's main treaties-or those parts to which the British government has agreed-Union legislation becomes part of the law and takes precedence over domestic leg-islation, although the latter may sometimes be required to implement it. Accordingly, law which is inconsistent with Union law is repealed by implication and British citizens, like their counterparts elsewhere in the EU, become subject to the relevant Union laws (unless an 'opt-out' has been negotiated).

Whereas the provisions of the main treaties represent primary legislation, the regulations, directives and decisions emanating from the Union's institutions are secondary (or subordinate) legislation, made under the authority conferred by the Treaty of Rome (1957) and by subsequent Acts (e.g. the Single European Act 1986, the Maastricht Treaty 1992). As Chapter 3 indicated, regulations are of general application throughout the Member States and confer individual rights and duties which must be recognised by the national courts. Their purpose is to achieve uni-formity throughout the EU, as in the requirement for heavy goods vehicles to fit tachographs to control drivers' hours.

Directives, by contrast, are not directly applicable; they are addressed to member states and not individuals, although a directive may create rights enforceable by an individual citizen, as they become directly applicable if a member state fails to implement its provisions within the prescribed time limits. The aim of EU direc-tives is to seek harmonisation or approximation between national laws rather than to achieve uniformity; hence the method of implementation is left to the discre-tion of the individual state, usually within a given time limit (e.g. the Companies Act of 1981 implemented the Union's fourth directive on company accounts by allowing small and medium-sized companies to reduce the amount of information provided to the Registrar of Companies).

Decisions, too, are binding, but only on the member state, organisation or indi-vidual to whom they are addressed and not on the population generally. In practice, EU decisions become effective from the date stated in the decision, which is generally the date of notification, and they are enforceable in national courts if they impose financial obligations.

The Legal System: the Courts

A country's legal system can be said to have two main functions: to provide an enabling mechanism within which individuals and organisations can exist and operate (e.g. companies are constituted by law) and to provide a means of resolving conflicts and of dealing with those who infringe the accepted standards of behav-iour. These functions are carried out by a variety of institutions, including the government and the courts, and a detailed analysis of the legal system within a state would require consideration of the interrelationship between politics and law. Since the political system has been examined in Chapter 3, the focus here is on the courts as a central element of a country's legal system, with responsibility for inter-preting the law and administering justice in democratic societies. It is worth remembering, however, that political and governmental activity take place within a framework of law and that framework is itself a product of the political process at a variety of spatial levels.

The English Legal System

Under the English legal system, a useful distinction can be made between courts on the basis of their status. The superior courts are the House of Lords, the Court of Appeal and the High Court. Law reports generally emanate from the higher courts-these cases involve a major point of law of general public interest (e.g. *R v R*, 1991). Inferior courts, in contrast, have limited jurisdiction and are subject to the supervi-sory jurisdiction of the High Court. The current hierarchy of courts is illustrated in Figure 7.1. For domestic purposes (i.e. not concerning EU legislation), the highest court is the House of Lords, which is the final court of appeal for both civil and criminal cases. Decisions reached by the Law Lords are binding on all other courts, though not necessarily on their Lordships themselves.

Like the House of Lords, the Court of Appeal has only appellate jurisdiction. In the case of the Civil Division of the court, its decisions bind all inferior courts and it is bound by its own previous decisions and by those of the House of Lords. The Criminal Division similarly is bound by the decisions of the Law Lords, but not by the Court of Appeal's Civil Division; nor is it bound by its own previous decisions where these were against a defendant, as exemplified in a number of celebrated cases in recent years.

The High Court is divided into three separate divisions, Chancery, Queen's Bench and Family, and has virtually unlimited original jurisdiction in civil matters, many of which are of direct relevance to business organisations. The Family court deals with such things as adoption, wardship and contested divorce cases, while the Chancery court deals with cases concerning trusts, property and taxation. Claims in contract and tort are the responsibility of the Queen's Bench division, which has two specialist courts to deal with commercial matters and with ships and aircraft. It also exercises the criminal jurisdiction of the High Court-the latter being entirely appellate in instances referred to it by the magistrates' courts or the Crown Court.

In criminal cases the Crown Court has exclusive original jurisdiction to try all indictable offences and can hear appeals against summary conviction or sentence from magistrates' courts. Broadly speaking, the latter largely deal with less serious offences (especially motoring offences), where trial by judge and jury is not permit-ted-an issue still under discussion following the publication of the Runciman Report (1993). Whereas magistrates' courts have both criminal and civil jurisdiction-with the emphasis towards the former-the jurisdiction of the county courts is entirely civil and derived solely from statute. Amongst the issues they deal with are conflicts between landlords and tenants and disputes involving small claims (e.g. concerning consumer matters) where a system of arbitration provides for a rela-tively inexpensive and quick method of resolving problems.

In disputes with a supranational dimension-involving EU member states, insti-tutions, organisations, companies or individuals-ultimate jurisdiction rests with the European Court of Justice. Under Article 220 (ex 164) of the Treaty of Rome, the court is required to ensure that in the application and interpretation of the Treaty the law is observed. As indicated elsewhere, in carrying out this function, the court has adopted a relatively flexible approach in order to take account of chang-ing circumstances. Few would dispute that its judgments have had, and will continue to have, a considerable influence on the development of EU law.

MINI CASE: JEAN-MARC BOSMAN-A CASE OF FOUL PLAY?

An example of how EU law affects individuals and organisations in member states is provided by the case of Jean-Marc Bosman, a Belgian football player who successfully challenged the transfer fee system operated by Europe's football authorities in the mid-1990s.

Bosman, who had been under contract to the Belgian club Liège, had sought a transfer to a French team when his contract expired but had his ambitions thwarted when Liège demanded a very high transfer fee. In the judgment of the European Court of Justice, clubs could no longer demand a fee for players out of contract if the player was headed for another EU member state. According to the judges, the system allowing for a fee to be imposed violated the right enshrined in the Treaty of Rome that European citizens could go from one EU country to another in pursuit of work. They also held that the rule limiting the number of foreign players a club could field in European matches violated the principle of the free movement of workers.

As a final comment, it is perhaps worth stating that while conflict remains an enduring feature of daily life, many disputes are settled without recourse to the courts, often through direct negotiation between the parties concerned (e.g. Richard Branson's attempts to reach a negotiated settlement with British Airways over its alleged 'dirty tricks' campaign). Moreover, even where negotiations fail or where one party declines to negotiate, a dispute will not necessarily result in court action, but may be dealt with in other ways. Disputes over employment contracts, for example, tend to be dealt with by a specialist tribunal, set up by statute to exer-cise specific functions of a quasi-legal nature. Similarly, complaints concerning maladministration by public (and increasingly private) bodies are generally dealt with by a system of 'ombudsmen', covering areas as diverse as social security bene-fits and local authority services. Financial services such as banking and insurance are covered by the Financial Services Ombudsman.

BUSINESS ORGANISATIONS AND THE LAW

Business organisations have been described as transformers of inputs into output in the sense that they acquire and use resources to produce goods or services for con-sumption. As Table 7.1 illustrates, all aspects of this transformation process are influenced by the law.

It is important to emphasise from the outset that the law not only constrains busi-ness activity (e.g. by establishing minimum standards of health and safety at work which are enforceable by law), but also assists it (e.g. by providing a means by which a business unit can have an independent existence from its members), and in doing so helps an enterprise to achieve its commercial and other objectives. In short, the legal environment within which businesses operate is an enabling as well as a regula-tory environment and one which provides a considerable degree of certainty and stability to the conduct of business both within and between democratic states. Given the extensive influence of the law on business organisations, it is clearly impossible to examine all aspects of the legal context within which firms function. Accordingly, in the analysis below attention is focused primarily on contract law, agency, and some of the more important statutes enacted to protect the interests of the consumer, since these are areas fundamental to business operations. Laws relat-ing to the establishment of an enterprise and to the operation of markets are discussed in Chapters 8 and 15 respectively.

Law and the business organisation

Business activity	*Examples of legal influences*
Establishing the organisation	Company laws, partnerships, business names
Acquiring resources	Planning laws, property laws, contract, agency
Business operations	Employment laws, health and safety laws, contract, agency
Selling output for consumption	Consumer laws, contract, agency

CONTRACT LAW: THE ESSENTIALS

All businesses enter into contracts, whether with suppliers or employees or finan-ciers or customers, and these contracts will be important-and possibly crucial-to the firm's operations. Such contracts are essentially agreements (oral or written) between two or more persons which are legally enforceable, provided they com-prise a number of essential elements. These elements are: offer, acceptance, consideration, intention to create legal relations and capacity.

Offer

An offer is a declaration by the offeror that they intend to be legally bound by the terms stated in the offer if it is accepted by the offeree (e.g. to supply component parts at a particular price within a specified time period). This declaration may be made orally or in writing or by conduct between the parties and must be clear and unambiguous. Furthermore it should not be confused with an 'invitation to treat', which is essentially an invitation to make an offer, as is generally the case with advertisements, auctions and goods on display. Tenders are offers; a request for ten-ders is merely an invitation for offers to be made.

Termination of an offer can happen in several ways. Clearly an offer is ended when it is accepted but, that apart, an offer may be revoked at any time up to acceptance. It is of no consequence, legally, that an offer may be kept open for a certain time. It is only when some consideration is paid for 'buying the option' that the time factor is important and this 'buying the option' would generally be a sepa-rate contract in any case. If an offer is for a certain length of time, then later acceptance is ineffective, and even where there is no specified time limit, the courts will imply a reasonable time. Thus, in *Ramsgate Victoria Hotel v Montefiore* (1866), shares in the hotel were offered for sale. After several months the offer was 'accepted' but the court held that too much time had passed, bearing in mind that the purpose of the shares offer was to raise money.

Another way for an offer to come to an end is by the failure of a condition. Although a genuine offer is always held to be firm and certain, sometimes it may be conditional and not absolute. Thus, should A wish to buy a model car from B, B may agree but impose conditions on the deal, such as stating that A must collect at a specific time on a certain day at a particular place and must pay in cash. This is known as a 'condition precedent' and failure to complete the conditions will nul-lify the agreement. There is another type of condition, called a 'condition subsequent' where there is a perfectly good contract which runs until something happens. For instance, a garage may have a good contract with an oil company to buy petrol at £x per 1000 litres until the price of oil at Rotterdam reaches \$x per barrel. It is only when oil reaches the stipulated price that the contract ends.

Acceptance

Just as an offer must be firm and certain, the acceptance of an offer by the person(s) to whom it was made must be unequivocal and must not contain any alterations or additions. Accordingly, any attempt to alter the terms of an offer is regarded as a counter-offer and thus a rejection of the original offer, leaving the original offeror free to accept or decline as he or she chooses.

While acceptance of an offer normally occurs either in writing or verbally, it may also be implied by conduct. In the case of *Brogden v Metropolitan Railways Co.* (1877) Mr Brogden had supplied the company for many years without formalities. It was then decided to regularise the position and a draft agreement was sent to him. He inserted a new term, marked the draft 'approved' and returned it to the company where it was placed in a drawer and forgotten about, although both parties traded with each other on the terms of the draft for more than two years. Following a dis-pute, Mr Brogden claimed there was no contract. The House of Lords decided differently, saying that a contract had been created by conduct.

Inferring the acceptance of an offer by conduct is quite different from assuming that silence on the part of the offeree constitutes acceptance: silence cannot be construed as an acceptance. Equally, while the offeror may prescribe the method of acceptance (although this is regarded as permissive rather than directory), the offeree may not prescribe a method by which he or she will make acceptance. For instance, an offer may be made by fax, thus implying that a fast response is required; therefore a reply accepting the offer which is sent by second-class mail may well be treated as nugatory.

There are some rules about acceptance which are important. Postal acceptance, for example, is a good method of communication and one which is universally used by businesses; but to be valid for contractual purposes a communication must be properly addressed and stamped and then placed into the hands of the duly authorised person (i.e. the post box or over the counter). An acceptance sent to a home address may be nullified if there has been no indication that this is acceptable. Similarly, acceptance of the offer must be effectively received by the offeror where modern, instantaneous methods of communication are used. Thus if a telephone call is muffled by extraneous sound, then the acceptance must be repeated so that the offeror hears it clearly.

Consideration

Together, offer and acceptance constitute the basis of an 'agreement' or meeting of minds, provided the parties are clear as to what they are agreeing about (i.e. a *con-sensus ad idem* exists). Central to this agreement will be a 'consideration' which has been defined as some right, interest, profit or benefit accruing to one party or some forbearance, detriment, loss or responsibility given, suffered or undertaken by the other. In commercial contracts, the consideration normally takes the form of a cash payment in return for the goods or services provided (i.e. the 'price' in a contract of sale). In contracts involving barter, however, which are sometimes used in interna-tional trade, goods are often exchanged for goods or for some other form of non-pecuniary consideration (e.g. information or advice).

Intention to Create Legal Relations

Not every agreement is intended to create a legally binding relationship. For exam-ple, most domestic agreements-such as the division of household chores-would not constitute a contract recognised in law. In commercial agreements, however, it is generally accepted that both parties intend to make a legally binding contract and therefore it is unnecessary to include terms to this effect. Should such a pre-sumption be challenged, the burden of proof rests with the person who disputes the presumption.

Capacity

A contract may be valid, voidable or void and one of the factors which determines this is the contractual capacity of the respective parties to the agreement. Normally speaking, an adult may make a contract with another adult which, if entered into freely and without any defects, and which is not contrary to public policy, is bind-ing upon them both (i.e. valid). However, the law provides protection for certain categories of persons deemed not to have full contractual capacity (e.g. minors, drunks and the mentally disordered); hence the practice by firms of excluding people under the age of 18 from offers of goods to be supplied on credit.

Concentrating on minors-those below voting age-the law prescribes that they can only be bound by contracts for 'necessaries' (e.g. food, clothing, lodging) and contracts of employment that are advantageous or beneficial, as in the case of a job which contains an element of training or education. In most other instances, con-tracts with minors are void or voidable and as such will be either unenforceable or capable of being repudiated by the minor.

In the case of business, legal capacity depends on the firm's legal status. Unincorporated bodies (e.g. sole traders, partnerships) do not have a distinct legal personality and hence the party to the agreement is liable for their part of the bar-gain. Limited companies, by contrast, have a separate legal identity from their members and hence contractual capacity rests with the company, within the limits laid down in the objects clause of its Memorandum of Association.

Other Factors

To be enforceable at law a contract must be legal (i.e. not forbidden by law or con-trary to public policy). Similarly, the agreement must have been reached voluntarily and result in a genuine meeting of minds. Consequently, contracts involving mis-takes of fact, misrepresentation of the facts, or undue influence or duress may be void or voidable, depending on the circumstances. In insurance contracts, for instance, the insured is required to disclose all material facts to the insurer (e.g. health record, driving record), otherwise a policy may be invalidated. In this con-text a 'material fact' is one which would affect the mind of a prudent insurer, even though the materiality may not be appreciated by the insured.

AGENCY

As business activity has become more specialised and complex, firms have increas-ingly turned to outside individuals to carry out specialist functions such as freight forwarding, overseas representation, insurance broking and commercial letting. These individuals (known as agents) are authorised by the individual or organisation hiring them (known as the principal) to act on their behalf, thus creating an agency rela-tionship. As in other areas of commercial activity, special rules of law have evolved to regulate the behaviour of the parties involved in such a relationship.

In essence, the function of an agent is to act on behalf of a principal so as to effect a contract between the principal and a third party. The agent may be a 'servant' of the principal (i.e. under their control as in the case of a sales representa-tive) or an 'independent contractor' (i.e. their own master as in the case of an estate agent) and will be operating with the consent of the principal whether by contract or implication. Having established a contractual relationship between the principal and the third party, the agent generally leaves the picture and usually has no rights and duties under the contract thus made.

With regard to an agent's specific obligations under an agency agreement, these are normally expressly stated under the terms of the agreement, although some may also be implied. Traditionally the common law of agency prescribes, however, that agents:

- *Obey the lawful instruction of the principal,* otherwise they may be in breach of contract.
- *Exercise due care and skill,* in order to produce a deal which is to the principal's best advantage.
- *Act personally,* rather than delegate, unless expressly or implicitly authorised to do so.
- *Act in good faith,* thus avoiding conflicts of interest or undisclosed profits and bribes.
- *Keep proper accounts,* which separate the principal's funds from those which belong personally to the agent.

Moreover, in so far as an agent is acting under the principal's authority, the princi-pal is bound to the third party only by acts which are within the agent's authority to make. Consequently ultra vires acts only affect the principal if he or she adopts them by ratification and the agent may be liable for the breach of the implied war-ranty of authority to the third party.

In addition to these common law duties owed by the principal, the Commercial Agents (Council Directive) Regulations 1993 apply when an agent falls within the definition of a commercial agent (Reg. 2(1)). They apply to transactions involving the sale or purchase of goods and they bestow certain rights and obligations upon both the principal and agent. It is clear that these duties overlap to some extent with the common law duties. Regulation 3 provides the agent's duties to their principal:

- a commercial agent must look after the interests of her/his principal and act dutifully and in good faith;
- make proper efforts to negotiate and, where appropriate, conclude the transac-tions;
- communicate to their principal all the necessary information available to them;
- comply with reasonable instructions given by the principal.

Regulation 4 specifies the duties of the principal:

- to act dutifully and in good faith;
- to provide the commercial agent with the necessary documentation relating to the goods in question;
- to obtain necessary information for the agent. This is a higher standard, perhaps requiring searching for data, than under the common law, where all the princi-pal needs to do is to disclose information in their possession;
- to notify the agent within a reasonable period of time if the usual volume of trade is likely to be significantly reduced;
- to inform the agent within a reasonable period of time of the principal's accept-ance, refusal, or non-acceptance of a commercial transaction arranged by the agent.

LAW AND THE CONSUMER

Economic theory tends to suggest that laws to protect the consumer are unneces-sary. If individuals are behaving rationally when consuming goods and services, they would arrange their consumption to maximise their satisfaction (or 'utility'), in the words of an economist. Products which because of poor quality or some other factor reduced a consumer's utility would be rejected in favour of those which proved a better alternative and this would act as an incentive to producers (and retailers) to provide the best products. In effect, market forces would ensure that the interest of the consumer was safeguarded as suppliers in a competitive market arranged their production to meet the needs and wants of rational consumers.

The 'ideal' view of how markets work is not always borne out in practice. Apart from the fact that consumers do not always act rationally, they often do not have access to information which might influence their choice of products; in some cases they may not even have a choice of products (e.g. where a monopoly exists) although this situation can change over time (e.g. through privatisation of state monopolies). Also, given the respective resources of producers and consumers, the balance of power in the trading relationship tends to favour producers who can influence consumer choices using a range of persuasive techniques, including advertising. Taken together, these and other factors call into question the assumption that the consumer is 'sovereign' and hence the extent to which individuals have inherent protection in the marketplace from powerful (and, in some cases, unscrupulous) suppliers. It is in this context that the law is seen to be an important counterbalance in a contractual relationship where the consumer is, or may be, at a disadvantage, and this can be said to provide the basis of legal intervention in this area.

Existing laws to protect consumers are both civil and criminal and the relevant rights, duties and liabilities have been created or imposed by common law (espe-cially contract and tort) or by statute. Significantly, as the examples below illustrate, a large element of current consumer law has resulted from statutory inter vention, much of it in the last 30 years. Indeed, a sizeable quality of consumer pro-tection law comes from the EU by way of directives. These laws-covering areas as diverse as trade descriptions, the sale of goods and services, and consumer credit and product liability-indicate a growing willingness on the part of governments to respond to the complaints of consumers and their representative organisations and to use legislation to regulate the relationship between business organisations and their customers. Europe is keen to encourage consumers to take advantage of cross-border EU markets by harmonising consumer protection. As suggested elsewhere, such intervention could reasonably be construed as a political response to some of the socially unacceptable characteristics of a capitalist economy

Trade Descriptions Act 1968

The main aim of the Trade Descriptions Act is to protect consumers from traders who deliberately misdescribe goods or give a false description of services in the process of trade. Under the Act-which imposes an obligation on local authorities to enforce its provisions (via Trading Standards Officers)-a trader can be convicted of a criminal offence in three main areas:

1 Making a false trade description of goods.

2 Making a false statement of price.

3 Making a false trade description of services.

The penalty for such offences can be a fine on summary conviction and/or impris-onment following conviction on indictment.

With regard to goods, the Act applies both to goods which have been sold and to those which are offered for sale and to which a false description, or one which is misleading to a material degree, has been applied. It can also apply to advertise-ments which are 'economical with the truth', such as claims regarding a used car for sale by a local dealer. Similarly, with services it is an offence to make false or misleading statements as to the services offered to consumers and it is possible for an offence to be committed even if the intention to mislead is not deliberate.

In the case of price, the Act outlaws certain false or misleading indications as to the price of goods, such as claims that prices have been reduced from previously higher levels (sham sales). For this claim to be within the law, a trader needs to show that the goods have been on sale at the higher price for a period of 28 consec-utive days during the preceding six months. If not, this must be made quite clear to the consumer when a price reduction is indicated.

The Consumer Credit Act 1974

The Consumer Credit Act, which became fully operational in May 1985, controls transactions between the credit industry and private individuals (including sole traders and business partnerships) up to a limit of £15 000. Under the legislation consumer credit agreement is defined as a personal credit providing the debtor with credit up to the accepted limit. This credit may be in the form of a cash loan or some other type of financial accommodation (e.g. through the use of a credit card). The Act also covers hire purchase agreements (i.e. a contract of hire which gives the hirer the option to purchase the goods), conditional sale agreements for the sale of goods or land, and credit sale agreements, where the property passes to the buyer when the sale is effected. The main aim of this consumer protection measure is to safeguard the public from trading malpractices where some form of credit is involved. To this end the Act provides, among other things, for a system of licensing controlled by the Office of Fair Trading which must be satisfied that the person seeking a licence is a fit person and the name under which he or she intends to be licensed is neither misleading nor undesirable. Providing credit or acting as a credit broker without a licence is a criminal offence, as is supplying a minor with any document inviting them to borrow money or obtain goods on credit. (Note that the Consumer Credit Bill has been re-introduced in 2005 and so the above rules may change.)

A further protection for the consumer comes from the requirements that the debtor be made fully aware of the nature and cost of the agreement and his or her rights and liabilities under it. The Act stipulates that prior to the contract being made the debtor must be supplied with certain information, including the full price of the credit agreement (i.e. the cost of the credit plus the capital sum), the annual rate of the total charge for credit expressed as a percentage (i.e. the annual percentage rate), and the amounts of payments due and to whom they are payable. In addition, the debtor must be informed of all the other terms of the agreement and of their right to cancel if this is applicable. In the case of the latter, this applies to credit agreements drawn up off business premises, and is designed to protect individuals from high-pressure doorstep sellers who offer credit as an incentive to purchase. Some companies, aware of the rights of cancellation on cold calls at home, have adopted a practice of writing to potential customers, making specific claims such as discounts and inviting the customer to book an appointment. Thus any subsequent home visit is not technically a cold call. This practice has raised some concern and is almost cer-tain to be outlawed, either by legislation or under a code of practice.

Sale of Goods Act 1979

Under both the Sale of Goods Act 1979 (as amended) and the Unfair Contract Terms Act 1977 consumers are essentially seen as individuals who purchase goods or services for their own personal use from other individuals or organisations sell-ing them in the course of business. A computer sold, for example, to a student is a consumer sale, while the same machine sold to a secretarial agency is not, since it has been acquired for business purposes. This legal definition of a consumer is important in the context of laws designed specifically to provide consumer protec-tion, as in the case of the Sale of Goods Act which governs those agreements whereby a seller agrees to transfer ownership in goods to a consumer in return for a monetary consideration, known as the 'price'. Where such an agreement or con-tract is deemed to exist the legislation provides consumers with rights in respect of items which are faulty or which do not correspond with the description given to them, by identifying a number of implied conditions to the sale. In the case of con-tracts for the supply of services (e.g. repair work) or which involve the supply of goods and services (e.g. supplying units and fitting them in a bathroom or kitchen), almost identical rights are provided under the Supply of Goods and Services Act 1982 (as amended).

The three main implied conditions of the 1979 Act are relatively well known. Under section 13, goods which are sold by description must match the description given to them and it is of no significance that the goods are selected by the pur-chaser. This description may be on the article itself or on the packaging or provided in some other way, and will include the price and possibly other information (e.g. washing instructions) which the consumer believes to be true. A shirt described as 100 per cent cotton, for instance, must be just that, otherwise it fails to match the description given to it and the consumer is entitled to choose either a refund or an exchange.

The second condition relates to the quality of the goods provided. Under section 14(2) of the Act goods had to be of 'merchantable quality', except where any defects are drawn specifically to the attention of the purchaser before the contract is made or where the buyer has examined the goods before contracting and the examination ought to have revealed such defects. As 'merchantable quality' was a matter of some controversy the phrase was amended to 'satisfactory quality' and this is defined in section 1 of the Sale of Goods and Services Act 1994, but the gen-eral expectation is that a product should be fit for the purpose or purposes for which it is normally bought, bearing in mind questions of age, price and any other relevant factors (e.g. brand name). A new top-of-the-range car should have no sig-nificant defects on purchase, whereas a high-mileage used car sold for a few hundred pounds could not reasonably evoke such expectations in the mind of the consumer. Thus, while the implied condition of 'satisfactory' applies to sale goods and used goods as well as to full-price purchases of new goods, it needs to be judged in light of the contract description and all the circumstances of a particular case, including the consumer's expectations.

The third implied condition derives from section 14(3) of the legislation, namely that goods are fit for a particular purpose (i.e. capable of performing the tasks indi-cated by the seller). Section 14(3) comes into its own when a use or range of uses is made known to the seller. Accordingly, if the seller, on request from the purchaser, confirms that goods are suitable for a particular purpose and this proves not to be the case, this would represent a breach of section 14(3). Equally, if the product is unsuitable for its normal purposes, then section 14(2) would also be breached and the consumer would be entitled to a refund of the price.

It is worth noting that 'satisfactory' and 'fitness for a purpose' are closely related and that a breach of one will often include a breach of the other. By the same token, failure in a claim for a breach of section 14(2) is likely to mean that a claim for a breach of section 14(3) will also fail. Moreover, if, on request, a seller disclaims any knowledge of a product's suitability for a particular purpose and the consumer is willing to take a chance, any subsequent unsuitability cannot be regarded as a breach of section 14(3). The same applies if the buyer's reliance on the skill or judgement of the seller is deemed 'unreasonable'.

The remedies available for breach of these implied terms was rejection, or dam-ages if the right to reject the goods had been lost, such as by the lapse of an unreasonable period of time. The only exception to this has traditionally been that of durability that is, where the goods have failed before goods of that type could reasonably be expected to fail. Durability has always been treated as a damages only breach, so as to avoid overcompensating the buyer.

However, the Sale and Supply of Goods to Consumers Regulations 2002 has granted the consumer/buyer new remedies. The Regulations come from the European Consumer Guarantees Directive (1999/44/EC) and seek to continue the move towards harmonising the cross-border sale of consumer goods. The DTI, keen not to reduce the pre-existing levels of consumer protection, added the new reme-dies to those already existing. The result is that the consumer still retains the short-term right to reject the goods for nonconformity. The period of time to exer-cise this option is quite short, normally a number of weeks at most. However, if this remedy is lost due to lapse of time, the consumer now has four new remedies in pairs: repair or replace, price reduction or rescission. It must be noted that the dam-ages awarded for rescission, the last remedy, will include a sum knocked off for 'beneficial use', reflecting the amount of use the consumer managed to get out of the goods. Until these Regulations the consumer had no right to require a repair or a replacement, and could only sue for damages. Moreover, the Regulations now remove the problem of goods damaged in transit. Under the old law, the risk passed to the consumer/buyer once the goods had been handed over to a third-party carrier. The result being that the purchaser would find both the carrier and the seller blaming one another for the loss. Ultimately, the con-sumer would go uncompensated unless they decided to sue both parties. The Regulations now require that goods must actually be received by the consumer/buyer in conformity with the contract, so risk passes later. Lastly, the manufacturer must bear the return cost for any defective goods under a manufacturer's guarantee.

These new remedies only apply to consumers/buyers of goods sold in the course of a business. Section 15A of the Sale of Goods Act applies to business-to-business sales where there is only a slight breach of an implied condition of description or quality. The provision seeks to prevent a business buyer from rejecting goods due to a technical breach, and imposes an award of damages only. As damages are based on loss, damages for a technical breach will probably be very low. As a result, busi-ness which find that they can get the goods cheaper elsewhere will no longer be encouraged to seek to reject goods for minor breaches. This also recognises that rejections of goods is not the norm in business; normally a recalculation of the price takes place. Having theoretical rights is one thing, but in business one may need to trade with the other party again.

As a final comment, under the Sale and Supply of Goods and Services Act 1982, section 3, there is an implied condition that a supplier acting in the course of busi-ness must carry out the service with reasonable care and skill and within a reasonable time, where a specific deadline is not stated in the contract. Reasonable care and skill tends to be seen as that which might be expected of an ordinary com-petent person performing the particular task, though this will, of course, depend on the particular circumstances of the case and the nature of the trade or profession. As in the case of the Sale of Goods Act, any attempt to deprive the consumer of any of the implied conditions represents a breach both of the Unfair Contract Terms Act 1977 and the Unfair Terms in Consumer Contracts Regulations 1999.

Exclusion or limitation clauses in consumer contracts are subject to the Unfair Contract Terms Act 1977 and the Unfair Terms in Consumer Contracts Regulations 1999, which currently operate as a dual regime, giving the consumer the choice of actions. Under the former any clause seeking to exclude or limit liability for personal injury/death is void while all other clauses are subject to the test of reasonableness. Under the latter regulations a term that has not been individually negotiated will be unfair if it is contrary to good faith by causing a significant imbalance between the parties. The situation is a little different in business deals although personal injury/death still cannot be excluded. Thus, where a reference is made on a product or its container or in a related document to a consumer's rights under sections 13 to 15 of the Sale of Goods Act, there must be a clear and accessible notice informing consumers that their statutory rights are not affected when returning an item deemed unsatisfactory. It is an offence under the Fair Trading Act 1974 to display notices stat-ing 'no refunds' or 'no refunds on sale goods'. The aim is to ensure that buyers are made fully aware of their legal rights and are not taken advantage of by unscrupulous traders who seek to deny them the protection afforded by the law.

The Consumer Protection Act 1987

The Consumer Protection Act 1987 came into force in March 1988 as a result of the government's obligation to implement EC Directive 85/374 which concerned product liability. In essence the Act provides for a remedy in damages for any consumer who suffers personal injury or damage to property as a result of a defective product by imposing a 'strict' liability on the producers of defective goods (including substances, growing crops, ships, aircraft and vehicles). Naturally, the onus is on the complainant to prove that any loss was caused by the claimed defect and a claim can be made where damage to property, personal injury or death has occurred. In the case of the latter, for example, a relative or friend could pursue an action and, if American expe-rience is anything to go by, could be awarded very substantial damages if liability can be proven. As far as property is concerned, damage must be to private rather than commercial goods and property and must exceed £275 for claims to be considered.

While the Act is intended to place liability on the producers of defective goods, this liability also extends to anyone putting a name or distinguishing mark on a product which holds that person out as being the producer (e.g. supermarkets' own-brand labels). Similarly, importers of products from outside the EU are also liable for any defects in imported goods, as may be firms involved in supplying components or parts of the process of manufacture of a product. To prevent a firm escaping its liability as a supplier claiming it is unable to identify its own suppliers, the legislation provides a remedy: any supplier unable or unwilling to identify the importing firm or previous supplier becomes liable itself for damages under the Act.

Firms seeking to avoid liability for any claim have a number of defences under section 4 of the Act. Specifically these are:

- That the defendant did not supply the product in question.
- That the product was not manufactured or supplied in the course of business.
- That the defect did not exist at the time the product was distributed.
- That where a product has a number of components, the defect is a defect of the finished product or due to compliance with any instructions issued by the man-ufacturer of the finished product.
- That the defect is attributable to the requirement to comply with existing laws.
- That the state of scientific and technical knowledge at the time the product was supplied was not sufficiently advanced for the defect to be recognised.

Of these, the last-the so-called development risks or 'state of the art' defence-is the most contentious, given that it applies largely to products such as new drugs and new technology where the implications of their usage may not be apparent for some years. As recent cases have shown, manufacturers faced with damages from claimants who appear to have suffered from the use of certain products often decide to settle out of court without accepting liability for their actions.

The annual Report of the Office of Fair Trading (OFT) contains useful commentary on consumer protection issues, including codes of practice and the powers of the OFT.

CODES OF PRACTICE

Alongside the protection provided by the law, consumers may be afforded a further measure of security when the organisation they are dealing with belongs to a trade association which is operating under a code of practice (e.g. the Association of British Travel Agents). In essence, codes of practice represent an attempt by trade associations to impose a measure of self-discipline on the behaviour of their mem-bers by establishing the standards of service customers should expect to receive and by encouraging acceptable business practices.

In addition, such codes of conduct invariably identify how customer complaints should be handled and many offer low-cost or no-cost arbitration schemes to help settle disputes outside the more formal legal process.

While codes of practice do not in themselves have the force of law, they are nor-mally seen as a useful mechanism for regulating the relationship between business organisations and their customers and accordingly they have the support of the Office of Fair Trading, which often advises trade associations on their content. Businesses, too, usually find them useful, particularly if through the establishment of a system of self-regulation they are able to avoid the introduction of restrictions imposed by the law.

SYNOPSIS

All business activities, from the establishment of the organisation through to the sale of the product to the customer, are influenced by the law. This legal environment within which businesses exist and operate evolves over time and is a key influence on firms of all sizes and in all sectors, as illustrated by an examination of some of the main laws gov-erning the relationship between a business and its customers. The majority of consumer laws are of relatively recent origin and derive from the attempts by successive govern-ments to provide individuals with a measure of protection against a minority of firms which behave in ways deemed to be unacceptable. Concomitantly, they also provide rep-utable organisations with a framework within which to carry out their business and, as such, act as an incentive to entrepreneurial activity in market-based economies.

SUMMARY OF KEY POINTS

- The legal rules within which businesses exist and operate are an important part of the external environment of business organisations.
- Laws affecting businesses derive from a variety of sources including custom, the decisions of the courts and legislation.
- Laws are sometimes made at international and supranational level (including Europe).
- Contract, agency and consumer protection are three key areas governing the day-to-day work of businesses.
- Offer, acceptance, consideration, intention to create legal relations and capacity are central elements of contract law.
- Agency relationships are a common feature of business practice.
- The relationship between businesses and their customers is governed by a variety of laws, many of which derive from statute.
- In addition to the protection provided to consumers by the law, many organisations also operate under agreed codes of conduct.

CASE STUDY: THE SALE OF GOODS ON THE INTERNET

The sale of consumer goods on the Internet (particularly those between European member states) raises a number of legal issues. First, there is the issue of trust, with-out which the consumer will not buy; they will need assurance that the seller is genuine, and that they will get the goods that they believe they have ordered.

Second, there is the issue of consumer rights with respect to the goods in question: what rights exist and do they vary across Europe? Last, the issue of enforcement: what happens should anything go wrong?

Information and Trust

Europe recognises the problems of doing business across the Internet or telephone and it has attempted to address the main stumbling blocks via Directives. The Consumer Protection (Distance Selling) Regulations 2000 attempts to address the issues of trust in cross-border consumer sales, which may take place over the Internet (or telephone). In short, the consumer needs to know quite a bit of infor-mation, which they may otherwise have easy access to if they were buying face to face. Regulation 7 requires *inter alia* for the seller to identify themselves and an address must be provided if the goods are to be paid for in advance. Moreover, a full description of the goods and the final price (inclusive of any taxes) must also be provided. The seller must also inform the buyer of the right of cancellation available under Regulations 10-12, where the buyer has a right to cancel the con-tract for seven days starting on the day after the consumer receives the goods or services. Failure to inform the consumer of this right automatically extends the period to three months. The cost of returning goods is to be borne by the buyer, and the seller is entitled to deduct the costs directly flowing from recovery as a restocking fee. All of this places a considerable obligation on the seller; however, such data should stem many misunderstandings and so greatly assist consumer faith and confidence in non-face-to-face sales.

Another concern for the consumer is fraud. The consumer who has paid by credit card will be protected by section 83 of the Consumer Credit Act 1974, under which a consumer/purchaser is not liable for the debt incurred, if it has been run up by a third party not acting as the agent of the buyer. The Distance Selling Regulations extend this to debit cards, and remove the ability of the card issuer to charge the consumer for the first £50 of loss (Regulation 21). Moreover, section 75 of the Consumer Credit Act 1974 also gives the consumer/buyer a like claim against the credit card company for any misrepresentation or breach of contract by the seller. This is extremely important in a distance selling transaction, where the seller may disappear.

What Quality and what Rights?

The next issue relates to the quality that may be expected from goods bought over the Internet. Clearly, if goods have been bought from abroad, the levels of quality required in other jurisdictions may vary. It is for this reason that Europe has attempted to standardise the issue of quality and consumer rights, with the Consumer Guarantees Directive (1999/44/EC), thus continuing the push to encour-age cross-border consumer purchases.

The implementing Sale and Supply of Goods to Consumer Regulations 2002 came into force in 2003, which not only lays down minimum quality standards, but also provides a series of consumer remedies which will be common across Europe. The Regulations further amend the Sale of Goods Act 1979. The DTI, whose job it was to incorporate the Directive into domestic law (by way of delegated legislation) ensured that the pre-existing consumer rights were maintained, so as not to reduce the overall level of protection available to con-sumers. The Directive requires goods to be of 'normal' quality, or fit for any purpose made known by the seller.

This has been taken to be the same as our pre-existing 'reasonable quality' and 'fitness for purpose' obligations owed under sections 14(2) and 14(3) of the Sale of Goods Act 1979. Moreover, the pre-existing remedy of the short-term right to reject is also retained. This right provides the buyer a short period of time to discover whether the goods are in conformity with the contract. In practice, it is usually a matter of weeks at most. After that time has elapsed, the consumer now has four new remedies that did not exist before, which are provided in two pairs. These are repair or replacement, or price reduction or rescission. The pre-existing law only gave the consumer a right to damages, which would rarely be exercised in practice. (However, the Small Claims Court would ensure a speedy and cheap means of redress for almost all claims brought.) Now there is a right to a repair or a replacement, so that the consumer is not left with an impractical action for damages over defective goods.

The seller must also bear the cost of return of the goods for repair. So such costs must now be factored into any business sales plan. If neither of these remedies is suitable or actioned within a 'rea-sonable period of time' then the consumer may rely on the second pair of remedies. Price reduction permits the consumer to claim back a segment of the pur-chase price if the goods are still useable. It is effectively a discount for defective goods. Rescission permits the consumer to reject the goods, but does not get a full refund, as they would under the short-term right to reject. Here money is knocked off for 'beneficial use'. This is akin to the pre-existing treatment for breaches of durability, where goods have not lasted as long as goods of that type ought reason-ably be expected to last. The level of compensation would take account of the use that the consumer has (if any) been able to put the goods to and a deduction made off the return of the purchase price. However, the issue that must be addressed is as to the length of time that goods may be expected to last. A supplier may state the length of the guarantee period, so a £500 television set guaranteed for one year would have a life expectancy of one year. On the other hand, a consumer may expect a television set to last ten years. Clearly, if the set went wrong after six months, the consumer would only get £250 back if the retailer's figure was used, but would receive £475 if their own figure was used. It remains to be seen how this provision will work in practice.

One problem with distance sales has been that of liability for goods which arrive damaged. The pre-existing domestic law stated that risk would pass to the buyer once the goods were handed over to a third-party carrier. This had the major problem in practice of who would actually be liable for the damage. Carriers would blame the supplier and vice versa. The consumer would be able to sue for the loss, if they were able to determine which party was responsible. In practice, consumers usually went uncompensated and such a worry has put many consumers off buying goods over the Internet. The Sale and Supply of Goods to Consumer Regulations also modify the transfer of risk, so that now the risk remains with the seller until actual delivery. This will clearly lead to a slight increase in the supply of goods to consumers, with the goods usually now being sent by insured delivery. However, this will avoid the prob-lem of who is actually liable and should help to boost confidence.

Enforcement

Enforcement for domestic sales is relatively straightforward. Small-scale consumer claims can be dealt with expeditiously and cheaply under the Small Claims Court. Here claims under £5000 for contract-based claims are brought in a special court intended to keep costs down by keeping the lawyers' out of the court room, as a victorious party cannot claim for their lawyers' expenses. The judge will conduct the case in a more 'informal' manner, and will seek to discover the legal issues by questioning both parties, so no formal knowledge of the law is required. The total cost of such a case, even if it is lost, is the cost of issuing the proceedings (approximately 10 per cent of the value claimed) and the other side's 'reasonable expenses'. Expenses must be kept down, and a judge will not award value which has been deliberately run up, such first-class rail travel and stays in five star hotels. Residents of Northampton have hosted a trial of an online claims procedure, so that claims may now be made via the Internet. (*www.courtservice.gov.uk* outlines the procedure for MCOL, or Money Claims Online.) Cases will normally be held in the defendant's court, unless the complainant is a consumer and the defendant a business.

Enforcement is the weak point in the European legislation, for there is, as yet, no European-wide Small Claims Court dealing with transnational European transac-tions. The consumer is thus forced to contemplate expensive civil action abroad in a foreign language, perhaps where no such small claims system exists-a pointless measure for all but the most expensive of consumer purchases. The only redress lies in EEJ-Net, the European Extra-Judicial Network, which puts the complainant in touch with any applicable professional or trade body in the supplier's home member state. It does require the existence of such a body, which is unlikely if the transac-tion is for electrical goods, which is one of the most popular types of Internet purchase. Therefore, until Europe provides a Euro Small Claims Court, the consumer cross-border buyer may have many rights, but no effective means of enforcement. Until then it would appear that section 75 of the Consumer Credit Act 1974, which gives the buyer the same remedies against their credit card company as against the seller, is the only effective means of redress.

7

Legal Structures

INTRODUCTION

Business organisations can be classified in a variety of ways, including:

- size (e.g. small, medium, large);
- type of industry (e.g. primary, secondary, tertiary);
- sector (e.g. private sector, public sector); and
- legal status (e.g. sole trader, partnership, and so on).

These classifications help to distinguish one type of organisation from another and to focus attention on the implications of such differences for an individual enterprise. In the discus-sion below, business organisations are examined as legal structures and the consequences of variations in legal status are discussed in some detail. Subsequent chapters in this sec-tion investigate alternative structural perspectives in order to highlight how these too have an important bearing on the environment in which businesses operate.

PRIVATE SECTOR ORGANISATIONS IN THE UK THE SOLE TRADER

Many individuals aspire to owning and running their own business-being their own boss, making their own decisions. For those who decide to turn their dream into a reality, becoming a sole trader (or sole proprietor) offers the simplest and eas-iest method of trading.

As the name suggests, a sole trader is a business owned by one individual who is self-employed and who may, in some cases, employ other people on either a full-time or a part-time basis. Normally using personal funds to start the business, the sole trader decides on the type of goods or services to be produced, where the busi-ness is to be located, what capital is required, what staff (if any) to employ, what the target market should be and a host of other aspects concerned with the estab-lishment and running of the enterprise. Where the business proves a success, all profits accrue to the owner and it is common for sole traders to reinvest a consider-able proportion of these in the business and/or use them to reduce past borrowings. Should losses occur, these too are the responsibility of the sole trader, who has unlimited personal liability for the debts of the business.

Despite this substantial disadvantage, sole proprietorship tends to be the most popular form of business organisation numerically. In the United Kingdom, for example, it is estimated that about 80 per cent of all businesses are sole traders and in some sectors-notably personal services, retailing, building-they tend to be the dominant form of business enterprise. Part of the reason for this numerical domi-nance is the relative ease with which an individual can establish a business of this type. Apart from minor restrictions concerning the use of a business name-if the name of the proprietor is not used-few other legal formalities are required to set up the enterprise, other than the need to register for Value Added Tax if turnover exceeds a certain sum (e.g. £58000 in 2004/5) and/or to fulfil any special requirements laid down by the local authority prior to trading (e.g. some businesses require licences). Once established, of course, the sole trader, like other forms of business, will be subject to a variety of legal requirements (e.g. contract law, con-sumer law, employment law)-though not the requirement to file information about the business in a public place. For some, this ability to keep the affairs of the enterprise away from public scrutiny provides a further incentive to establishing this form of business organisation-some of which may operate wholly or partly in the 'black economy' (i.e. beyond the gaze of the tax authorities).

A further impetus towards sole ownership comes from the ability of the individ-ual to exercise a considerable degree of control over their own destiny. Business decisions-including the day-to-day operations of the enterprise as well as long-term plans-are in the hands of the owner and many individuals evidently relish the risks and potential rewards associated with entrepreneurial activity, preferring these to the relative 'safety' of employment in another organisation. For others less fortunate, the 'push' of unemployment rather than the 'pull' of the marketplace tends to be more of a deciding factor and one which clearly accounts for some of the growth in the number of small businesses in the United Kingdom in the later part of the twentieth century.

Ambitions and commitment alone, however, are not necessarily sufficient to guarantee the survival and success of the enterprise and the high mortality rate among businesses of this kind, particularly during a recession, is well known and well documented. Part of the problem may stem from developments largely outside the control of the enterprise-including bad debts, increased competition, higher interest rates, falling demand-and factors such as these affect businesses of all types and all sizes, not just sole traders. Other difficulties, such as lack of funds for expansion, poor marketing, lack of research of the marketplace and insufficient management skills are to some extent self-induced and emanate, at least in part, from the decision to become a sole proprietor rather than some other form of busi-ness organisation. Where such constraints exist, the sole trader may be tempted to look to others to share the burdens and the risks by establishing a partnership or co-operative or limited company or by seeking a different approach to the business venture, such as through 'franchising'. These alternative forms of business organisa-tion are discussed in detail below.

The Partnership

The Partnership Act 1890 defines a partnership as 'the relation which subsists between persons carrying on a business in common with a view to profit'. Like the sole trader, this form of business organisation does not have its own distinct legal personality and hence the owners-the partners-have unlimited personal liability both jointly and severally. This means that in the case of debts or bankruptcy of the partnership, each partner is liable in full for the whole debt and each in turn may be sued or their assets seized until the debt is satisfied. Alternatively, all the partners may be joined into the action to recover debts, unless by dint of the Limited Partnership Act 1907, a partner (or partners) has limited liability. Since it tends to be much easier to achieve the same ends by establishing a limited company, limited partnerships are not common; nor can all partners in a partnership have limited liability. Hence in the discussion below, attention is focused on the partnership as an unincorporated association, operating in a market where its liability is effec-tively unlimited.

In essence, a partnership comes into being when two or more people establish a business which they own, finance and run jointly for personal gain, irrespective of the degree of formality involved in the relationship. Such a business can range from a husband and wife running a local shop as joint owners, to a very large firm of accountants or solicitors, with in excess of a hundred partners in offices in various locations. Under the law, most partnerships are limited to 20 or less, but some types of business, particularly in the professions, may have a dispensation from this rule (Companies Act 1985, s 716). This same Act requires businesses which are not exempt from the rule and which have more than 20 partners to register as a company.

While it is not necessary for a partnership to have a formal written agreement, most partnerships tend to be formally enacted in a Deed of Partnership or Articles since this makes it much easier to reduce uncertainty and to ascertain intentions when there is a written document to consult. Where this is not done, the Partnership Act 1890 lays down a minimum code which governs the relationship between partners and which provides, amongst other things, for all partners to share equally in the capital and profits of the business and to contribute equally towards its losses.

In practice, of course, where a Deed or Articles exist, these will invariably reflect differences in the relative status and contribution of individual partners. Senior partners, for example, will often have contributed more financially to the partner-ship and not unnaturally will expect to receive a higher proportion of the profits. Other arrangements-including membership, action on dissolution of the partner-ship, management responsibilities and rights, and the basis for allocating salaries-will be outlined in the partnership agreement and as such will provide the legal framework within which the enterprise exists and its co-owners operate.

Unlike the sole trader, where management responsibilities devolve on a single individual, partnerships permit the sharing of responsibilities and tasks and it is common in a partnership for individuals to specialise to some degree in particular aspects of the organisation's work-as in the case of a legal or medical or veterinary practice. Added to this, the fact that more than one person is involved in the own-ership of the business tends to increase the amount of finance available to the organisation, thus permitting expansion to take place without the owners losing control of the enterprise. These two factors alone tend to make a partnership an attractive proposition for some would-be entrepreneurs; while for others the rules of their professional body-which often prohibits its members from forming a company-effectively provide for the establishment of this type of organisation.

On the downside, the sharing of decisions and responsibilities may represent a problem, particularly where partners are unable to agree over the direction the part-nership should take or the amount to be reinvested in the business, unless such matters are clearly specified in a formal agreement. A more intractable problem is the existence of unlimited personal liability-a factor which may inhibit some individuals from considering this form of organisation, particularly given that the actions of any one partner are invariably binding on the other members of the business. To overcome this problem, many individuals, especially in manufacturing and trading, look to the limited company as the type of organisation which can combine the benefits of joint ownership and limited personal liability-a situation not necessarily always borne out in practice. It is to this type of business organisa-tion that the discussion now turns.

Limited Companies

In law a company is a corporate association having a legal identity in its own right (i.e. it is distinct from the people who own it, unlike in the case of a sole trader or partnership). This means that all property and other assets owned by the company belong to the company and not to its members (owners). By the same token, the per-sonal assets of its members (the shareholders) do not normally belong to the business. In the event of insolvency, therefore, an individual's liability is limited to the amount invested in the business, including any amount remaining unpaid on the shares for which they have subscribed. One exception to this would be where a com-pany's owners have given a personal guarantee to cover any loans they have obtained from a bank or other institution-a requirement for many small, private limited com-panies. Another occurs where a company is limited by guarantee rather than by shares, with its members' liability being limited to the amount they have undertaken to contribute to the assets in the event of the company being wound up. Companies of this type are normally non-profit-making organisations-such as professional, research or trade associations-and are much less common than companies limited by shares. Hence in the discussion below, attention is focused on the latter as the domi-nant form of business organisation in the corporate sector of business.

Companies are essentially business organisations consisting of two or more indi-viduals who have agreed to embark on a business venture and who have decided to seek corporate status rather than to form a partnership. Such status could derive from an Act of Parliament or a Royal Charter, but is almost always nowadays achieved through 'registration', the terms of which are laid down in the various Companies Acts. Under the legislation, enacted in 1985 and 1989, individuals seek-ing to form a company are required to file numerous documents, including a Memorandum of Association and Articles of Association, with the Registrar of Companies. If satisfied, the Registrar will issue a Certificate of Incorporation, bring-ing the company into existence as a legal entity. As an alternative, the participants could buy a ready-formed company 'off the shelf, by approaching a company reg-istration agent who specialises in company formations. In the United Kingdom, advertisements for ready-made companies appear regularly in magazines such as *Exchange and Mart* and *Dalton's Weekly*.

Under British law a distinction is made between public and private companies. Public limited companies (PLCs)-not to be confused with public corporations, which in the UK are state-owned businesses are those limited compa-nies which satisfy the conditions for being a 'PLC. These conditions require the company to have:

- a minimum of two shareholders;
- at least two directors;
- a minimum (at present) of £50000 of authorised and allotted share capital;
- the right to offer its shares (and debentures) for sale to the general public;
- a certificate from the Registrar of Companies verifying that the share capital requirements have been met; and
- a memorandum which states it to be a public company.

A company which meets these conditions must include the title 'public limited company' or 'PLC in its name and is required to make full accounts available for public inspection. Any company unable or unwilling to meet these conditions is therefore, in the eyes of the law, a 'private limited company', normally signified by the term 'Limited' or 'Ltd'. Like the public limited company, the private limited company must have a mini-mum of two shareholders, but its shares cannot be offered to the public at large, although it can offer them to individuals through its business contacts. This restriction on the sale of shares, and hence on their ability to raise considerable sums of money on the open market, normally ensures that most private companies are either small or medium sized, and are often family businesses operating in a relatively restricted market; there are, however, some notable exceptions to this general rule (e.g. Virgin). In contrast, public companies-many of which began life as private companies prior to 'going public'-often have many thousands, even millions, of owners (shareholders) and normally operate on a national or international scale, producing products as diverse as computers, petro-chemicals, cars and banking services. Despite being out-numbered by their private counterparts, public companies dwarf private companies in terms of their capital and other assets, and their collective influence on output, invest-ment, employment and consumption in the economy is immense.

Both public and private companies act through their directors. These are indi-viduals chosen by a company's shareholders to manage its affairs and to make the important decisions concerning the direction the company should take (e.g. invest-ment, market development, mergers and so on). The appointment and powers of directors are outlined in the Articles of Association (the 'internal rules' of the organisation) and so long as the directors do not exceed their powers, the share-holders do not normally have the right to intervene in the day-to-day management of the company. Where a director exceeds his or her authority or fails to indicate clearly that they are acting as an agent for the company, they become personally liable for any contracts they make. Equally, directors become personally liable if they continue to trade when the company is insolvent and they may be dismissed by a court if it considers that an individual is unfit to be a director in view of their past record (Company Directors Disqualification Act 1985).

It is usual for a board of directors to have both a chairperson and a managing director, although many companies choose to appoint one person to both roles. The chairperson, who is elected by the other members of the board, is usually chosen because of their knowledge and experience of the business and their skill both internally in chairing board meetings and externally in representing the best interest of the organisation. As the public face of the company, the chairperson has an important role to play in establishing and maintaining a good public image and hence many large public companies like to appoint well-known public figures to this important position (e.g. ex-Cabinet ministers). In this case knowledge of the business is less important than the other attributes the individual might possess, most notably public visibility and familiarity together with a network of contacts in government and in the business world.

The managing director, or chief executive, fulfils a pivotal role in the organisation, by forming the link between the board and the management team of senior execu-tives. Centrai to this role is the need not only to interpret board decisions but to ensure that they are put into effect by establishing an appropriate structure of dele-gated responsibility and effective systems of reporting and control. This close contact with the day-to-day operations of the company places the appointed individual in a position of considerable authority and they will invariably be able to make important decisions without reference to the full board. This authority is enhanced where the managing director is also the person chairing the board of directors and/or is responsi-ble for recommending individuals to serve as executive directors (i.e. those with functional responsibilities such as production, marketing, finance).

Like the managing director, most, if not all, executive directors will be full-time executives of the company, responsible for running a division or functional area within the framework laid down at board level. In contrast, other directors will have a non-executive role and are usually part-time appointees, chosen for a vari-ety of reasons, including their knowledge, skills, contacts, influence, independence or previous experience. Sometimes, a company might be required to appoint such a director at the wishes of a third party, such as a merchant bank which has agreed to fund a large capital injection and wishes to have representation on the board. In this case, the individual tends to act in an advisory capacity-particularly on mat-ters of finance-and helps to provide the financing institution with a means of ensuring that any board decisions are in its interests.

In Britain the role of company directors and senior executives in recent years has come under a certain amount of public scrutiny and has culminated in a number of enquiries into issues of power and pay. In the Cadbury Report (1992), a committee, with Sir Adrian Cadbury as chairperson, called for a non-statutory code of practice which it wanted applied to all listed public companies. Under this code the com-mittee recommended:

- a clear division of responsibilities at the head of a company to ensure that no individual had unfettered powers of decision;
- a greater role for non-executive directors;
- regular board meetings;
- restrictions on the contracts of executive directors;
- full disclosure of directors' total enrolments;
- an audit committee dominated by non-executives.

The committee's stress on the important role of non-executive directors was a theme taken up in the Greenbury Report (1995) which investigated the controver-sial topic of executive salaries in the wake of a number of highly publicised pay rises for senior company directors. Greenbury's recommendations included:

- full disclosure of directors' pay packages, including pensions;
- shareholder approval for any long-term bonus scheme;
- remuneration committees consisting entirely of non-executive directors;
- greater detail in the annual report on directors' pay, pensions and perks;
- an end to payments for failure.

Greenbury was followed by a further investigation into corporate governance by a committee under the chairmanship of ICI chairman Ronald Hampei. The Hampel Report (1998) called for greater shareholder responsibility by companies and increased standards of disclosure of information; it supported Cadbury's recom-mendation that the role of chairperson and chief executive should normally be separated. As might have been anticipated, the Hampel Report advocated self-regu-lation as the best approach for UK companies.

As far as the issue of non-executive directors was concerned, this was investi-gated further by the Higgs Committee which was set up in 2002 and which reported the following year. In essence the Higgs Report set down a code of non-binding corporate guidelines regarding the role of non-executive directors on company boards. Like the Cadbury Report, Higgs recommended that the role of chairperson and chief executive should be kept separate and that the former should be independent, though not necessarily non-executive. As for non-executive direc-tors, Higgs recommended that at least half the board should be independent and that non-executives should play key roles in areas such as strategy, performance, risk and the appointment and remuneration of executive directors. The latter issue, in particular, has been an area of considerable controversy in the UK in recent years and seems destined to remain so for some time.

MINI CASE: DAIMLER-BENZ UNDER PRESSURE

Public companies have to satisfy the conflicting demands of a range of stakeholder groups (*see* below), not least their shareholders who expect the organisation to operate in their interest. On the whole, individual shareholders are usually relatively quiescent, leaving the strategic and day-to-day decisions to the organisation's directors and senior executives. As an increasing number of public companies have found, however, many shareholders are becoming more actively involved in corporate decisions which affect their investments and have been willing to voice their feelings at shareholders' meetings and to the media. This is particularly true of large corporate investors.

Daimler-Benz, Germany's biggest industrial group, is an example of a company which has experienced this rise in shareholder militancy. At its centenary annual meeting held in Stuttgart in May 1996, the company's senior personnel faced around 10000 shareholders, a significant number of whom expressed concern over record losses, allegations of executive deceit and plans to shed another aerospace subsidiary. Both the board of directors and the supervisory board were accused of failure by small shareholders who had recently experienced no dividends on the back of the largest loss in German corporate history. Claims by board chairperson Jürgen Schrempp that he was seeking to turn the situation around and to promote 'shareholder value' did little to placate the critics who were keen to see heads roll.

Apart from allegations of incompetence and abuse of position, the directors were subjected to criticisms from environmentalist shareholders and those campaigning against the company's sales of military hardware. This only serves to demonstrate that *within* any one stakeholder group there will tend to be a range of different opinions and interests-a fact which can make the task of satisfying stakeholder aspirations considerably more difficult.

Consumer Co-operative Societies

Consumer societies are basically 'self-help' organisations which have their roots in the anti-capitalist sentiment which arose in mid-nineteenth-century Britain and which gave rise to a consumer co-operative movement dedicated to the provision of cheap, unadulterated food for its members and a share in its profits. Today this movement boasts a multibillion-pound turnover, a membership numbered in millions and an empire which includes thousands of food stores (including the Alldays convenience chain purchased in 2002), numerous factories and farms, dairies, travel agencies, opti-cians, funeral parlours, a bank and an insurance company, and property and development business. Taken together, these activities ensure that the Co-operative Group remains a powerful force in British retailing into the early twenty-first century.

Although the co-operative societies, like companies, are registered and incorporated bodies-in this case under the Industrial and Provident Societies Act-they are quite distinct trading organisations. These societies belong to their members (i.e. invariably customers who have purchased a share in the society) who elect Area Committees to oversee trading areas. These committees have annual elections and meetings for all members and these in turn appoint members on to regional boards and elect individual member directors to the Group Board. The Group Board also includes directors of corporate members who are representatives of other societies. Individual stores may also have member forums. Any profits from the Group's activities are supposed to benefit the members. Originally this took the form of a cash dividend paid to members in relation to their purchases, but this was subse-quently replaced either by trading stamps or by investment in areas felt to benefit the consumer (e.g. lower prices, higher-quality products, modern shops, and so on) and/or the local community (e.g. charitable donations, sponsorship). The twice-yearly cash dividend has, however, recently been reintroduced. The societies differ in other ways from standard companies. For a start, shares are not quoted on the Stock Exchange and members are restricted in the number of shares they can purchase and in the method of disposal. Not having access to cheap sources of capital on the stock market, co-operatives rely heavily on retained surpluses and on loan finance, and the latter places a heavy burden on the societies when interest rates are high. The movement's democratic principles also impinge on its operations and this has often been a bone of contention as members have complained about their increasing remoteness from decision-making centres. Some societies have responded by encouraging the development of locally elected com-mittees, to act in an advisory or consultative capacity to the society's board of directors and it looks likely that others will be forced to consider similar means of increasing member participation, which still remains very limited.

The movement's historical links with the British Labour Party are also worth noting and a number of parliamentary candidates are normally sponsored at gen-eral elections. These links, however, have tended to become slightly looser in recent years, although the movement still contributes to Labour Party funds and contin-ues to lobby politicians at both national and local level. It is also active in seeking to influence public opinion and, in this, claims to be responding to customer demands for greater social and corporate responsibility. Among its initiatives are the establishment of a customer's charter (by the Co-operative Bank) and the deci-sion to review both its investments and the individuals and organisations it does business with, to ascertain that they are acceptable from an ethical point of view.

Workers' Co-operatives

In Britain, workers' co-operatives are found in a wide range of industries, includ-ing manufacturing, building and construction, engineering, catering and retailing. They are particularly prevalent in printing, clothing and wholefoods, and some have been in existence for over a century. The majority, however, are of fairly recent origin, having been part of the growth in the number of small firms which occurred in the 1980s.

As the name suggests, a workers' co-operative is a business in which the owner-ship and control of the assets are in the hands of the people working in it, having agreed to establish the enterprise and to share the risk for mutual benefit. Rather than form a standard partnership, the individuals involved normally register the business as a friendly society under the Industrial and Provident Societies Acts 1965-78, or seek incorporation as a private limited company under the Companies Act 1985. In the case of the former, seven members are required to form a co-opera-tive, while the latter only requires two. In practice, a minimum of three or four members tends to be the norm and some co-operatives may have several hundred participants, frequently people who have been made redundant by their employers and who are keen to keep the business going.

The central principles of the movement-democracy, open membership, social responsibility, mutual co-operation and trust-help to differentiate the co-operative from other forms of business organisation and govern both the formation and operation of this type of enterprise. Every employee may be a member of the organ-isation and every member owns one share in the business, with every share carrying an equal voting right. Any surpluses are shared by democratic agreement and this is normally done on an equitable basis, reflecting, for example, the amount of time and effort an individual puts into the business. Other decisions, too, are taken jointly by the members and the emphasis tends to be on the quality of goods or services provided and on creating a favourable working environment, rather than on the pursuit of profits-although the latter cannot be ignored if the organisation is to survive. In short, the co-operative tends to focus on people and on the relationship between them, stressing the co-operative and communal tradi-tions associated with its origins, rather than the more conflictual and competitive aspects inherent in other forms of industrial organisation.

Despite these apparent attractions, workers' co-operatives have never been as popular in Britain as in other parts of the world (e.g. France, Italy, Israel), although a substantial increase occurred in the number of co-operatives in the 1980s, largely as a result of growing unemployment, overt support across the political spectrum and the establish-ment of a system to encourage and promote the co-operative ideal (e.g. Co-operative Development Agencies). More recently however, their fortunes have tended to decline, as employee shareholding and profit schemes (ESOPs) have grown in popularity. It seems unlikely that workers' co-operatives will ever form the basis of a strong third sector in the British economy, between the profit-oriented firms in the private sector and the nationalised and municipal undertakings in the public sector.

PUBLIC SECTOR BUSINESS ORGANISATIONS IN THE UK

Public sector organisations come in a variety of forms. These include:

- central government departments (e.g. Department of Trade and Industry);
- local authorities (e.g. Lancashire County Council);
- regional bodies (e.g. Regional Development Agencies);
- non-departmental public bodies or quangos (e.g. the Arts Council);
- central government trading organisations (e.g. The Stationery Office); and
- public corporations and nationalised industries (e.g. the BBC).

Public Corporations

Private sector business organisations are owned by private individuals and groups who have chosen to invest in some form of business enterprise, usually with a view to personal gain. In contrast, in the public sector the state owns assets in various forms, which it uses to provide a range of goods and services felt to be of benefit to its citizens, even if this provision involves the state in a 'loss'. Many of these serv-ices are provided directly through government departments (e.g. social security benefits) or through bodies operating under delegated authority from central gov-ernment (e.g. local authorities, health authorities). Others are the responsibility of state-owned industrial and commercial undertakings, specially created for a variety of reasons and often taking the form of a 'public corporation'.

These state corpora-tions are an important part of the public sector of the economy and have contributed significantly to national output, employment and investment. Their numbers, however, have declined substantially following the wide-scale 'privatisa-tion' of state industries which occurred in the 1980s and this process has continued through the 1990s and beyond with the sale of corporations such as British Coal, British Rail and British Energy.

Public corporations are statutory bodies, incorporated (predominantly) by special Act of Parliament and, like companies, they have a separate legal identity from the individuals who own them and run them. Under the statute setting up the corpora-tion, reference is made to the powers, duties and responsibilities of the organisation and to its relationship with the government department which oversees its opera-tions. In the past these operations have ranged from providing a variety of national and international postal services (the Post Office), to the provision of entertainment (the BBC), an energy source (British Coal) and a national rail network (British Rail). Where such provision involves the organisation in a considerable degree of direct contact with its customers, from whom it derives most of its revenue, the corpora-tion tends to be called a 'nationalised industry'. In reality, of course, the public corporation is the legal form through which the industry is both owned and run and every corporation is to some degree unique in structure as well as in functions.

As organisations largely financed as well as owned by the state, public corpora-tions are required to be publicly accountable and hence they invariably operate under the purview of a 'sponsoring' government department, the head of which (the Secretary of State) appoints a board of management to run the organisation. This board tends to exercise a considerable degree of autonomy in day-to-day deci-sions and operates largely free from political interference on most matters of a routine nature. The organisation's strategic objectives, however, and important questions concerning reorganisation or investment, would have to be agreed with the sponsoring department, as would the corporation's performance targets and its external financing limits.

The link between the corporation and its supervising ministry provides the means through which Parliament can oversee the work of the organisation and permits ordi-nary Members of Parliament to seek information and explanation through question time, through debates and through the select committee system. Additionally, under the Competition Act 1980, nationalised industries can be subject to investigation by the Competition Commission, and this too presents opportunities for further parliamentary discussion and debate, as well as for government action. A further opportunity for public scrutiny comes from the establishment of indus-try-specific Consumers' or Consultative Councils, which consider complaints from customers and advise both the board and the department concerned of public atti-tudes to the organisation's performance and to other aspects of its operations (e.g. pricing). In a number of cases, including British Rail before privatisation, pressure on government from consumers and from other sources has resulted in the estab-lishment of a 'Customers' Charter', under which the organisation agrees to provide a predetermined level of service or to give information and/or compensation where standards are not achieved. Developments of this kind are already spreading to other parts of the public sector and in future may be used as a means by which gov-ernments decide on the allocation of funds to public bodies, as well as providing a vehicle for monitoring organisational achievement.

It is interesting to note that mechanisms for public accountability and state regu-lation have been retained to some degree even where public utilities have been 'privatised' (i.e. turned into public limited companies). Industries such as gas, elec-tricity, water and telecommunications are watched over by newly created regulatory bodies which are designed to protect the interests of consumers, particu-larly with regard to pricing and the standard of service provided. Ofgas, for example, which used to regulate British Gas, monitored gas supply charges to ensure that they reasonably reflected input costs and these charges could be altered by the 'regulator' if they were seen to be excessive. Similarly, in the case of non-gas services, such as maintenance, the legislation privatising the industry only allowed prices to be raised to a prescribed maximum, to ensure that the organisation was not able to take full advantage of its monopoly power.

An additional source of government influence has come through its ownership of a 'golden share' in a privatised state industry which effectively gives the govern-ment a veto in certain vital areas of decision making. This notional shareholding-which is written into the privatisation legislation-tends to last for a number of years and can be used to protect a newly privatised business from a hostile takeover, particularly by foreign companies or individuals. Ultimately, however, the expectation is that this veto power will be relinquished and the organisation con-cerned will become subject to the full effects of the market-a point exemplified by the government's decision to allow Ford to take over Jaguar in 1990, having origi-nally blocked a number of previous takeover bids.

The existence of a 'golden share' should not be equated with the decision by government to retain (or purchase) a significant proportion of issued shares in a privatised (or already private) business organisation, whether as an investment and/or future source of revenue, or as a means of exerting influence in a particular industry or sector. Nor should it be confused with government schemes to attract private funds into existing state enterprises, by allowing them to achieve notional company status in order to overcome Treasury restrictions on borrowing imposed on public bodies. In the latter case, which often involves a limited share issue, gov-ernment still retains full control of the organisation by owning all (or the vast majority) of the shares-as in the case of Consignia (formerly known as the Post Office). In March 2001 Consignia was incorporated as a government-owned public company. This change in legal status allowed the company more freedom to borrow and invest in the business, to make acquisitions and to enter into joint ven-tures and to expand internationally. Since the last edition was published the name Consignia has been dropped in favour of the original name.

Municipal Enterprises

UK local authorities have a long history of involvement in business activity. In part this is a function of their role as central providers of public services (e.g. education, housing, roads, social services) and of their increasing involvement in supporting local economic development initiatives. But their activities have also traditionally involved the provision of a range of marketable goods and services, not required by law but provided voluntarily by a local authority and often in direct competition with the private sector (e.g. theatres, leisure services, museums). Usually such provision has taken place under the aegis of a local authority department which appoints staff who are answerable to the council and to its committees through the department's chief officer and its elected head. Increasingly, though, local authorities are turning to other organisational arrangements-including the establishment of companies and trusts-in order to separate some of these activities from the rest of their responsibilities and to create a means through which private investment in the enterprise can occur.

One example of such a development can be seen in the case of local authority controlled airports which are normally the responsibility of a number of local authorities who run them through a joint board, representing the interests of the participating district councils (e.g. Manchester International Airport). Since the Airports Act 1986, local authorities with airports have been required to create a lim-ited company in which their joint assets are vested and which appoints a board of directors to run the enterprise. Like other limited companies, the organisation can, if appropriate, seek private capital and must publish annual accounts, including a profit and loss statement. It can also be 'privatised' relatively easily if the local authorities involved decide to relinquish ownership (e.g. the former East Midlands Airport now renamed Nottingham East Midlands Airport and part of the Manchester Airports Group).

Such developments, which have parallels in other parts of the public sector, can be seen to have had at least four benefits:

1. They have provided a degree of autonomy from local authority control that is seen to be beneficial in a competitive trading environment.
2. They have given access to market funds by the establishment of a legal structure that is not fully subject to central government restrictions on local authority borrowing.
3. They helped local authority organisations to compete more effectively under the now defunct system of compulsory competitive tendering (CCT), by removing or reducing charges for departmental overheads that are applied under the normal arrangements.
4. They have provided a vehicle for further private investment and for ultimate privatisation of the service.

Given these benefits and the current fashion for privatisation, there is little doubt that they will become an increasing feature of municipal enterprise in the foresee-able future. That said, local authorities are restricted in their degree of ownership of companies following the passage of the 1990 Local Government and Housing Act.

BUSINESS ORGANISATIONS IN MAINLAND EUROPE

Sole traders, partnerships, co-operatives and limited companies are to be found throughout Europe and beyond, and in many cases their legal structure is similar to that of their British counterparts. Where differences occur, these are often a reflec-tion of historical and cultural factors which find expression in custom and practice as well as in law. Examples of some of these differences are contained in the discus-sion below, which focuses on France, Germany, Denmark and Portugal.

France

Numerically, the French economy is dominated by very small businesses (i.e. fewer than ten employees), the majority of which are sole traders. As in Britain, these are owner-managed-and-operated enterprises, with a husband and wife often assuming joint responsibility for the business. Formal requirements in this type of organisa-tion tend to be few, although individuals as well as companies engaging in a commercial business are required to register before trading officially begins. Since this process is relatively simple and there are no minimum capital requirements nor significant reporting obligations, sole traderships tend to be preferred by the vast majority of individuals seeking to start a business and they are particularly preva-lent in the service sector. They carry, however, unlimited personal liability for the owner, whose personal assets are at risk in the event of business failure.

Most of the remaining French business organisations are limited companies, many of which are Petites et Moyennes Entreprises (PMEs)-small and medium enterprises-employing between 10 and 500 employees. These companies come in a variety of legal forms, but two in particular predominate: the Société à Responsabilité Limitée (SARL) and the Société Anonyme (SA). A new company form, the Société Anonyme Simplifée was created by statute in 1994 and combines the legal status of a corporation with the flexibility of a partnership.

The SARL tends to be the form preferred by smaller companies, whose owners wish to retain close control of the organisation; hence many of them are family businesses-an important feature of the private sector in France. This type of enter-prise can be established (currently) with a minimum capital of €7500, cannot issue shares to the general public, has restrictions on the transfer of shares and is run by individuals appointed by the shareholders-usually the shareholders themselves and/ or relatives. In practice, these various restrictions help to ensure that the owner-managers remain dominant in the organisation and the appointed head of the company will invariably be the most important decision maker. Concomitantly they help to provide the organisation with a defence against hostile takeover, par-ticularly by overseas companies looking for a French subsidiary in order to avoid the special rules which apply to branches and agencies (e.g. a foreign parent com-pany has unlimited liability for the debts of its branch or agency, since these do not have a separate legal identity).

The SA is the legal form normally chosen by larger companies seeking access to substantial amounts of capital. In the case of a privately owned company, the mini-mum capital requirement is currently €37 000; if publicly owned the minimum is €225 000 million. Where capital assets are substantial, this tends to ensure that financial institutions are large shareholders in SAs and many of them have interests in a wide range of enterprises which they often manage through a holding com-pany (see below). One advantage of this arrangement is that it provides the financial institution with a means of managing its investments and of exerting influence over companies in which it has a large minority stake. Another is that it provides a means of defending French companies from hostile takeovers and hence small and medium enterprises often seek backing from holding companies to help fend off foreign predators.

As in Britain, the legal basis of the SA provides for a clear distinction between the roles of the owners (the shareholders) and the salaried employees, and it is the former who appoint the company's board of directors. In smaller companies, the chairperson and managing director is often the same person and many smaller French companies continue to have extremely strong central control, often by the head of the owning family. In larger companies, the two roles are normally sepa-rated, with the managing director assuming responsibility for the day-to-day operations of the enterprise and forming the link between the board and the com-pany's senior executives and managers, some of whom may have considerable delegated authority.

It is worth noting that in companies with more than 50 employees, there is a legal requirement to have elected work councils, and workers' delegates have the right to attend board meetings as observers and to be consulted on matters affect-ing working conditions. In companies with more than ten employees, workers have the right to elect representatives to look after their interests and regular meetings have to take place between management and workers, over and above the obliga-tion of employers to negotiate annually on pay and conditions. Despite these arrangements and the legal right for unions to organise on a company's premises, trade union membership-outside state-run companies-remains low and hence union influence tends to be limited. Recent steps to encourage local agreements on pay and conditions seem destined to reduce this influence even further-a situa-tion which has parallels in Britain.

Germany

All major forms of business organisation are to be found in Germany, but it is the limited company which is of particular interest. Some of these are of relatively recent origin, having formerly been East German state-owned enterprises which have undergone 'privatisation' following the reunification of the country.

In numerical terms it is the private limited company *(Gesellschaft mit beschränkter Haftung*-GmbH) which predominates and which is the form chosen by most foreign companies seeking to establish an enterprise in Germany. As in Britain, this type of organisation has to be registered with the authorities and its founding members must prepare Articles of Association for signature by a public notary. The Articles include information on the purpose of the business, the amount of capital subscribed, the members' subscriptions and obligations and the company's name and registered address. Once the registration process is complete-usually a matter of a few days-the personal liability of the members becomes limited to the amount invested in the business. Currently, the minimum amount of subscribed share capital required for registration is €25 000, half of which must be paid up by the company itself.

Large numbers of GmbHs are owned and run by German families, with the banks often playing an influential role as guarantors of part of the initial capital and as primary sources of loan finance. As in France, this pattern of ownership makes hostile takeovers less likely, as well as ensuring that the management of the enterprise remains in the hands of the owners. Significantly, the management of a proposed GmbH is subject to quality control, being required to prove that they are qualified for the task prior to trading. This requirement stands in stark contrast to arrangements in Britain, where no such guarantees are needed, other than those implicit in a bank's decisions to help finance a proposed venture on the basis of a business plan. The procedures for establishing other types of business organisation are similar to those of the GmbH, although in the case of the public limited company *(Aktiengesellschaft*-AG), the current minimum amount of capital required at start-up is €50 000 in negotiable share certificates. Unlike British companies, the AG usually consists of two boards of directors, one of which (the supervisory board) decides on longer-term strategy, while the other (the managing board) concentrates on more immediate policy issues, often of an operational kind. Normally half the members of the supervisory board *(Aufsichtrat)* are elected by shareholders, while the other half are employees elected by the workforce, and it is the responsibility of the board to protect the interests of employees as well as shareholders.

Such worker representation at senior levels is an important element of the German system of business organisation and even in smaller enterprises workers have the right to establish works councils and to be consulted on social and person-nel issues and on strategic decisions. Equally, all employees have a constitutional right to belong to a trade union-most of which are organised by industry rather than by craft or occupation, as is largely the case in the United Kingdom. Consequently, German companies typically negotiate with only one union; usually in an atmosphere which stresses consensus and an identity of social and economic interests, rather than conflict and confrontation.

Corporate finance is another area in which German experience differs from that in the United Kingdom, although the situation has changed to some degree in recent years. Historically, in Britain a substantial amount of company finance has been raised through the stock market and this is also the case in the United States and Japan. In Germany (and for that matter in France, Italy and Spain), the banks and a number of other special credit institutions play a dominant role, with bank loans far outstripping joint-stock financing as a source of long-term capital. Traditionally, German banks have been willing to take a longer-term view of their investment, even at the expense of short-term profits and dividends, and this has benefited German companies seeking to expand their operations. In return, the banks have tended to exert a considerable amount of influence in the boardrooms of many German companies, usually by providing a substantial number of mem-bers of a company's supervisory board, including the chairperson.

Denmark

Denmark, like France, is a country whose economy is dominated by small busi-nesses, many of which are sole traders. As in other countries, there are very few regulations governing the establishment of this type of enterprise, other than the need to register for VAT if turnover exceeds a predetermined limit and to meet taxa-tion and social security requirements. In keeping with practice throughout Europe and beyond, sole traders have unlimited personal liability and this imposes a con-siderable burden on the organisation's owner and family, who often run the business jointly. The same conditions also apply in the case of Danish partnerships-whether formal or informal-with the joint owners having full and unlimited lia-bility for all debts accruing to the organisation.

Limited companies in Denmark also reflect practice elsewhere, being required to reg-ister under the Companies Act and having a legal existence separate from the owners and employees. Three main types of limited liability company can be distinguished:

1 The *Anpartselskaber* (ApS), which is a private joint-stock company, often run by a family and owned and controlled by a handful of individuals, one of whom may simultaneously occupy the roles of main owner, chairperson and managing director. Many of these companies began life as sole traders, but for reasons of taxation and liability have registered as an ApS.

2 The *Aktieselskaber* (A/S), which is a quoted or (more regularly) unquoted public limited company, subject essentially to the same regulations as the ApS, but having a much larger minimum capital requirement on registration. A large number of A/S companies are still small businesses, run by family members who wish to retain control of the enterprise as an increase in assets occurs.

3 The AMBA is a special kind of limited company-in essence a tax-free co-opera-tive with its own regulations. Many of these companies have grown over the years through merger and acquisition and some of them belong to larger Danish companies and employ a substantial number of workers. They tend to be con-centrated in farm-related products, but can also be found in the service sector, especially wholesaling and retailing.

Portugal

A brief look at Portuguese business organisations reveals a range of legal structures which includes sole traders, joint ventures, complementary groups, unlimited com-panies, limited partnerships and public and private limited companies. In the case of the latter, capital requirements tend to be an important distinguishing feature with the Public Limited Company or Corporation *(Sociedade Anonima*-SA) having a much larger minimum capital requirement than the private company *(Sociedade Por Quotas or Limitada*-LDA) as in other countries.

THE PUBLIC SECTOR IN MAINLAND EUROPE

Given the number of countries involved, it is impossible to survey the whole of the public sector in the rest of Europe. Students with an interest in this area are encour-aged to read further and to consult the various specialist sources of information covering the countries they wish to investigate. A number of general points, how-ever, are worthy of note:

1. Public sector business organisations can be found in all countries and invariably exist because of the decision by the state to establish a particular organisation under state ownership and control, or to nationalise an existing private business (or industry).
2. In some countries (e.g. France, Greece, Portugal) the state has traditionally played an important role in business and still controls some key sectors of the economy.
3. State involvement in business often includes significant shareholdings in a number of large enterprises, not only by the national government but also by regional and/or local government (e.g. in Germany).
4. State intervention often occurs in organisations or industries which can be deemed 'problematic' (e.g. in Greece).
5. Privatisation of state-owned enterprises has occurred throughout Europe and in other parts of the world. In the former East Germany, for example, most of the state-owned companies have been transferred to private ownership, by turning them initially into trusts which became the vehicle for privatisation and/or joint ventures. Similarly in Portugal, the wholesale nationalisation of the economy after the 1974 Revolution has

been reversed and the government is committed to a phased programme of privatisation, involving employees and small investors as well as large national and international organisations.

This latter point serves to re-emphasise that the business environment is subject to change over time and the fashions of today may tomorrow become things of the past. This fluctuating environment is as applicable to the public sector as it is to the private sector of the economy.

LEGAL STRUCTURE: SOME IMPLICATIONS

For businesses in the private sector, the choice of legal structure has important implications. Among the factors which the aspiring entrepreneur has to take into account when deciding what form of business enterprise to establish are:

- the degree of personal liability;
- the willingness to share decision-making powers and risks;
- the costs of establishing the business;
- the legal requirements concerning the provision of public information;
- the taxation position;
- commercial needs, including access to capital; and
- business continuity.

For some, retaining personal control will be the main requirement, even at the risk of facing unlimited personal liability and reducing the opportunities for expansion. For others, the desire to limit personal liability and to provide increased capital for growth will dictate that the owner seeks corporate status, even if this necessitates sharing decision-making powers and may ultimately result in a loss of ownership and/or control of the enterprise.

This link between an organisation's legal structure and its subsequent operations can be illustrated by examining three important facets of organisational life: the organisation's objectives, its sources of finance and its stakeholders. As the analysis below illustrates, in each of these areas significant differences occur between alterna-tive forms of business organisation, both *within* the private sector and *between* the state and non-state sectors of the economy. In some cases, these differences can be attributed directly to the restraints (or opportunities) faced by an organisation as a result of its legal status, suggesting that the legal basis of the enterprise conditions its operations. In other cases operational considerations tend to dictate the organisation's legal form, indicating that these are as much a cause of its legal status as a result of it-a point well illustrated by the workers' co-operative and the public corporation.

Organisational Objectives

All business organisations pursue a range of objectives and these may vary to some degree over time. New private sector businesses, for example, are likely to be con-cerned initially with survival and with establishing a position in the marketplace, with profitability and growth seen as less important in the short term. In contrast, most well-established businesses will tend to regard profits and growth as key objectives and may see them as a means towards further ends, including market domination, maximising sales revenue and/or minimising operating costs.

Organisational objectives are also conditioned by the firm's legal structure. In sole traders, partnerships and some limited companies, control of the enterprise rests in the hands of the entrepreneur(s) and hence organisational goals will tend to coincide with the personal goals of the owner(s), whatever the point in the organisation's life cycle. In public companies, however-where ownership tends to be separated from control-the goals of the owners (shareholders) may not always correspond with those of the directors and senior managers who run the organisa-tion, particularly when the latter are pursuing personal goals to enhance their own organisational position, status and/or rewards.

It is worth noting that the possibility of goal conflict also occurs where an indi-vidual company becomes a subsidiary of another organisation, whether by agreement or as a result of a takeover battle. This parent-subsidiary relationship may take the form of a holding company which is specially created to purchase a majority (sometimes all) of the shares in other companies, some of which may operate as holding companies themselves. Thus, while the individual subsidiaries may retain their legal and commercial identities and may operate as individual units, they will tend to be controlled by a central organisation which may exercise a considerable degree of influence over the objectives to be pursued by each of its subsidiaries. It is not inconceivable, for example, that some parts of the group may be required to make a loss on paper, particularly when there are tax advantages to be gained by the group as a whole from doing so.

Workers' co-operatives and public corporations provide further evidence of the relationship between an organisation's legal status and its primary objectives. In the case of the former, the establishment of the enterprise invariably reflects a desire on the part of its members to create an organisation which emphasises social goals (e.g. democracy, co-operation, job creation, mutual trust) rather than the pur-suit of profits-hence the choice of the 'co-operative' form. Similarly in the case of the public corporation, a decision by government to establish an entity which operates in the interests of the public at large (or 'national interest') favours the cre-ation of a state-owned-and-controlled organisation, with goals laid down by politicians and generally couched in social and financial terms (e.g. return on assets, reinvestment, job creation) rather than in terms of profit maximisation.

This apparent dichotomy between the profit motive of the private sector and the broader socio-economic goals of public bodies has, however, become less clear-cut over the last decade, as an increasing number of state-owned organisations have been 'prepared' for privatisation and successive governments have sought to bring private money into public projects by creating public/private partnerships.

Equally, in other parts of the public sector-including the health service and local government-increasing stress is being laid on 'best value' and on operating within budg-ets-concepts which are familiar to businesses in the private sector. While it is not inconceivable that a change in government could reverse this trend, current evi-dence suggests that a shift in cultural attitudes has occurred and public bodies can no longer rely on unconditional government support for their activities. If this is the case, further convergence is likely to occur between state and privately owned bodies, with the former moving towards the latter rather than vice versa.

Finance

Business organisations finance their activities in a variety of ways and from a range of sources. Methods include reinvesting profits, borrowing, trade credit and issuing shares and debentures. Sources include the banks and other financial institutions, individual investors and governments, as well as contributions from the organisa-tion's original owners.

In the context of this chapter it is appropriate to make a number of observations about the topic as it relates generally to the business environment:

1 All organisations tend to fund their activities from both internal (e.g. owner's capital, reinvested profits) and external sources (e.g. bank borrowing, sale of shares).
2 Financing may be short term, medium term or longer term, and the methods and sources of funding chosen will reflect the time period concerned (e.g. bank borrowing on overdraft tends to be short term and generally needed for immedi-ate use).
3 Funds raised from external sources inevitably involve the organisation in certain obligations (e.g. repayment of loans with interest, personal guarantees, paying divi-dends) and these will act as a constraint on the organisation at some future date.
4 The relationship between owner's capital and borrowed funds-usually described as an organisation's gearing-can influence a firm's activities and prospects in a variety of ways (e.g. high-geared firms with a large element of borrowed funds will be adversely affected if interest rates are high).
5 Generally speaking, as organisations become larger many more external sources and methods of funding become available and utilising these can have implica-tions for the structure, ownership and conduct of the organisation.

This latter point is perhaps best illustrated by comparing sole traders and partner-ships with limited companies. In the case of the former, as unincorporated entities neither the sole trader nor the partnership can issue shares (or debentures) and hence their access to large amounts of external capital is restricted by law. Companies have no such restrictions-other than those which help to differentiate a private company from a public one-and consequently they are able to raise larger amounts by inviting individuals (and organisations) to subscribe for shares. Where a company is publicly quoted on the stock market, the amounts raised in this way can be very large indeed and the resultant organisation may have millions of owners who change on a regular basis as shares are traded on the second-hand market.

Organisations which decide to acquire corporate status in order to raise funds for expansion (or for some other purposes) become owned by their shareholders, who may be the original owners or may be individual and institutional investors hold-ing equity predominantly as an investment and with little, if any long-term commitment to the organisation they own. As indicated above, in the latter case, a separation tends to occur between the roles of owner (shareholder) and controller (director) and this can lead to the possibility of conflicting aims and objectives or differences in opinion over priorities within the enterprise-a problem discussed in more detail below under 'Stakeholders'.

A further illustration of the relationship between an organisation's legal structure and its ability to raise finance is provided by the public corporation. In this case, as a public body accountable to Parliament and the public via government, the public corporation is required to operate within a financial context largely controlled by government and normally conditioned by the government's overall fiscal policy, including its attitude to the size of the Public Sector Borrowing Requirement (PSBR). One aspect of this context in Britain has been the establishment of external financing limits (EFLs) for each nationalised industry, arrived at by negotiation between government and the board running the public corporation, and used as a means of restraining monetary growth and hence the size of the PSBR. Unfortunately this has also tended to prevent the more financially sound corpora-tions, such as British Telecom before privatisation, from borrowing externally on a scale necessary to develop their business-a restriction which tends to disappear when the corporation becomes a fully fledged public company, either through pri-vatisation or by some other means.

Stakeholders

All organisations have stakeholders; these are individuals and/or groups who are affected by or affect the performance of the organisation in which they have an interest. Typically they would include employees, managers, creditors, suppliers, shareholders (if appropriate) and society at large. As Table 8.1 illustrates, an organi-sation's stakeholders have a variety of interests which range from the pursuit of private gain to the more nebulous idea of achieving public benefit. Sometimes these interests will clash as, for example, when managers seek to improve the organisation's cash flow by refusing to pay suppliers' bills on time. On other occa-sions, the interests of different stakeholders may coincide, as when managers plan for growth in the organisation and in doing so provide greater job security for employees and enhanced dividends for investors.

The legal structure of an organisation has an impact not only on the type of stakeholders involved but also to a large degree on how their interests are repre-sented. In sole traders, partnerships and smaller private companies, the coincidence of ownership and control limits the number of potential clashes of interest, given that objectives are set by and decisions taken by the firm's owner-manager(s). In larger companies, and, in particular, public limited companies, the division between ownership and control means that the controllers have the responsibility of representing the interests of the organisation's shareholders and creditors and, as suggested above, their priorities and goals may not always correspond.

Organisational stakeholders and their interests

Types of stakeholder	*Possible principal interests*
Employees	Wage levels; working conditions; job security; personal development
Managers	Job security; status; personal power; organisational profitability; growth of the organisation
Shareholders	Market value of the investment; dividends; security of investment; liquidity of investment
Creditors	Security of loan; interest on loan; liquidity of investment
Suppliers	Security of contract; regular payment; growth of organisation; market development
Society	Safe products; environmental sensitivity; equal opportunities; avoidance of discrimination

A similar situation occurs in public sector organisations, where the interest of taxpayers (or ratepayers) is represented both by government and by those individuals chosen by government to run the organisation. In this case, it is worth recalling that the broader strategic objectives of the enterprise and the big decisions concern-ing policy, finance and investment tend to be taken by politicians, operating with advice from their officials (e.g. civil servants, local government officers) and within the context of the government's overall economic and social policies.

The organisa-tion's board of management and its senior executives and managers are mainly responsible for the day-to-day operations of the business, although the board and the person chairing it would normally play a key role in shaping overall objectives and decisions, through regular discussions with government and its officials.

One important way in which public sector organisations differ from their private sector counterparts is in the sanctions available to particular groups of stakeholders who feel that the organisation is not representing their best interests. Shareholders in a company, for example, could withdraw financial support for a firm whose directors consistently disregard their interests or take decisions which threaten the security and/or value of their investment, and the possibility of such a reaction normally guarantees that the board pays due attention to the needs of this important group of stakeholders.

The taxpayer and ratepayer have no equivalent sanction and in the short term must rely heavily on government and its agencies or, if possible, their power as consumers to represent their interest *vis-à-vis* the organisation. Longer term, of course, the public has the sanction of the ballot box, although it seems highly unlikely that the performance of state enterprises would be a key factor in determin-ing the outcome of general or local elections.

The relative absence of market sanctions facing state-owned organisations has meant that the public has had to rely on a range of formal institutions (e.g. parlia-mentary scrutiny committees, consumer consultative bodies, the audit authorities) and on the media to protect its interest in areas such as funding, pricing and quality of service provided. As these organisations are returned to the private sector, the expectation is that the sanctions imposed by the free market will once again operate and shareholders in privatised utilities will be protected like any other group of share-holders in a privately owned enterprise. To what extent this will occur in practice, of course, is open to question, while the newly privatised public corporations face little, if any, competition. Government, it seems, prefers to hedge its bets on this question, at least in the short term-hence the establishment of 'regulators' with powers of investigation into performance and some degree of control over pricing.

MINI CASE: BIG MAC GETS BIGGER

Growth through franchising has become a preferred option for many organisations, typified by McDonald's, which is the world's biggest fast food chain. Established in 1955 when Raymond Croc opened his first burger restaurant, McDonald's was estimated to have had in excess of 20000 outlets spread across the globe by the end of 1996. Contrary to popular predictions, the organisation has continued to expand at a significant rate and has benefited from the opening of new markets in eastern Europe and the Far East. In the mid-1990s, for example, it was estimated that at its current rate of growth, a new McDonald's was opening somewhere in the world every three hours.

When considering applicants for a coveted McDonald's franchise the company has always been concerned to ensure that its reputation for quality and service is maintained. Potential franchisees have to demonstrate not only a successful track record in a previous occupation, but also that they have the necessary financial resources and a willingness to commit themselves to the organisation. Individuals making the grade have traditionally been offered two kinds of franchise scheme. The conventional franchise involves a 20-year agreement between the franchisee and the company under which the latter buys and develops the site which the former takes over and operates for an agreed price, as well as paying McDonald's a royalty fee based on a pre-agreed percentage of turnover. Under the other option-the business facilities lease-the individual leases the restaurant normally for a three-year period, prior to being offered the opportunity to convert to a conventional franchise if funds permit.

As far as future expansion in parts of western Europe is concerned it remains to be seen how far the 'beef scare' will affect market demand in the medium to long term, and hence the opportunities available to aspiring franchisees. Elsewhere in the world, there appears to be ample scope for would-be entrepreneurs to trade under the McDonald's brand name and to take advantage of the seemingly inexorable global demand for Big Macs and associated products.

Postscript In late October 2002 McDonald's announced its intention of sharply cutting back on its expansion plans and redirecting its efforts towards supporting its existing chain of restaurants (see the *Guardian,* 23 October 2002). By 2005, McDonalds claimed to have over 30000 local restaurants serving nearly 50 million people each day in more than 119 countries.

FRANCHISING, LICENSING AND JOINT VENTURES

To complete this review of the legal structure of business organisations, it is useful to consider three developments which have a legal aspect: franchising, licensing and joint ventures. All three may be seen as a means of carrying out a business ven-ture in a way that reduces some of the risks normally faced by the entrepreneur.

Franchising

Franchising, which has grown significantly in recent years, is an arrangement where one party (the franchiser) sells the right to another party (the franchisee) to market its product or service. In terms of their legal status the parties involved could be any of the forms described above, but in practice it is usually the case that the franchiser is a company while the franchisee tends to be a sole trader or part-nership. Both parties in law have a separate legal identity, but the nature of the contract between them makes their relationship interdependent and this has important implications for the operation of the franchise.

Franchise arrangements come in a variety of forms. Probably the best known is the 'business format franchise' (or 'trade name franchise') under which the fran-chiser agrees to allow the franchisee to sell the product or service with the help of a franchise package which contains all the elements needed to set up and run a busi-ness at a profit. These would typically include the brand name, any associated supplies, promotional material and other forms of support and assistance. In return the franchisee usually pays an initial sum or fee for the use of the service and its various elements, remits royalties based on sales and/ or profits, agrees to make a contribution for consultancy, training and promotion, and undertakes to maintain standards. Wimpy, Kentucky Fried Chicken, Burger King, Prontaprint and Dynarod are examples of this type of franchise.

Other forms include manufacturer/retailer franchises (e.g. car dealers), manufac-turer/wholesaler franchises (e.g. Coca-Cola, Pepsi) and wholesaler/retailer franchises (e.g. Spar and Mace) and it is estimated by the industry's trade body-the British Franchise Association-that in retailing alone franchising accounts for over 20 per cent of sales in the

United Kingdom. One indication of its growing significance is the spread of franchising into further and higher education, with universities and other colleges of higher education franchising some of their courses to local further education colleges, which in turn may franchise some of their courses to schools and/or sixth-form colleges. Another indicator is the decision by many clearing banks and firms of accountants to establish franchise sections to help and advise individuals who want to open a franchise or who have already done so and are seeking further guidance.

Undoubtedly the mutual benefits to be derived from a franchise arrangement help to explain its popularity as a way of doing business in both domestic and external markets and it has proved an attractive vehicle for some companies seek-ing rapid overseas expansion, without undertaking substantial direct investments-although this is sometimes necessary to support the operation (e.g. McDonald's had to invest in a plant to make hamburger buns in the United Kingdom). Equally, many would-be entrepreneurs find the security of a franchise more attractive than other methods of starting a business, especially as there is some evidence to suggest that franchises have better survival rates than the more conventional forms of independent enterprise (e.g. sole traders).

Current indications are that this popularity is likely to continue into the foresee-able future, although it is more likely that greater selectivity of potential franchisees will occur as the franchise industry becomes more mature and attempts to gain an increased degree of public respectability. Franchisees, too, are likely to become more particular about the businesses they agree to deal with, as they endeavour to join the enterprise culture. It is, after all, the franchisee who has to bear the financial risk of the business in return for a share in the profits; the fran-chiser has a reputation to think about.

Licensing

Licensing is another form of non-equity agreement under which a firm in one country (the licensor) authorises a firm in another country (the licensee) to use its intellectual property (e.g. patents, copyrights, trade names, know-how) in return for certain considerations, usually royalty payments. Licences may be granted to individuals, independent companies, subsidiaries of a multinational company or to government agencies and the rights granted may be exclusive or non-exclusive.

Companies invariably enter into licensing agreements to gain certain advan-tages. These might include:

- Reducing competition by sharing technology.
- Seeking overseas profits without direct foreign investment.
- Protecting an asset from potential 'pirates'.
- Avoiding restrictions on foreign investment or imports imposed by other countries.
- Recouping some research and development costs.
- Gaining a share of an overseas market.

Needless to say, most organisations granting licences tend to be based in the advanced industrial economies and are frequently multinationals which regard their trade marks and technologies as an integral part of their asset base. One prob-lem of transferring the use of such assets to another firm is that the owner loses a degree of control over the asset, including the quality of production, and this may affect the product's image and sales elsewhere. Another is the possibility of the licensee dominating the market after the agreement ends, even to the extent of excluding the licensor from the marketplace by aggressive competition or the development of an alternative product.

Joint Ventures

The term 'joint venture' tends to be used in two ways: to describe a contractual agreement involving two or more parties; or to describe a jointly owned and inde-pendently incorporated business venture involving more than one organisation. It is the latter usage which is mainly applied here.

Joint ventures-which are popular with international companies-can take a variety of legal forms and almost every conceivable type of partnership may exist, ranging from two companies joining together in the same domestic market (e.g. Sainsbury's and British Home Stores set up the Savacentre chain), to joint private/public sector ventures between participants from different countries. Sometimes numerous organisations may be involved and these may be based in one country or in several. Where this occurs the term 'consortium' is often used, as in the case of TransManche Link (TML), the international joint venture which built the Channel Tunnel.

As with licensing and franchising, joint ventures have increased in popularity in the last 25-30 years and have been one of the ways in which international compa-nies have sought to develop an overseas market, particularly in the face of import restrictions, or heavy research and development costs.

Multinational car companies have been active in this field-as evidenced by past links between General Motors and Toyota, Ford and Mazda-and these arrangements look likely to continue as markets become more global.

For western companies wishing to exploit the gradual 'privatisation' of the former planned economies of eastern Europe, joint ventures with indigenous producers are likely to prove a safer bet than direct inward invest-ment, particularly given the degree of economic and political uncertainty. They are also likely to prove more politically acceptable in states seeking to establish their own economic independence and identity after almost 50 years of regional domination.

SYNOPSIS

Market-based economies throughout Europe and beyond have a range of business organisations with broadly similar legal structures. These legal structures help to deter-mine not only the ownership and control of the enterprise, but also other aspects of its operations, including its objectives, its access to finance and its external relationships and obligations. Viewing businesses as legal entities provides a useful insight into a number of the external influences which impinge upon their daily existence and high-lights some of the consequences faced by organisations which transfer from public (i.e. state) to private ownership. It also sheds light on other important developments in entrepreneurial activity, including franchising, licensing and joint ventures.

SUMMARY OF KEY POINTS

- Business organisations have a legal structure.
- The three commonest forms of business in the private sector are sole traders, part-nerships and limited companies.
- Whereas the owners of the first two types of business organisation face unlimited personal liability, in companies the legal separation of the firm from its owners affords the latter limited personal liability.

- Companies are normally run by directors who are appointed to represent the interest of the owners (the shareholders). In public companies this separation of ownership and control is a key distinguishing feature.
- Other forms of business organisation exist in the public sector (e.g. the public corpo-ration) and the 'third sector' (e.g. the co-operative).
- Government-owned businesses are increasingly adopting private sector forms of organisation to provide for greater flexibility and freedom of action.
- The legal status of the organisation has implications for the objectives of the enter-prise, how it is financed and for its stakeholder relationships.

CASE STUDY : THE ENTERPRENEURIAL SPIRIT

Business studies textbooks teach us that new businesses invariably come into exis-tence to satisfy the needs and ambitions of their owners. Once established, it is assumed that an enterprise will begin to grow and that the owner(s) will sanction this and take steps to bring it about. As the two case studies below illustrate, these assumptions may be correct or not, according to specific circumstances. Arguing from the particular to the general needs to be approached with caution in business, as in any other field of study.

T & S Stores PLC

Like many medium-to large-sized businesses, T & S Stores started from relatively modest origins and was the brainchild of one individual, Kevin Threlfall, a Wolverhampton entrepreneur.

A barrow boy by background, Threlfall received his early business training work-ing from the age of 12 on his parents' pitch in West Midlands markets. Despatched to public school, Threlfall soon found this market background was treated contemptuously by his fellow pupils and this made him determined to prove his worth in the business world. On leaving school he began providing pet-foods in bulk, before selling out his business and founding the Lo Cost food chain in 1972. This was subsequently bought for £1.5 million by Oriel Foods, later owned by the Argyll Group.

Threlfall's T & S Stores grew from the Wolverhampton market stalls and quickly expanded into retail outlets, with their emphasis on discount tobacco and conven-ience shopping. Using day-glo starbursts offering low-priced cigarettes, Threlfall cleverly attracted customers into his stores where they were tempted by the use of colourful confectionery gondolas and other techniques into impulse purchases of products carrying high margins. By keeping costs to a minimum, Threlfall was able to turn his company into a highly profitable enterprise with a stock market capitali-sation of almost £140 million by 1991 and a chain of almost 600 stores.

In 1989, T & S acquired the Dillons and Preedy chains from Next for £54 million and subsequently purchased 22 stores from Johnson News Group for £4.25 million in February 1991, thus helping to increase the organisation's interest in conven-ience stores, which Threlfall believed would be the company's main area of future growth. Trading from outlets larger than most of the T & S shops and offering an extended range of grocery and frozen-food lines, Threlfall's One Stop convenience stores generally achieved higher gross margins than the core tobacco shops and helped to contribute to the company's strong net cash position in the early 1990s. Despite these developments, Threlfall maintained close contacts with what was happening on the ground and attempted to maintain a degree of individual cus-tomer attention in a field of retailing which is rapidly changing.

Threlfall's entrepreneurial skills, coupled with the gains from introducing National Lottery and other facilities in many of the group's outlets, continued to strengthen the organisation's financial and trading position. With hundreds of stores and increasing turnover and pre-tax profits, T & S attracted outside invest-ment from reputable fund managers who expressed confidence in the management's strategy of refocusing the business towards the growing convenience store market. Turnover by 2001 was recorded at £933 million; in 1995 it had been £445 million.

Postscript: T & S was acquired by Tesco in January 2003. It now trades under the One Stop brand and some stores have been converted to the Tesco Express format.

Dave Noble (Windsurfing)

Unlike Kevin Threlfall, Dave Noble came from a non-business background and had no ambitions as a child to seek a career in industry or commerce. Following A-levels at the local grammar school in Woking, Noble went to Aberystwyth University where he obtained a degree in philosophy, before continuing his studies at post-graduate level. After a brief spell doing research, he left university and worked on building sites, subsequently returning to study for a postgraduate certificate of edu-cation, a move which was to take him into teaching in Loughborough.

With the start of a family, Noble gave up his full-time teaching post to look after the children, continuing as a supply teacher as and when circumstances allowed. As a keen windsurfer, with an established reputation in the sport, he decided to use some of his time at home to make his own boards, buying the necessary fittings from suppliers to the trade. As requests from friends for similar equipment began to grow, Noble found himself dealing with suppliers on a larger scale and spending an increasing amount of his time making and equipping windsurfing boards. Before he had fully realised what was happening, Noble found himself in business as a sole trader, operating in the leisure industry, a growing sector in the UK economy.

With an initial injection of his own capital, supported by a weekly income from the government's Enterprise Allowance Scheme, Noble established his own venture in late 1986/early 1987, operating from home in Shepshed in Leicestershire. Despite only limited expenditure on advertising, the business began to grow quickly, allowing the venture to become totally self-financing. Before long, it became obvious that new premises would be needed and so in 1989 the Noble family (now five in total) moved to a Georgian house in the village of Wymeswold on the Leicestershire/Nottinghamshire border. Apart from providing adequate space for a growing family, the new house had numerous outbuildings suitable for making and selling equipment and for storing supplies and material. It was also suf-ficiently close to Shepshed to allow Noble to keep his existing customer and supplier bases which were fundamental to the success of the business. Noble's initial enthusiasm at working from his village home-in a manner reminis-cent of a traditional cottage industry-was soon to be dampened following complaints from neighbours who objected to the traffic from customers seeking boards and other equipment. Consequently, the business was forced to relocate to the nearby Wymeswold Airfield Industrial Estate, where Noble acquired two units from which to operate. Like other units on the estate, Noble's premises were rela-tively basic, but provided sufficient space for production, storage and sales and had more than adequate parking for customers and suppliers. Being in a rural location, with no houses in the immediate vicinity, complaints concerning disturbance ceased to be a problem for the business.

Despite the successive moves, Noble's business continued to grow, even in the recession years in the early 1990s. Part of this growth was manifestly attributable to the increased demand for leisure products, and the decision to add mountain bikes and ski equipment to the range of items on offer was clearly beneficial, although by no means part of a deliberate strategy of diversification. The most significant factor in the firm's success, however, and one which resulted in the need to hire addi-tional staff to meet the increased demand, appears to have been Noble's deliberate policy of keeping customers and suppliers happy. By paying all his bills on time, Noble was able to strike good bargains with suppliers and to pass savings on to the customer in the form of highly competitive prices which other traders could not meet. In addition, Noble and his staff did their best to meet their customers' needs individually, even if it meant working extra hours and incurring some additional expense.

By the mid-1990s Dave Noble (Windsurfing) had become a formidable operator in the marketplace, with a dominant share of the market in the East Midlands and a loyal and extensive customer base. As the firm continued to prosper, Noble even-tually decided to sell his business to the staff and to go into semi-retirement. He has, however, maintained an interest in the leisure industry, importing snowboards which he sells to the trade via mail order.

8

Size Structure of Firms

INTRODUCTION

There has been an increase in the level of industrial concentration in the United Kingdom over the last one hundred years. In 1909 the largest hundred companies pro-duced 16 per cent of manufacturing output; by 1990 this had risen to around 30 per cent. Such an increase in the size of business organisations gives rise to worries about the concentration of power in the hands of a few producers and abuses of this power. If the companies are multinationals, they may be beyond the control even of national governments. More recently the trend towards greater concentration has been reversed, and there seems to be a movement towards employment in smaller units. This chapter will look at the size structure of British industry and the reasons for such a structure, with some international comparisons. It will consider the role of small and large firms in the economy. It will also examine the reasons for growth, the ways in which organisations grow, the financing of growth and the limits to growth. It will also consider the relatively more recent trend towards co-operation in production, rather than competition, through activities like joint ventures and networking.

THE SIZE STRUCTURE OF UK INDUSTRY

When looking at the size of firms it is important to define the terms used in official data. The firm, or 'enterprise', is the organisation as a whole, and it might be com-prised of several units or 'establishments'. Small firms like the corner shop will mostly be enterprises with only one establishment. Large firms like Sainsbury's will have many establishments as they have branches in most towns.

There are many different ways to measure the size of firms. Common measures used are turnover, the value of output, the capital employed or the level of employ-ment. Such measurement is beset by problems, not least the difficulty of defining the small firm, as will be seen later in this chapter.

The three measures mentioned above might give conflicting pictures, as an industry which is becoming increas-ingly mechanised will probably have rising levels of average capital employed and output but falling average levels of employment. Table 9.1 shows the 'top ten' com-panies in the United Kingdom using two of these measures and it illustrates the point that different measures of the size of a firm will give different rankings.

Some of these names will be familiar to the reader while others are less so. Compass Group plc, for example, is a food service organisation which provides catering and support services to its clients.

The most common measure of size used is the level of employment. Table 9.2 shows the size structure of units in all industries by the number of employees in the United Kingdom in 2003. The table shows that smaller firms predominate in terms of numbers, with 98.5 per cent of firms employing fewer than 100 employ-ees. In terms of employment, however, these firms account for only 34.2 per cent of the total level of employment in manufacturing. At the other end of the scale establishments with over 500 employees account for only 0.4 per cent of the total number but 53.8 per cent of total employment. The pattern of size structure varies across industries and over time. In the last 20 years there seems to have been an increase in the importance of small firms and a decline in the importance of large firms in their contribution to employment.

In 1980 establishments with fewer than 200 employees accounted for 31.9 per cent of total employment and establish-ments with more than 500 employees accounted for 49.8 per cent. The comparable figures from Table 9.2 are 39.3 per cent and 53.8 per cent. Even the short period of time from 1991 to 2000 saw a shift in the importance of small firms. There was an increase of 188968 in the number of units employing fewer than 20 people, while there was a decrease of 13 332 in the number of units employing more than 20 employees. A similar pattern emerges with employment, with an increase in employment of

313 800 in the smaller units and a decrease in employment of 882 800 in the larger units.

Many of the large companies listed in Table 9.1 operate in more than one coun-try and are therefore multinationals. Multinational corporations strictly defined are enterprises operating in a number of countries and having production or service facilities outside the country of their origin. Multinationals pose particular prob-lems for governments and economies because of their size.

The ten largest companies in the UK, 2004

Ranking by turnover
1 Vodafone Group plc
2 Tesco plc
3 Aviva plc
4 Unilever plc
5 Glaxosmithkline plc
6 Tesco Stores Ltd
7 BT group plc
8 British Telecommunications plc
9 Centrica plc
10 CGU International Insurance plc
Ranking by employment
1 Compass Group plc
2 Unilever plc
3 Tesco plc
4 HSBC Holdings plc
5 Royal Mail Holdings plc
6 Royal Mail Group plc
7 Anglo American plc
8 Tesco Stores Ltd
9 J Sainsbury plc
10 Safeway Stores Ltd

Source: *Key British Enterprises*, 2005

Table : Size structure of UK industry by employment, 2003

Employment size group	*Number of units*	*% of total*	*Employment (000s)*	*% of total*
1-9	1 018120	83.0	3 828	15.4
10-19	112 780	9.2	1 575	6.4
20-49	59 015	4.8	1822	7.4
50–99	17 740	1.5	1 241	5.0
100-199	9 155	0.8	1 274	5.1
200-499	5 625	0.5	1 731	7.0
500 and over	4485	0.4	13300	53.8

Source: Adapted from Table 1, *www.sbs.gov.uk/content/analytical/statistics/'UKIndustry Summary'!A1*

ORGANISATIONAL GROWTH

The Reasons for Organisational Growth

Firms grow in size for many reasons; growth could be an explicit objective of man-agement or could be necessary for the successful operation of the firm:

- Growth could be a managerial objective if it brings benefits to management such as greater security and higher remuneration.
- It could be that the market in which the business operates is expanding and growth is necessary to maintain market share. This is especially the case as mar-kets become more international.
- Growth enables the organisation to reap the benefits of economies of scale.
- Growth enables firms to diversify into other markets, which means that risk can be spread further.
- Industries which are capital intensive will of necessity be comprised of large firms.
- In the area of product development it is possible that the necessary research and development could only be carried out by large companies.
- Growth could be pursued as a defensive strategy, as a reaction to the activities of competitors.

An illustration of how the stated objectives of EU firms for engag-ing in merger activity can change over time and gives some indication of the reasons for growth. Much of this shift can be explained by changing market conditions which have resulted from the creation of the Single European Market in 1992. The relaxation of trade restrictions in the run-up to 1992 encouraged much greater com-petition, and hence expansion and strengthening of market position have assumed much greater importance since 1985, together accounting for nearly 75 per cent of mergers. It was expected that the increased competition would force companies to concentrate more upon their core activities and as a result diversification as a motive for merger fell from 17.6 per cent in 1985 to 2.1 per cent of cases in 1992.

Table : Main motives for mergers in Europe, 1985-1992

Motive	*% of times mentioned*			
	1985-86	*1989-90*	*1990-91*	*1991-92*
Expansion	17.1	26.9	27.7	32.4
Diversification	17.6	3.0	2.8	2.1
Strengthening market position	10.6	45.3	48.2	44.4
Rationalisation and synergies	46.5	17.7	13.3	16.2
Research and development	2.4	0.6	0	0
Other	5.9	6.4	8.0	5.0

Source: *European Economy*, no. 57, 1994. Reproduced by permission of the Office for Official Publications of the European Communities

In industrial economics firm size is seen as a function of growth. It is suggested that although there is no limit on the size of a firm there are limits on the rate of expansion. Growth rates are seen to depend on different things by different theo-rists, including the availability of finance, the level of consumer demand and the limitations of management.

These theories, however, are primarily concerned with large firms and their development. Small firms are seen as potentially large firms that failed to grow for some reason or other. One interesting theory of growth is the stages model, where the firm is seen as passing through various stages in its development from small sole proprietor/partnership through the decision to expand into a large organisation. This again is a 'grow or fail' theory which does not apply well to industries which are dominated by successful small firms, as will be seen later in the chapter.

MINI CASE: MERGERS IN COMMERCIAL RADIO

The year 2005 saw the merger between the two biggest commercial radio groups in the UK-GWR and Capital-to form GCap Media plc. This merger is a good example of the motives for merging and the benefits that can accrue from merger.Commercial radio is distinguished from public service broadcasting (which is financed through the government) by the fact that it derives most of its revenue from advertising. The share of display advertising in the UK going to radio grew from 5.5 per cent in 1999 to 6.8 per cent in 2003. It is possible to target audiences much more precisely using the radio since the socio-demographic characteristics of listeners is well known and constant. Table 9.4 shows the market leaders in the UK together with their percentage shares of listening hours and advertising revenue in 2003. As can be seen, the merger took place between the two market leaders as measured in both ways.

A number of changes have occurred in the radio market which have provided the motivation for structural change. The Communications Act 2003 liberalised the restrictions on mergers in the communications sector and made changes in the way that licences are granted. The advent of digital technology has opened new doors with respect to both listening and advertising.The GWR Group had a presence at both the national level (Classic FM, Core and Planet X) and at the local level with 32 local stations. Capital Radio Group was a local radio provider. A high number of radio stations will bring high economies of scale-post merger, GCap Media have control of 57 radio stations out of a total of 242 in the UK. This places them in a prefect position to take advantage of the opportunities offered by digital technology. GCap Media emphasises the development of a relationship with listeners through diversification into other areas like concerts and local merchandising.

The Office of Fair Trading considered the proposed merger but decided that it would not be referred for investigation. It ruled that, although the merger would give the new company a 40 per cent share in advertising revenue, this was not a good measure of the degree of competition in the market since there are alternatives to radio advertising and that the radio stations owned by the two companies largely covered different parts of the country.

METHODS OF GROWTH

Internal Growth

Growth is a natural process for many firms that start small, capture a segment of the market and then continue to expand either by producing more of the same goods or by extending their product lines. The advantage of internal growth over external growth is that the company grows within the existing structure of management; there are none of the problems of bringing together two different management sys-tems. There might also be economies of scale from building a bigger plant that might not be available when companies merge and plant size does not change. Set against these, internal growth has certain disadvantages and this is why most of the growth in the size of organisations has occurred through external growth.

External Growth

Growth by acquisition is called external growth and occurs through takeover or merger. A merger is the voluntary coming together of two companies with the agreement of the management of both companies, the result of which is the cre-ation of a new legal identity. A takeover is where one company makes an offer to the shareholders of another. If the management of the threatened company resist it is called a hostile takeover, but if the price offered to shareholders is high enough they will accept. Takeover bids can be and have been successfully fought off by the management of the second firm. A holding company is a new company that is formed to acquire assets in other companies. The acquired companies retain their independent identities but are directed by the holding company. External growth can be seen to have a number of advantages:

1 It is fast, so that productive capacity can be increased very quickly.

2 The acquiring firm has access to an established management team and system.

3 If the shares of the acquiring company have sufficiently high values relative to the acquired firm, there might be no need for additional cash to be raised.

4 The purchase of existing assets could be cheaper than building new productive capacity.

But set against these is the fact that the process might not be an easy one; it is a dif-ficult job to merge two companies smoothly and successfully and there are likely to be many teething problems. Research by Coopers & Lybrand (now PriceWaterhouse Coopers) found that top executives regarded half of the takeovers in which they had been involved as failures. The main reasons for failure were lack of planning and managerial problems.

Although the definitions of merger and takeover are clear enough, it is often dif-ficult to tell them apart in practice and they are usually put together in official publications under the heading of acquisitions. In order to understand fully the motivation for mergers and takeovers it is important to recognise that there are dif-ferent types of mergers.

Horizontal Mergers

A horizontal merger is where a combination between firms at the same stage in a production process takes place; for example, between two car manufacturers or between two brewers. The vast majority of mergers that take place are of this type and many of our largest companies have been formed through horizontal merger. Examples include mergers between banks and building societies. The motives for this type of merger are:

- *To benefit from economies of scale.* Horizontal mergers allow the merged firms a greater level of specialisation and the benefits of other economies of scale.
- *Greater market share.* When firms come together there will be a reduction in com-petition in the market and the resulting firm will have a much larger share of the market.
- *Rationalisation of output.* If the level of demand for a good is shrinking, merger between the producers could be necessary in order to rationalise output.
- *Reaction to competitors.* In markets where mergers are taking place, companies may feel that they have to do the same in order to maintain their market position.

Vertical Mergers

A vertical merger involves firms at different stages of the same production process. It is vertical since it runs along the production process from extraction of raw mate-rials to distribution. An example would be a merger between a car manufacturer and a metal-pressing company. Vertical integration can take place 'backwards' towards the beginning of the production process or 'forwards' towards the end of it and it can occur for several reasons:

1. In the case of backwards integration, to control the supplies of raw materials with respect to their quantity and quality. This brings greater security to the acquiring firm.
2. To restrict supplies of the raw materials to competitors.
3. In the case of forwards integration, to control the quality of the outlets for the finished product. Manufacturers finance the majority of advertising and they might well feel that a forwards merger would enable them to ensure that the good was being sold in the most appropriate setting.
4. In both cases, economies of scale are possible if different parts of the production process are brought together.
5. Again, vertical mergers can be carried out as a reaction to the activities of com-petitors.

Conglomerate Mergers

These mergers are neither vertical nor horizontal but involve a merger between firms involved in producing different goods. An example would be the failed merger proposal between Kingfisher (general retailing) and Asda (grocery retailing) in 1999. The main motivation for this type of merger is diversification. It reduces the risk involved in producing for only one market and allows the firm to spread risk further. It can also provide the firm with another option if the original market declines in size.

As far as the economy is concerned, the main gains of mergers are in increased efficiency resulting from economies of scale and also the increased scope for research and development. A common view is that merger and takeover activity serves the purpose of rationalising business. The weak businesses go and the strong survive. Even when a takeover is carried out for the purpose of asset stripping this will be the case.

Growth by Merger and Takeover

Growth through merger and takeover first appeared in the USA over a hundred years ago and merger activity tends to come in waves.

Five periods of heightened merger activity have been identified in the USA:

- The period 1880 to 1905-this coincided with the proliferation of the joint stock company and the international establishment of stock exchanges. This period was characterised by mergers of a horizontal nature.
- The 1920s-at this time the mergers were largely vertical in nature, as manufac-turers took control of both suppliers and distributors.
- The 1960s-mergers in this period were mainly about diversification and the establishment of conglomerates.
- The post-1980 period-this wave of activity took place in a period of recession and was largely about cost-cutting and rationalisation.
- The late 1990s-as companies in mature industries attempted to become global operators. The pace of this surge of activity slowed for a period after September 11th 2001, but by 2004 the boom in activity had restarted.

The first two periods of heightened merger activity in the USA had little effect in Europe; however, there were waves of activity in Europe which coincided with the last two. The first wave of merger activity in Europe came in the 1960s after obsta-cles to trade were removed by the establishment of the EEC in 1957. The second wave of mergers came in the 1980s in the run-up to the establishment of the Single European Market in 1992. As yet there is little evidence of an increase in merger activity as a result of EMU in Europe. The most recent surge of activity in the USA did not reach the EU until 2005-the value of mergers and acquisitions in Europe in the first quarter of 2005 was three times higher than the same period in 2004 and there are several pending large deals. The motivation for this activity seems to be the synergies achieved through mergers with similar companies-it seems that national companies are trying to become European companies.

FINANCE FOR GROWTH

Internal Sources

As part of its operation the firm will generate income in the form of profit. Part of this profit will be distributed in the form of dividends to shareholders, the rest can be used for reinvestment and to finance growth.

Although this is seen as a relatively easy and cheap source of finance, it does carry an opportunity cost and therefore should be judged on its rate of return like any other source of finance. Table 9.5 shows that inter-nal funds were the largest single source of finance for industry in 1990, 1994 and 1997. It also shows that the totals available and the pattern of sources vary a great deal from year to year. (This data is no longer compiled by the Office for National Statistics.)

Sources of funds for industry, 1990, 1994 and 1997 (£million)

Source	*1990*	*1994*	*1997*
Internal funds	33838	61 406	56363
Banks and other short-term borrowing	19911	-4 841	6 630
Loans and mortgages	9120	4557	4384
Ordinary shares	1 880	8495	19616
Debentures and preference shares	6367	1 008	10 640
Other capital issues	7485	5 067	10526
Other overseas investment	11 233	-1 400	25938
Other	1 444	3 766	953
Total	91 278	78056	135 050

Source: *Financial Statistics,* January 1993, 1996 and 1999. Crown copyright 1999. Reproduced by permission of the Controller of HMSO and of the Office for National Statistics, UK

External Sources

As the size and availability of retained earnings will be limited, most firms will also have to seek other sources of finance for expansion. There are many external sources of finance and a typical firm's capital structure will comprise a combination of these. The sources are as follows.

Banks

Banks provide short-and medium-term finance to companies in the form of loans or overdrafts. The relative cost of these depends upon how the firm wishes to use the funds. Loans carry a lower rate of interest but the interest is paid on the whole amount, while the interest on overdrafts is only paid on the amount drawn. British banks have been criticised by many for failing to provide longer-term finance for business, as banks do in other countries.

Capital Market

The capital market is the place where stocks and shares are traded and is therefore a key provider of long-term finance to firms. The main institution in the capital market is the Stock Exchange. The capital market is made up of two parts: the pri-mary part which involves the buying and selling of new stocks and shares; and the secondary part which involves the buying and selling of existing stocks and shares. It is therefore the primary part of the market that is the source of finance for firms.

The secondary part of the market is, however, also important in this process as indi-viduals and organisations are more likely to buy stocks and shares with the knowledge that there is a ready market on which they can be traded at a later date.

The main institutions that buy stocks and shares are the insurance companies, pension funds, investment trusts, unit trusts and other large financial institutions such as building societies.

A new issue of shares takes place when an existing company needs extra finance or when a company becomes a public limited company.

Types of Stocks and Shares

1 *Preference shares.* These are shares in a company which carry a fixed dividend. Holders have preference over other shareholders in the payment of dividends and on the liquidation of the firm. Preference shares usually carry no voting rights, and so holders have little influence over how the company is run.

2 *Ordinary shares.* Ordinary shares are called the 'equity' of the company. They do not usually carry a fixed dividend; the company declares a dividend, depending upon its performance in that year. This means that in good years ordinary share-holders could receive high dividends, while in bad years possibly none at all. Ordinary shares are therefore more risky than preference shares, and in recogni-tion of this they usually carry voting rights, so that holders can exercise some influence over how the company is run.

3 *Debentures.* Debentures or loan stock are bonds which are given in exchange for a loan to the company. The company agrees to repay the borrowed amount at some date in the future and to make annual payments of interest in the mean-time. Interest on debentures is paid before payment of any dividends and the interest is allowable against tax. A debenture holder is a creditor of the company, a shareholder is an owner of the company.

New Issue of Shares

A company will go to an issuing house or merchant bank which will advise it on the type and number of shares to issue, the price at which they should be offered and other matters. They will often carry out the issue of shares on behalf of the firm. A new issue of shares is not a big source of finance for growth as it is fairly expensive; retained earnings are more convenient and cheaper. Also the amount of information that is required from companies which issue shares to the general public can act as a disincentive.

It is worth noting that in the UK the Stock Market essentially comprises three main elements: the main market, the Alternative Investment Market (AIM) and off-exchange share matching and trading facility (OFEX). The main market deals in the shares of the large and well-established companies. The Alternative Investment Market provides an opportunity for growing smaller companies to raise capital and have their shares traded in a market without the considerable expense of a full market listing. OFEX tends to be used by companies seeking relatively small amounts of capital, mainly from private investors, and has to be seen as a stepping stone to a listing on a more senior market (e.g. the Official List, AIM, NASDAQ).

Money Market

The money markets provide short-term finance for companies, often for as brief a period as overnight.

Government and other Institutions

The government is a source of finance for firms. Through its regional policy it gives tax allowances, loans, grants and training allowances to firms in certain parts of the country. It has many schemes for helping business, particularly small businesses. This will be covered more fully later in this chapter.

Other Sources

Other sources include trade credit and hire purchase (i.e. receiving assets now and paying later). This is only a small source of finance for companies. As Table 9.5 shows, industry draws a fairly high proportion of its funding from overseas. This includes finance from many different sources, including individuals, governments, financial institutions overseas and companies.

Firms will typically go for a mixture of different types of finance. The exact com-bination will depend upon many factors, including their relative costs, their availability and the desired capital structure of the firm. A firm's desired capital structure will largely depend upon the type of market in which it operates. The dif-ferent types of finance are classified under the two headings of debt and equity. Debt refers to all types of capital on which payments have to made each year regardless of how the firm has performed; this would include loans and preference shares. Equity refers to ordinary shares where the payment of a dividend depends upon the performance of the firm. As a source of finance, debt is generally cheaper but it is also more risky since in bad years the firm will have to meet the interest payments. The ratio of debt to equity is called the gearing of the company. Debt is not well suited to firms in industries where profits fluctuate and such firms will have lower gearing than those in more stable markets.

Limits to Growth

Several factors tend to act as a limit to organisational growth:

- To finance growth, excessive borrowing might have taken place and the firm may have trouble meeting debt repayments; therefore there is increased risk of bankruptcy.
- A serious constraint to growth might be the abilities of management. As organi-sations grow in size they may experience diseconomies of scale, which are mainly to do with managerial problems, like communication and control. If the size of the market for the product is stagnant or declining it may be both unnecessary and impossible for the firm to grow.
- Government policies, too, can have an important impact on growth. Every gov-ernment has policies on competition which seek to limit anti-competitive practices and which normally regulate merger activity.

Merger Activity in the United Kingdom

There are two common ways of measuring the level of merger activity-by the number of transactions or by the total value of the transactions. Figure 9.1 shows the level of merger activity in the UK according to the number of companies acquired in the UK by UK companies. It can be seen that there was a sharp rise in merger activity in the mid-1980s and a downturn in 1989. The cyclical pattern con-tinues into the 1990s but the amplitude is reduced. This cyclical pattern is repeated in other countries and in the EU as a whole and it implies that the level of mergers is in some way related to the state of the economy. The rise in the mid-1980s was due partly to an improvement in the state of the economy and partly to the liberalisation of the financial markets, which made finance for takeover bids more freely available. The fall in 1989 was due partly to the recession and partly to the problems that some companies subsequently experienced by over-stretching themselves in the mid-1980s. The subsequent rise in the level of merger activity was due to the restructuring which took place in many diverse industries in the 1990s like the financial services sector and the public utilities.

The level of merger activity in the UK according to the value of the transactions, and the same cyclical path can be discerned although the peaks and troughs do not exactly coincide with the number of transactions. The use of the value of the transactions as a measure of merger activity is problematic in that it will be distorted by any very high-value deals that take place, as in 1995-7 and 2000 when the number of transactions fell but their value rose.

Merger activity in Europe

The number and value of cross-border mergers and acquisitions in the EU between 1999 and 2005. As in the UK, there was a fall in activity by both measures after 2001 but a sharp rise in the first half of 2005.

Cross-border mergers and acquisitions in the EU, 1999-2005, by value and by number

The total value of cross-border mergers and acquisitions in the EU in the first half of 2005 was €286.6 billion. The most important acquirer was France (21 per cent of total) followed by the USA (19 per cent), Italy (10 per cent) and the UK (9 per cent).

Global Merger Activity

T'e value of outflows from and inflows to OECD countries for merger and acquisitions between 1999 and 2005. The pattern is 'e same as for the UK and the EU-flows fell after 2001 and increased sharply at the beginning of 2005. It is predicted that in 2006 the number of global cross-border mergers and acquisitions will be in excess of 700 and their total value in excess of $720 billion.

It can be seen that the same pattern presents itself for the UK on its own, the EU and the world as a whole-a decline in merger and acquisition activity followed by a surge in activity in 2005. During the 1990s the boom in merger and acquisition activity was dominated by the telecommunications sector. In 2004/5 recovery activity was taking place mainly in the financial services sector-the two largest deals were the takeover of Abbey National Bank (UK) by Banco Santander Central Hispano (Spain) and the takeover of John Hancock Financial Services (USA) by Manulife Financial Corporation (Canada).

SMALL FIRMS

There are serious problems in the analysis of the small-firm sector, including the lack of data over a long period of time and the problem of defining exactly what is a small firm.

Size of companies by turnover across different industries, 2004 (%)

Industry	*Turnover size ('000)*		
	up to £250	*£250-£500*	*over £500*
Agriculture, forestry and fishing	87	8	5
Mining and quarrying and public utilities	40	10	50
Manufacturing	54	14	32
Construction	71	12	17
Wholesaling	48	14	38
Retailing	65	19	16
Financial services	51	11	38
Business services	77	10	13

Source: Adapted from Table B5.1, PA1003, 2004, Office for National Statistics

The Bolton Report, published in 1971, was the report of a committee set up to look into the role of small firms in the UK economy. It used various definitions for statistical purposes, depending upon the industry being considered, on the grounds that what is small in one industry might be large in another. Table 9.7 shows the size distribution of firms based on their turnover for a selection of industries for 2004.

It is clear from Table 9.7 that the definition of 'big' will vary with the industry. In the Bolton Report the definition used for small firms in manufacturing was 'less than 200 employees', while in construction it was 'less than 25 employees'. In some industries turnover limits were chosen while in others a m. .ture of employment and turnover was used. Although this is confusing and makes comparison between industries and countries difficult, it was accepted that there could not be a single definition which would apply to all sectors. The EU in 1994 recommended to its members that they use 'less than 250 employees' as the definition of a small to medium-sized enterprise (SME), in order to facilitate the easy comparison of data across member states. A further refinement of the definition used by Eurostat based on numbers employed is shown in Table 9.8.

Classification of firms by employment size

Number of employees	*Type of firm*
0-9	micro businesses
10-99	small enterprises
100-499	medium-sized enterprises
500+	large enterprises

Applying this definition to Table 9.2, it can be seen that 83 per cent of manufac-turing firms in the UK are micro businesses, 15.5 per cent are small, 1.3 per cent are medium sized and 0.4 per cent are large. Although there are some national differ-ences (the southern-most countries have relatively more micro businesses than the northern countries) the pattern of size structure is similar in the EU as a whole- 92 per cent of all enterprises are micro businesses, 7.4 per cent are small, 0.5 per cent are medium sized and 0.1 per cent are large.

It is important to note that the definition of SME used within the EU changed in 2005. For grant-aid purposes an SME must have no more than 25 per cent of its capital owned by a larger enterprise and must meet specific criteria with regard to numbers of employees, turnover or balance sheet totals. A 'micro firm' is one with 0-9 employees, a maximum annual turnover of 2 million euros or a maximum bal-ance sheet total also of 2 million euros. The equivalent figures for a 'small firm' are 10-49 employees, 10 million euros turnover or 10 milion euros balance sheet total; for a 'medium-sized firm' 50-249 employees, 50 million euros turnover or 43 mil-lion euros balance sheet total. Using these definitions it is estimated that 99 per cent of all enterprises in the EU (prior to enlargement) were SMEs and that they provided around 65 million jobs.

No matter how small firms are defined, they will suffer from similar problems, which are very different from those faced by larger companies.

Trends in the Small-firm Sector

Figure 9.4 shows how the share of small establishments in total manufacturing employment changed between 1930 and 1990. The definition used here is fewer than 200 employees. The establishment is the reporting unit. It can be seen that the small-firm sector was in decline up to the late 1960s and early 1970s, since when its importance has increased.

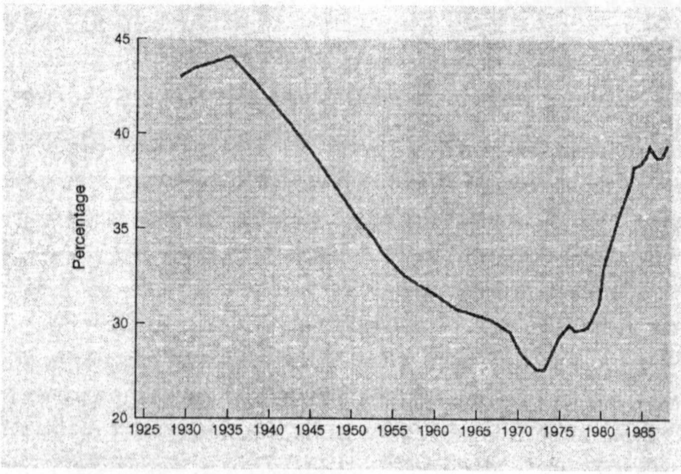

Share of small establishments in total manufacturing employment, 1930-1990

Source: Stanworth, J. and Gray, C. (eds), *Bolton 20 Years On: The Small Firm in the 1990s,* Chapman, 1991, Table 1.1

For manufacturing industries small firms are very important in terms of the numbers of companies, accounting for 99 per cent of total firms according to the Bolton Report definition. Even though they were less important in terms of employment they still accounted for 47 per cent of total employment. This tends to understate their importance because it does not include the service sector, many parts of which are heavily dominated by small firms due to the nature of the production process. Although there is a great deal of information available from official sources on the manufacturing sector, the same depth of information is not available for the service sector, so accurate information is difficult to obtain.

Reasons for the Growth in the Small-firm Sector

There has clearly been a resurgence in the importance of the small-firm sector which appears to have been more pronounced in the United Kingdom than in other countries. Why? Some causal factors are as follows:

- *The changing pattern of industry.* There has been a change in the industrial structure of the United Kingdom away from manufac-turing and towards services. Since many services are dominated by small firms, there will be a corresponding change in average firm size. However, this does not provide the full explanation as there has been a growth in the share of small firms even in the manufacturing sector. And it does not explain the international differences since there have been similar changes in industrial structure in other countries too.
- *Changes in consumer spending habits.* A move from mass-produced goods to more specialised products puts small firms at an advantage as they can react more quickly to changes in demand and shorter product life cycles.
- *Flexible specialisation and the growth of subcontracting.* A debate which started in the late 1980s centres round the idea of the 'flexible firm'. As a result of the recession of the early 1980s there was a drive by firms to reduce their costs in order to remain competitive. One way of reducing overhead costs was to move to a flexible firm structure whereby the firm's activities are divided into core and peripheral activities. The core activities, which are central to the activities of the firm, would be kept

'in-house' and carried out by full-time permanent workers. The peripheral activities would be carried out by temporary workers or would be subcontracted. The firm has then reduced its overheads and can react to peaks in demand by increasing the amount of temporary labour it uses or increasing the amount of subcontracting. This might also have had the effect of increasing the relative importance of the small-firm sector.

- *Reorganisation and job reduction.* There has been an increase in the phenomenon of downsizing by organisations in an attempt to reduce costs. Ninety per cent of large companies have reorganised and cut jobs since 1985.
- *Government policy.* After the Bolton Report there was a much greater interest in the role of the small firm in the regeneration of the economy and in the provi-sion of jobs. But most of the initiatives designed to help the small firm came after the start of the resurgence of the small-firm sector in the early 1970s.
- *The growth in self-employment. A* part of the growth in the small-firm sector has been due to the growth in the number of self-employed. The self-employed accounted for 9.8 per cent of the workforce in 1984 and 11.7 per cent in 2004. This represents a 19 per cent increase in the number of those self-employed over this period.

Percentage of workforce self-employed, 1984-2004 (UK)

Year	*% self-employed*
1984	9.8
1985	10.0
1986	10.0
1987	10.9
1988	11.3
1989	12.1
1990	12.3
1991	11.9
1992	11.3
1993	11.2

1994	11.7
1995	11.6
1996	11.6
1997	11.5
1998	10.9
1999	10.8
2000	10.6
2001	11.3
2002	11.2
2003	11.6
2004	11.7

Source: Adapted from *Annual Abstract of Statistics* (various), ONS, UK

The level of self-employment is likely to be related to the level of unemploy-ment, so that as unemployment rose during the 1970s and 1980s there was an increase in the level of self-employment. This goes a long way to explaining theinternational differences as the growth in self-employment in the United Kingdom has far outstripped that in other countries. Again, however, it does not provide the full explanation as business births were growing in the late 1960s when unemployment was falling.

- *Technological change.* Changes in technology, particularly information technology and the miniaturisation of components, has made it possible for small firms to benefit to a similar extent to large firms. This has had the effect of reducing the importance of economies of scale and enabling small firms to compete more effectively with large ones.
- *Competitive forces.* As far as the international differences are concerned, the Bolton Report found that industry in the United Kingdom was biased towards large size in comparison with other countries. So what may have happened as a result of competitive forces is that the balance of industry in the United Kingdom has moved towards the norm of other countries.

The Role of the Small-firm Sector

The growing importance of the small-firm sector implies that small firms do have a valuable role in the economy apart from being a mere provider of employment. The areas in which the small firm has advantages over large firms are those where there are:

- *Clearly defined small markets.* It is not worthwhile for large firms to enter such markets since there are no economies of scale and no scope for mass production.
- *Specialist, quality, non-standardised products.* Again it would not be worth a large firm entering such a market as the benefits of large-scale production cannot be reaped.
- *Geographically localised markets.* For example, the small corner shop.
- *Development of new ideas.* It is often argued that the small firm is the 'seedbed' of ideas and that, because of greater motivation and commitment on the part of the owner of the small firm, it is very conducive to invention and innovation.

Aid to the Small-firm Sector

The thinking on small firms has changed over time. Initially they were viewed favourably, but after the Second World War the dominant thinking was that large-scale production could take advantage of large economies of scale and that costs would be lower and production more efficient. It was not until more recently that the interest in the small-firm sector has increased again. The main reasons for the renewed interest are seen in the results of empirical studies which have shown that the role of the small firm is greater than previously thought in areas such as inno-vation, the balance of payments and employment.

The main argument for giving support to the small-firm sector is that it has a valuable role to play in the economy. In the 1980s and 1990s, for example, small firms were seen as a mechanism for reducing the very high levels of unemployment. Between 1983 and 1993 the small-firm sector created 2.5 million jobs. The basic premise for support is that small firms are at a disadvantage with respect to large businesses in areas such as raising capital, research and development and risk bear-ing. Two particular problems faced by small firms were highlighted in 1996: cash flow problems which stem from the late or non-payment of bills; and dealing with government red tape. These problems have been addressed by a number of recent developments. All public limited companies are now required by law to state in their annual reports the average length of time it takes them to pay their bills. The Federation of Small Businesses published a 'name and shame' list for the first time in April 1999 which is expected to apply peer pressure and thereby encourage firms to pay bills on time. It also provides information to help small firms decide who to trade with. The Federation of Small Businesses has estimated that 44 per cent of bills are paid more than 15 days after the normal 30-day credit period. The comparable figure is 35 per cent in the EU. It is also estimated that about £20 million is tied up in late payment, with a half of this owed by large firms to small firms. The govern-ment also publishes 'league tables' of government departments which are slow in paying their bills, with the pledge that this will be improved. To reduce the amount of red tape faced by firms, the government has, over the years, relaxed many of the rules and regulations involved in running a business. For example, from 1996 there has only been a single form for registration for income tax, national insurance and VAT, from April 1999 small employers have been able to move from monthly to quarterly payment of PAYE and National Insurance contributions.

Government Policy

Within the UK national policy for small firms has increasingly become a vital com-ponent of governmental attempts to create a competitive economy capable of achieving sustainable economic growth. To this end policy initiatives in recent years have become more focused and have tended to adopt a multi-agency approach, aimed at improving the environment in which small businesses emerge and grow, and at fostering enterprise and innovation. Key developments over the last decade or so have included:

- *Business Link*-a national network of 'one-stop shops' to provide information and support to small firms.
- *Direct Access Government*-a 'one-stop shop' on the Internet that provides busi-nesses with access to regulatory guidance and forms.
- *The Enterprise Zone*-another Internet-based initiative to help firms with finding information on issues such as finance, exporting, technology, innovation and management.
- *The Teaching Company Scheme (TCS)*-the government's premier technology transfer mechanisms for linking UK higher education establishments and busi-nesses.

- *The SMART Awards*-designed to promote technological development and inno-vation.

There have also been a number of legislative and fiscal changes aimed at reducing the burdens on small businesses (e.g. levels of corporation tax). Some of the most recent developments have included the launch of the University for Industry (UfI), the Enterprise Fund, the University Challenge Fund, the Small Business Service (SBS) and the EU SME Initiative.

The latter-introduced in December 1997-was designed to assist SMEs in rural areas or areas of industrial decline to become more competitive in overseas markets. There have also been attempts to reduce the flow and improve the quality of regulation affecting smaller businesses and an action plan to make the UK the number one location for starting and growing a business. This plan is available via the Small Business Service website *(www.sbs.gov.uk)*.

MINI CASE: THE SMALL FIRM SECTOR

In December 2002 the UK government published a document entitled *Small Business and Government-The Way Forward,* which set out an action plan designed to help the small firm sector. It has seven themes:

- building an enterprise culture-to provide everyone with the understanding of enterprise which will enable them to make an informed choice between employment and enterprise;
- encouraging a more dynamic start-up culture-to strengthen business support networks and create an environment which encourages enterprise;
- encouraging more enterprise in under-represented and disadvantaged groups-to increase the business start-up rate in both groups;
- improving the experience of small firms of government services-to improve the coherence, accessibility and quality of government services to small firms;
- developing better regulation and policy-to reduce unnecessary regulatory burdens on small firms;
- improving access to finance-to reduce the number of small businesses finding access to finance as a barrier to growth;

- building the capability for growth-to improve growth potential through raising performance in key areas such as management skills and the adoption of good practice.

Under each of these themes the document identifies policies and initiatives designed to address these objectives. The Confederation of British Industry (CBI) carried out an assessment of progress towards these objectives by 2005 in a report entitled *The Small Business Service Five Years On.* It found that the government had made significant progress towards three of these objectives-improving access to finance, improving the experience of government services and increasing the number of business start-ups. It found that for the other four objectives there is still much work to be done before the stated aim of the SBS-to make the UK the best place to start and grow a business-is achieved.

Networking between Firms

A more recent trend in industry which is well documented is towards co-operation rather than competition. This co-operation can take many forms: for example, subcontracting, networking (both formal and informal) and joint ventures. Such co-operation can be (and is) used by large as well as small and medium-sized enterprises. For large companies it is a way to grow and diversify without risk. For smaller firms it allows them to stay small but at the same time to benefit from some of the advantages of large-scale production like specialisation.

Subcontracting

There has been an increase in the amount of subcontracting, where firms do not carry out the whole of the production process themselves but subcontract some of their activities to other firms. This represents a rejection of vertical integration and it is related to the notion of the flexible firm mentioned earlier. Subcontracting goes some way to explaining the phenomenal growth rate in 'business services' that occurred in the 1980s. It is increasingly common for businesses to subcontract specialist work in areas such as human resource management to outside consultan-cies. 'Partnering' between companies and consultancies is becoming more common where the consultancy is retained on a semi-permanent basis to give advice on a whole range of human resource matters from recruitment to planning for succes-sion. This will obviously boost the small-firm sector. There has also been an increase in 'partnership sourcing' as large firms are developing long-term relation-ships between themselves and their suppliers. This phenomenon brings benefits to the large firms in the form of reducing stock levels and associated costs and facili-tating just-in-time production methods. It also brings benefits to small firms, many of which are the suppliers, in the form of greater security.

Networking

Networking refers to the relationships that exist between organisations and the people within those organisations. These relationships can be of different types, both formal and informal, and there is increasing recognition of the importance of these relationships, especially to small firms (e.g. they may be based on the exchange of goods and services, like the relationship between a firm and its sup-plier or client).

Subcontracting is an example of this kind of network but there are other links not based on exchange, like the relationship between a firm and the bank manager or other advisers. There are also informal links between the entrepre-neur and family and friends, and between entrepreneurs in different organisations. There might also be co-operative links between firms. This can be seen in the market for executive recruitment where there has been a growth in the links between consultancies, particularly for international work. The creation of the Single European Market and the increased internationalisation of business left the smaller consultancies in a weak position relative to the large international recruit-ment firms like Korn Ferry International, which have branches in most European countries. The smaller consultancies have reacted by forming networks. There are basically two types of network:

- Where firms are members of a network but where the network has a different name from the individual firms and the firms operate under their own name (i.e. the network has an identity of its own). The members are independent firms that co-operate in carrying out their business. There are 16 such groups in Europe including EMA Partners International and AMROP Heuer Group.
- Where firms are part of a network of independent firms but where the network does not have a separate identity and the

firms operate under their own names. There are ten such groups in Europe.

The firm is seen as existing within a spider's web of relationships, as Figure 9.5 shows. It is possible for two firms to be linked in a variety of ways; in one market they may be competitors, in the next co-operators, customers in another and sup-pliers in another.

Networking has taken on greater significance because of changes that are taking place in the economy, which include the reversal of the trend towards higher industrial concentration, the adoption of Japanese methods of production, the decline of 'mass markets' and technological change that requires greater specialisa-tion than previously. All of these changes favour the formation of networks.

The role of strategic alliances between firms has been recognised, especially in the small-firm sector where expansion through other means is often impossible and in the process of internationalisation.

The Virtual Organisation

The virtual organisation is a network-based structure built on partnerships where a small core operating company outsources most of its processes. It is a network of small companies which specialise in various aspects of production. The organisation can be very big in trading terms but very small in the numbers of permanent staff. The process is typically mediated by information technology.

The main benefit of the virtual structure is that it helps organisations to deal with uncertainty. When virtual organisations are managed properly they can simul-taneously increase efficiency flexibility and responsiveness to changes in market conditions. The organisation is reaping the benefits of specialisation without having to develop those specialisms itself. Therefore overhead costs are minimised, as too are training costs and support costs. Information technology assumes many of the co-ordinating and managing roles that managers and committees carry out in large organisations. Information technology enables communication and the sharing of information across geographical boundaries. It is often the case, how-ever, that the creation of a virtual organisation is driven solely by cost considerations rather than strategic considerations, in which case the benefits might not be realised. There will be a loss of control over outsourced activities and it may actually cost more to manage such activities. The organisation can become locked into contracts and specific relationships so that flexibility is reduced. There may be a lack of commitment of key resources (i.e. contractors) to the company and the loss of a contractor will be very serious.

There is some evidence that the incidence of virtual organisations is on the increase, facilitated by developments in information technology. It is a matter of 'wait and see' if this will become the dominant organisational structure in the future.

Joint Ventures

As indicated earlier in this chapter, oint ventures are a good way for firms to diver-sify and enter other countries' markets. Joint ventures benefit both parties as each can diversify with the benefit of the experience of the other, and the level of risk is minimised. Again, there are examples in the area of executive recruitment. The International Search Group, for instance, was set up as a joint venture between five companies in France, the UK, Austria, Germany and Italy in order to offer a European service to its customers.

Consortia

In some industries co-operative behaviour has come about for particular reasons. In process plant contracting, for example, the projects are often too large for single firms and so they form consortia in order to bid for the contract. The consortium will include contractors, suppliers and bankers who together will have the expertise and the resources to carry out the project.

Multinationals

At the opposite end of the scale from the very small business are companies which have the capability to produce goods or services in more than one country but where control usually resides in a central location. Multinationals are often well-known household names, as the examples below illustrate:

- UK multinationals-BP, Glaxosmithkline.
- European multinationals-Nestlé, Volkswagen.
- USA multinationals-General Motors, IBM.

These multinationals are huge organisations and their market values often exceed the GNP of many of the countries in which they operate. They are estimated to account for a quarter of the world's output.

The growth in the multinationals is due to relaxation of exchange controls making it easier to move money between countries, and the improvements in com-munication which make it possible to run a worldwide business from one country.

SYNOPSIS

This chapter has looked at the size structure of industry in the United Kingdom and Europe as a whole. It examined the motives for and the methods of growth, as well as the sources of finance for such growth. The role of the small firm was considered, as too was the role of the multinational. Although many industries are dominated by huge compa-nies, the trend seems to be moving away from growth towards a process of disintegration for a variety of reasons. As a result of this trend there has been an upsurge in the small-firm sector, and an increase in the level of co-operative behaviour between firms.

SUMMARY OF KEY POINTS

- The size structure of firms varies greatly within industries, within a country and between countries.
- Firms can grow internally through organic growth or externally through merger and takeover.
- There are many motivations for growth, including increased market share, the reap-ing of economies of scale, the diversification of risk.
- Growth can be financed internally through reinvested profits or externally through banks, the capital market and the money market.
- There are limits to organisational growth, such as diseconomies of scale.
- The level of merger activity in the UK and in Europe follows a cyclical pattern and is related to economic conditions.
- The small-firm sector is an important source of output and employment, and this importance has increased over time.
- Many factors have influenced the growth of the small-firm sector, including the changing pattern of industries, changes in demand, technological change, the trend towards increased subcontracting and government policy.

- At the other end of the size spectrum, multinational corporations have a massive impact on world output and employment through their activities.

CASE STUDY: EXECUTIVE SEARCH

As this chapter shows, the size of firms within an industry depends upon many fac-tors. The nature of the product and the production process are important in explaining why many service industries are dominated by small firms. Services have the following characteristics which differentiate them from goods and these characteristics have implications for the structure of the industry concerned:

- *Intangibility.* Services are intangible while goods are tangible. This means that it is impossible to sample a service before it is purchased.
- *Inseparability.* There is often no separation between consumption and production of services. Goods are produced, sold and then consumed. Services are sold, then production and consumption begin simultaneously.
- *Heterogeneity.* Given the nature of services, they are difficult to standardise; often each unit of a service sold is different. This stems from the central role that the buyer plays in service production.
- *Perishability.* Services are perishable, they are destroyed in the process of con-sumption and cannot be stored.
- *Irreversibility.* Many services are irreversible in that, once consumed, they cannot be returned and nor can faults be rectified.

These characteristics have an important impact upon the shape of the industry and the firms that constitute the industry. This case study looks at one such service industry, executive search.

Executive search (or headhunting) is one part of the executive recruitment market. It refers to the recruitment of candidates through direct and personal con-tact by a specialist recruitment consultancy acting as an intermediary between employer and potential candidate(s). Although there are some large international consultancies, such as Korn Ferry and Egon Zehnder, the industry is one which is dominated by small . Even the large international consultan-cies are small compared with firms in other industries. In 2000 the average number of consultants per firm was 5.4 and the most common firm size was 2 consultants. There are many reasons for this and some of these reasons apply equally to other services and are related to the services characteristics above. Some, however are spe-cific to executive search and selection:

- There is a large personal element in the service provided which means that the production process will be labour intensive. The only scope for technological change is through the computerisation of records and processes. This is likely to be true for many services and means that there is no scope for mass production and the typical firm size will remain small. The average number of assignments per consultant in 2000 was eight.
- The perishable nature of services means that stocks cannot be kept, and given that the demand for services will fluctuate, firms with large numbers of consult-ants will have to bear the cost of excess capacity when demand is low. There is therefore a tendency towards small size.

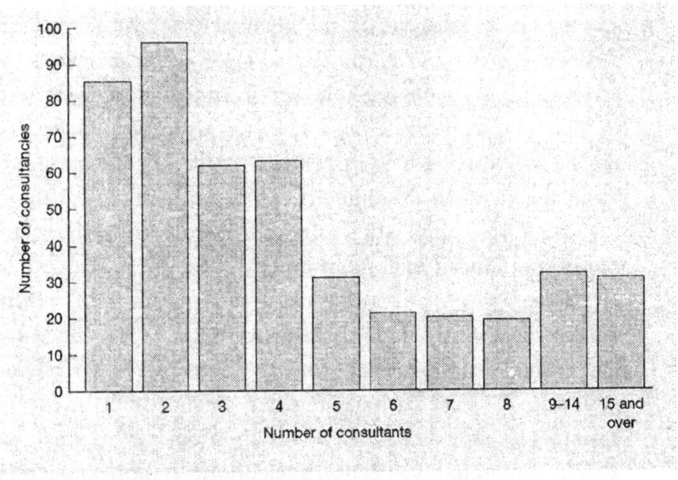

Figure : Size distribution of search consultancies, 2000

- The higher the number of consultants the greater the possibility of one or more leaving and starting a new consultancy in competition with the original, and taking their contacts with them. This is a fairly common method of entry for new firms in this industry. For this reason consultancies rarely have more than 14 consultants.

- Executive search is unique in that the greater the number of client companies, the smaller the pool of candidates. Most search firms offer an 'off-limits' guaran-tee-they will not approach someone they have placed for at least two years. Therefore the more people they place, the more restricted will be the pool of can-didates.
- It could be that there is little scope for economies of scale-there are many firms with only one consultant surviving and performing well. Although the size of the firms in the industry is small, greater specialisation in the task can take place than in a personnel department. Many consultancies specialise by function or by industry which may lead to reduced search times due to the consultants' easier access to candidates and data banks and better understanding of the industry. There is also the effect of repetition on the skills of the producer.
- Low barriers to entry and exit make the industry easy to enter and to leave. Because of the characteristics of services it is difficult for the quality of the serv-ice being provided to be ascertained. To overcome this lack of information, many service industries (accounting and law for example) have strong regulatory bodies which can enforce certain behaviour patterns upon the firms in the industry. This, however, is not the case for executive search. There is no regula-tory body, there are no pre-entry educational requirements and there are no legal limitations to entry, apart from the acquisition of a licence which can be obtained fairly easily for a small sum. Once a firm has entered there is little formal control over its operating methods; so legal barriers to entry are not high in executive search. The capital required to set up in business is small, since all that is required is a licence, a telephone, stationery, secretarial support and an office. The method of payment for assignments-which usually involves a part payment at the beginning of the assignment-reduces the 'break-in' period as loans can be quickly paid off. Consultancies become profitable after only a few assignments.

- The service characteristic of inseparability of production and consumption often places a geographical limit on markets that can be served, and this will impact upon firm size. Many services involve 'direct sales' with no intermediaries, and so firms are likely to locate near to the demand for their services or near to where the decision is taken to use that service. Executive search is seen as an extension of the management division of labour since it is the externalisation of previous internal personnel functions. Hence, if the location of search consultancies is close to its demand, and the decision to use recruitment consultancies is taken in head offices, then the location of these head offices plays an important part in the location of consultancies. In Britain this partly explains the geographical concentration of search consultancies (77.5 per cent of consultancies) in London and the south east.
- The inseparability of production and consumption in services means that the concept of vertical integration loses meaning when applied to services. Most services involve direct production, so the whole production process takes place when the service is performed. The existence of many business and other serv-ices represents a process of disintegration, as firms are increasingly shedding their peripheral functions and buying in these functions from external sources. Executive search is a good example of this process as recruitment and other per-sonnel functions are increasingly being contracted out. Indeed there is further disintegration in the industry, as researchers are setting up their own firms and consultants are buying in their services. There is no obvious reason why horizon-tal mergers should not take place in service industries. The motivation for and incidence of horizontal mergers will vary between the very different services which exist. As far as services with large personal inputs are concerned, there will be limited scope for economies of scale, and so this reason for mergers is removed. Similarly services which are geographically localised are less likely to be horizontally integrated. • The particular nature of service production makes diversification into other areas more difficult than in other types of production. The obvious directions for diversification are into products either produced with common

technology or through the development of existing technology, and into products that can be marketed though similar channels. Executive search consultancies diversify by offering other services to management, such as salary surveys or succession plan-ning. The development of executive search itself has partly been through a process of diversification as large accountancy firms have moved into the area of management consultancy, including recruitment.

CONCLUSION

Executive search (like many other services) is characterised by small firm size. For such industries, the traditional theories on the growth of firms, which see develop-ment as a 'grow or fail' process are not very helpful. They are clearly not true when small firms not only survive but are successful. A more fruitful approach is to look at the constraints which might prevent the growth of the firm. In executive search, the internal constraints include the personal nature of the production process which means that consultants can only handle a small number of assignments per year. There is some evidence that an increase in support staff does increase the output of consultants but not by a significant amount-the range remains narrow. Another internal constraint might be a lack of individuals with the right skills. The skills required in a consultant are good interpersonal and communication skills, possibly some experience of recruitment work and, more importantly, contacts. An external constraint is that the service can be carried out by clients, which might well limit the extent of the market. Also, unique to executive search, is that con-sultants will not normally approach an individual they have placed for at least two years. Therefore as the number of consultants rise in a firm the possible pool of candidates shrinks. The bigger the consultancy, the higher is the probability that one or more of the consultants would leave to set up in competition against the original consultancy, taking all of their contacts with them. There have been exam-ples of consultants doing this but taking with them researchers as well, leaving the original consultancy in a very weak position.

9

The Technological Environment: E-business

INTRODUCTION

We are on the verge of a revolution that is just as profound as the change in the econ-omy that came with the industrial revolution. Soon electronic networks will allow people to transcend the barriers of time and distance and take advantage of global markets and business opportunities not even imaginable today, opening up a new world of economic possibility and progress. (US Vice-President, Al Gore Jnr, July 1998)

This is undoubtedly an exciting time to be considering developments in the technologi-cal environment, with the emergence of new business terms and concepts such as electronic markets (e-markets), electronic business (e-business) and electronic com-merce (e-commerce). In the so-called 'new economy' digital networking and communication infrastructures provide a global platform through which enterprises and people interact, collaborate, communicate and search for information.

The potential growth for electronic business worldwide is impressive. A wealth of complementary digital technologies, including digital communications networks (Internet, intranets, extranets), computer hardware and software, and other related net-works, databases and information systems, distribution and supply chains, knowledge management and procurement are being merged into a powerful combination for busi-ness change using the World Wide Web (WWW) as the driving force. Starting more or less from zero in 1995, e-commerce has recently celebrated its tenth anniversary, and for many of us it is difficult to remember the pre-Internet business environment. In the US, it is estimated that the 200 million Americans with access to the web will soon be spending more than $145 billion annually online, equivalent to 7 per cent of all US retail sales. Similarly, in western Europe, a quarter of all Europeans do some shopping via the Internet. Globally, e-business has grown from $26 billion in 1997 to an estimated $1 tril-lion by 2005. Predicting the future growth of e-business is fraught with difficulty, but given that it has the potential to deliver a low-cost, universal, interactive and global medium that provides a simple and secure method for exchanging information instan-taneously, the business case appears compelling.

In addition, we might speculate that an Internet-based society will also notice a dra-matic change to other aspects of people's lives, outside of the workplace. For instance, changes such as new distance-learning methods and material are starting to emerge in education and many other areas of daily life are increasingly being affected by techno-logical developments.

However, we should also remember that while terms such as e-business and e-com-merce are relatively new, they are part of an evolutionary technology process dating back over 30 years. The concept of e-business has actually emerged from a fusion of various separate technologies, such as electronic data interchange (EDI), electronic fund transfer (EFT), electronic point-of-sale (EPOS) and smart cards that had previ-ously struggled in isolation to achieve mass acceptance.

Indeed, the terms 'electronic business' and 'electronic commerce' have no univer-sally accepted definitions, and confusingly are often used interchangeably. However, for our purposes there is a significant difference between the two terms.

Broadly, e-business means doing any element of business over the Internet, and embraces activities such as servicing customers and collaborating with partners, in addition to buying goods, services and information. E-business can be formally defined as the exchange of products, services or information, whether paid or unpaid, across electronic networks, at any stage within the value system, including the supply chain, the value chain and the distribution chain. There are a number of potential sub-sets within the general term 'e-business'.

E-commerce covers a narrower sphere of activities than e-business, and refers in particular to the process of electronic transactions involved in the exchange of prod-ucts, services and information between buyer and seller. The activities of e-retailers such as Amazon would fall under this category.

Within an organisation, there are several activities (for example, information and knowledge management, resource co-ordination etc.) that might be more effectively achieved through use of an intranet. Table 16.1 provides a common classification of e-business by nature of transaction. For the purposes of analysis, business organisations have been sub-divided into private sector (B), public sector (G) and third sector (T) organisations. There is also a column for consumers (C).

It can be seen from Table 16.1 that e-business encompasses a wide spectrum of potential external commercial and information exchanges and applications. However, the classifications business-to-business (B2B) and business-to-consumer (B2C) repre-sent the core of electronic commerce and these are the areas that have received the most interest and development to date. These classifications are now considered below in some detail.

BUSINESS APPLICATIONS 1: BUSINESS-TO-BUSINESS (B2B) COMMERCE

Features of B2B

Business-to-business (B2B) transactions account for, in terms of value, about 80 per cent of all Internet transactions. Both the buyer and seller are business organisa-tions. The technological and legal aspects of B2B commerce tend to be more complex than business-to-consumer (B2C) commerce, and it often requires sophis-ticated software. It can be arranged through either inter-organisational systems (IOS) or electronic markets.

B2B commerce is characterised by a number of key features, many of which dif-ferentiate it from B2C commerce. Turban and colleagues suggest that the following are some of its salient aspects:

- an automated trading process;
- high volumes of goods traded;
- high net value of goods traded;
- multiple forms of electronic payment and funds transfer are permitted, unlike B2C commerce, which tends to be restricted to credit cards and smart cards;

- high level of information exchange, including shared databases, between the dif-ferent trading partners. This often involves the use of extranets;
- prior agreements or contracts between the business partners requiring a higher level of documentation;
- different types of legal and taxation regimes depending on where the two parties are based, and what type of goods or services are the subject of the transaction;
- Business applications 1: business-to-business (B2B) commerce 435
- multiple levels of authorisation of purchases, each level having its own limits on expenditure or types of goods.

Benefits of B2B

On examination there appear to be a number of potential benefits and drivers of B2B commerce. The first of these is that it encourages the adoption of an Internet electronic data interchange (EDI) system to improve the efficiency of business processes. The DTI describes EDI as 'the computer-to-computer exchange of struc-tured data, sent in a form that allows for automatic processing with no manual intervention. This is usually carried out over specialist EDI networks'.

Using EDI to streamline business processes has a number of discernible benefits. These would include the following:

- A safe, secure and verifiable electronic environment that allows manufacturers or retailers to link their stock databases directly to suppliers. This reduces lead times by reducing the time taken in placing and receiving orders.
- Lower costs in creating, processing, distributing, storing, retrieving and destroy-ing paper-based information; fewer errors in data entry; improved inventory control, and reduced staff time involved in the process.
- Improved warehouse logistics, and improved co-ordination for moving goods to the appropriate place, at the defined time and in the correct quantities.
- Better and more efficient integration of support functions such as human resources, inventory control, order processing, accounting and payment processing.

- More efficient strategic alliances and partnering with suppliers, customers and competitors. For instance, in the motor industry, leading firms such as General Motors, Ford and Chrysler have set up a joint extranet with suppliers.

It should be recognised that EDI has been around since the 1960s, but before the development of an integrated Internet EDI system, it was seen to have some serious shortcomings that undermined the potential benefits. Two in particular are worth noting:

- It required an expensive private dedicated network connection between two estab-lished trading partners. According to Forrester Research *(www.forrester.research.com)* only 100000 of the 2 million companies in the USA employing 10 or more employ-ees chose to deploy traditional EDI. The rest felt that it was too expensive, was not interactive enough, and did not enable them to access or negotiate with their suppli-ers and other partners.
- The lack of agreed international standards for document formats meant that early EDI was based on proprietary technologies such as value added networks (VANs). Each EDI tended to be set up specifically for a single buyer and supplier, and consequently became heavily embedded deep within the organisation's IT systems. This served to inhibit change within the organisation, making it diffi-cult and expensive to change suppliers because of the difficulties of switching the existing system to a new supplier. It also meant that where a firm was multi-sourcing, a separate EDI might be needed for each supplier.

However, Internet-based EDI overcomes most of these shortcomings. Rather than using proprietary technology (VANs) it makes use of the public Internet. Therefore, Internet EDI, unlike traditional EDI, is ubiquitous, global, cheap, easy to use, and readily avail-able and accessible both within (intranet) and outside (extranet) the company.

In addition, Internet EDI standards are becoming increasingly compatible with eXtensible Mark-up Language (XML). XML is already the key international standard for transferring structured data, and has wide acceptance, having been championed by organisations such as Microsoft, Netscape and Sun Microsystems, as well as by the WorldWideWeb consortium. The widespread adoption of XML means that most companies are now able to use Internet-based EDI to exchange documents cheaply and quickly. The International Data Corporation (IDC) reported that Internet EDI's share of EDI revenues has risen from 12 per cent to 41 per cent over the period 1999-2003, with this trend likely to continue into the future.

A further potential benefit and driver of B2B commerce is that it provides for expansion from a local or national market to a global electronic market (e-market). For a relatively minimal capital outlay a business can access a wider range of (better and/or cheaper) suppliers, and contact a larger potential customer base.

B2B activities vary from firm to firm, and industry to industry, but as well as global electronic markets, where many buyers and sellers meet for the purposes of trading electronically together, other common types of markets include a sell-side marketplace (where one company does all the selling), and a buy-side market-place (where one company does all the buying).

Other benefits and drivers of B2B commerce include the following:

- That it provides an opportunity to market, sell and distribute goods and services to other businesses for 24 hours a day 365 days a year, the so-called 'martini effect'.
- That it can sometimes significantly reduce fixed costs, perhaps through savings on premises, where a website has effectively become the organisation's showroom.
- That it also has the potential to improve pull-type supply chain management, such as JIT manufacture and delivery based on integrated and fully-automatic supply chain management (SCM) and demand chain management (DCM) systems.
- That it can encourage organisations to adopt a more customer-centric approach, in which the business tracks consumers' preferences and re-engineers itself quickly to meet consumer needs. This might involve developing a mass cus-tomisation business model such as that adopted by Dell Computers, and discussed in the case study below.
- That it can facilitate the development of an integrated electronic customer rela-tionship management (eCRM) system, based on customer information gathering, data warehousing and other market intelligence.

- That it may improve knowledge management systems within the organisation as employees use the company intranet system to access organisation-wide know-how.

Many of these potential advantages of B2B can be illustrated by looking at the fol-lowing case study, based on Dell Computers. To facilitate your understanding of the issues discussed in the text an extended case study has been used in this chapter rather than two mini cases and there are additional questions at the end of the case study which you might like to attempt.

CASE STUDY

Dell Computers was developed in the early 1980s by Michael Dell; by 1990 Dell was assembling its own brand personal computers and sales were over $500 mil-lion, with an established reputation for both laptops and desktop computers. Sales efforts were focused on selling directly to business customers, including educational and government agencies.

In the early 1990s Michael Dell developed a small team to explore using the Internet as a way of communicating with customers, and selling products on-line. This team increasingly became convinced that the Internet was an ideal channel for Dell products. There were a number of reasons for this:

- The number of Internet users was 20 million in 1996, and this was expected to double every year.
- Dell's major customers-business users-were already involved in the Internet, both in their use of the Internet, and the development of intranets.

Dell Computer launched its on-line website in July 1996, selling computers direct to customers. Company sales at this point had reached $7.8 billion, with an operat-ing income in excess of $710 million. After six months Internet sales had reached about $1 million per day, and by autumn 1999, Internet sales accounted for 27 per cent of total revenue, at $15 million per day.

Dell is now the world's number one PC maker, having overtaken Compaq in July 2001, with a 13 per cent share of the market, and in the near future expects to see 50 per cent of its revenue come from Internet selling. So what are the critical suc-cess factors behind Dell's use of the Internet to grow its business, and why have rivals struggled to copy its business model?

First, Dell now sells all the items it produces via the Internet: desktops, worksta-tions, notebooks, network servers and storage devices, software, and add-ons (e.g., zip drive, printer, etc.). These items are also sold by telephone, fax and mail, with an additional call centre service that can complement the Internet home page. Service, support and an introduction to the company are also presented on the home page.

Second, Dell has achieved high price competitiveness, because its business model centres on having the lowest costs in the industry. For instance, its sales representa-tives need fewer calls to close a sale generated from an Internet lead, and achieve higher sales than the industry average. Furthermore, order processing via the Internet is more efficient. Each quarter Dell receives 200 000 visits to its website to check order status, 500 000 technical service visits and 400 000 library downloads. Each of these transactions would have cost between $5 and $15 in time if handled over the telephone. In addition, technical manuals are available on-line, instead of Dell having to print these out and mail them.

Third, Dell was the first Web-based computer seller, and already had significant experience in direct marketing. Some commentators suggest that this has given it a significant first-mover advantage over its rivals.

Fourth, Dell is a relatively young company, which was built on a business model based on direct telemarketing, so there was no need for Dell to change its business strategy to adopt Internet commerce. The Internet is simply another medium for contacting distant customers interactively. However, for other rival companies this was not the case. For them, changing business strategy fundamentally was difficult, expensive and time-consuming. Dell is also predominantly a one-product com-pany, unlike many others in the electronics and computer industry.

Fifth, Dell has readily invested in the most advanced technology available, to provide a fully integrated value network, linking end consumers all the way back through the supply chain. In 1999, Dell invested in i2 Technologies software. The software enables it to monitor practically every part, every day. Dell also uses the Web thoroughly and creatively. Dell allows business buyers to download Premier Pages, enabling customers to configure what information their employees can see, and even which employees can see it.

Sixth, Dell has pioneered the concept of mass customisation, with its adaptive build-to-order fashion manufacturing system. To keep the price competitive with-out longer delivery time, efficient procurement of small numbers of parts from vendors, flexible manufacturing systems, and economical distribution to customers are essential. Dell computers can be assembled to order in about four minutes, with a further 90 minutes needed to load the software. They are delivered, on average, within three days of order.

Seventh, Dell uses the Internet effectively to manage and enhance its relation-ships with its suppliers, as well as with its customers. It has a fully integrated supply chain management system, and consequently Dell has relatively few suppliers, fewer than 200 in total. Many of its main rivals have at least 2000 suppliers.

Eighth, Dell's direct relationship with all of its customers makes one-to-one database marketing more effective. Dell learns about its customers by monitoring how they use the website, and is able to identify new market trends through analysing changes it notes in new build-to-order specifications over time.

Ninth, Dell provides global reach and value-added services as a single contact point. It currently sells computers in more than 170 countries. Dell has more than 10 000 service providers around the world who provide technology planning and acquisition, system deployment, network and product maintenance. The Internet can provide an efficient single point of contact for these services backed by corpo-rate-level accountability for their products and services. The Internet makes it easier and reduces costs for customers to do business with Dell. Because the customers spend their own time to obtain service from the Internet, which previously required human agents in the call centre, the Internet has also reduced Dell's cost. Finally, Dell has worked hard to establish a high reputation for quality and relia-bility. For instance, Dell products such as OptiPlex and Dell Dimension Desktop computer have picked up over 174 industry awards for performance, reliability and service. Internet customers in particular will hesitate to order expensive and com-plicated items without a trial, unless they are satisfied by the prior reputation of the company concerned.

- Identify all the key elements of Dell's successful business model. Using a rating scale of 1-5 for each element identified (where

1 denotes the most important factor), summarise these into a single table.

- Critically examine the four most important (highest rated) elements that you believe explain Dell's success. Explain your rationale for selecting those particular factors.
- In your opinion, to what extent are other businesses (not just in the computer industry, but in any sector of the economy) able to successfully replicate Dell's business model? Illustrate your answer with appropriate examples.
- Draw up a list of potential 'opportunities' and 'threats' facing Dell over the next 5 years.

Potential Problems and Limitations of B2B

As we have illustrated, there are a number of significant advantages to the wide-spread adoption of B2B commerce. However, it should be noted that there are also some potential limitations or barriers that may serve to delay or hamper the growth in B2B commerce. These include:

- Internet technology is continually developing, encouraging some organisations to postpone investment in the short term;
- technical limitations such as lack of system security, reliability and protocols-there are also currently some problems with telecommunications bandwidth and speed;
- the cost and difficulty of integrating existing (legacy) IT applications and data-bases with Internet and related software;
- the slow progress made in achieving universal international standards for the electronic transfer of information documentation;
- many legal, taxation and regulatory issues remain unresolved.

Even successful companies such as Dell face challenges as the e-business market matures. In August 2005, Dell announced a slowdown on quarterly sales to 14.7 per cent, and saw its share price immediately fall by nearly 10 per cent as investors worried that it was running out of opportunities for further growth and was start-ing to face increasing competition from low-cost rivals such as the Asian company Lenovo, the Chinese manufacturer that recently acquired IBM.

Nevertheless, on balance the clear benefits of B2B commerce are likely to out-weigh the disadvantages, and we should expect to see continued dynamic growth in this area for some years to come.

BUSINESS APPLICATIONS 2: BUSINESS-TO-CONSUMER (B2C) COMMERCE

Key Features

The business-to-consumer (B2C) model was the first to mature on the Internet, and has generated the most publicity. It involves a simple, singular retailing transaction between a business and a consumer. About one-fifth of e-business is between businesses and consumers. One example of the successful development and use of a B2C business model is by the e-retailer Amazon.com, which we will look at in more detail later.

It has been estimated that retail sales over the Internet in the UK totalled £39.5 billion in 2004, while wider forms of IT sales, such as email, electronic data exchange and automated phone sales, accounted for £195.6 billion, which is equiv-alent to one-fifth of the UK economy.

B2C commerce can be characterised by a number of key features, including:

- Goods or services are offered for sale and purchased over the Internet; these may include both *digitised* products, such as music, airline tickets or computer soft-ware that can be delivered *virtually* direct on the Internet, or physical products such as books, flowers and groceries that are delivered by post or courier. Currently in the UK, two-thirds of Internet sales are in physical products rather than digitised products.
- Transactions are typically quick and interactive.
- There are no pre-established business agreements.
- Security is primarily an issue for the buyer, rather than the seller.
- Low volume between each individual purchaser and supplier, often for relatively inexpensive items and/or frequently purchased items such as groceries.
- Well known packaged items, which have standard specifications.
- Items backed by a security guarantee and/or high brand recognition. The remote-ness from the customer means that a strong reputation may be required to establish consumer confidence.
- Items whose operating procedures can be most effectively demonstrated by animation or video.

- Well designed websites, which are attractive and easy to use, are essential.

Emerging B2C and E-retailing Business Models

There are a number of ways of classifying the various B2C business models that are emerging:

- Direct marketing product websites-where manufacturers advertise and distribute their own products to customers via Internet-based stores, bypassing the use of intermediaries. Examples include Dell Computers, Nike, Cisco, The Gap and Sony.
- Pure electronic retailers (e-retailers) that have no physical stores, being purely cyber-based, such as Amazon.com.
- Traditional retailers with websites-sometimes called brick-and-click organisa-tions-where the Internet provides an additional distribution channel for an existing business. Examples include Wal-Mart, Tesco and Barnes & Noble.
- Best price searching agents-intermediaries, such as BestBuyBooks.com and Buy.com, that use software to search for the lowest prices available on the Net.
- Buyer sets the price-the customer nominates a price which they are willing to pay for certain goods or services, and the intermediary then tries to find a seller willing to sell at that price or lower. An example is Priceline.com.
- Electronic (on-line) auctions-host sites, such as eBay, act like brokers, offering website services where sellers post their goods for sale, thereby allowing buyers to bid on those items.
- Business applications 2: business-to-consumer (B2C) commerce

Benefits of B2C Commerce

There are a number of potential benefits and drivers of B2C commerce. Some of the more important are as follows:

- For existing business organisations, many of the benefits are similar to B2B com-merce, in that B2C commerce can expand the marketplace, lower costs, and improve management support systems, internal communications and knowledge sharing. It can also allow firms to focus more effectively on customer relation-ships. However, it might also promote more competition.

- For new businesses, the Internet can reduce barriers to entry, and thus make it easier to enter new markets. One example would be Amazon.com, which did not need to incur the expense of opening up high street shops in order to success-fully enter the retail book industry.
- For customers, B2C on average provides faster and more complete information, a wider choice, and cheaper products and services. It also allows greater interac-tion with other customers.
- For the wider community, an increase in B2C commerce may well have an impact in employment patterns, perhaps with an increase in home-working.

Possible Limitations

While B2C commerce has some obvious benefits for the parties involved in transac-tions of this kind, as one might anticipate there are a number of potential limitations to its future growth and development. These include:

- lack of trust and consumer resistance;
- unresolved security, legal and privacy issues;
- insufficient buyers and sellers on-line;
- technical issues such as poor reliability, insufficient bandwidth, and speed;
- hardware and software tools are rapidly evolving and changing;
- the very expensive off-line marketing costs involved in building brand recogni-tion for new on-line companies;
- lower barriers to entry will increase competition, and potentially increase rather than decrease consumer search and selection costs, as well as possible reduced industry profits overall;
- there are still significant distribution and storage costs involved for the sale of physical goods;
- existing bricks-and-mortar companies will not go away, and will continue to compete hard to maintain existing market share.

Many of the potential advantages and disadvantages of B2C can be illustrated by looking at the case study below, based on Amazon.com. As with the previous case study, you are encouraged to attempt at least some of the questions at the end of the text.

SYNOPSIS

Technology plays an important role in all areas of business operation and is increasingly providing opportunities for businesses to interact with their customers and suppliers.

With the development of the Internet there has been a revolution in the way in which business transactions are taking place and an increasing number of firms have begun to engage in electronic business-to-business and business-to-customer relationships alongside their traditional methods of doing business.

We have even seen the emer-gence of some new businesses which have only an electronic existence. While such electronic relationships can have their problems and limitations, this is an area of the business environment in which there is likely to be significant developments in the coming years.

SUMMARY OF KEY POINTS

- Technological developments have revolutionised the global marketplace and have spawned a whole new business vocabulary including the notion of e-business.
- The concept of e-business relates to the different aspects of doing business over the Internet and embraces a whole range of activities concerned with the exchange of products, services or information across electronic networks.
- E-commerce denotes a narrower range of activities related to the process of elec-tronic transactions between buyer and seller.
- B2B and B2C represent the core of the notion of electronic commerce and provide a number of potential benefits for the parties involved in the transaction process.
- Both B2B and B2C, however, have their limitations which may hamper the growth of these two types of commerce.
- In the field of retailing a number of B2C business models have begun to emerge.
- Developments in this field have implications for both the demand side and supply side of markets.
- Technological advancement is a never-ending process that continues to shape the business environment.

CASE STUDY

Bookselling over the Internet is one of the most sophisticated and successful B2C e-business sectors to have developed. The global cyber book market is expected to have grown beyond $1.1 billion by 2002.

Amazon is one of the most famous websites on the Internet, with 50 per cent of the cyber book market share. Amazon officially opened in July 1995, and had a turnover of $600 million by 1998, with an average monthly growth rate of 34 per cent.

As a pioneer, Amazon enjoyed considerable first-mover advantage, generating enormous publicity, which created awareness and established its brand name among the book buying public. Jeff Bezos, Amazon's founder, was convinced that consumers would enjoy the experience of browsing books electronically, reading reviews and excerpts from a particular book, and having it delivered a few days later. Bezos also felt that Amazon should be more profitable than traditional retail-ers in the longer term, on the basis that: 'We're short on real estate and long on technology. Technology gets cheaper every year and real estate more expensive.'

After initially gaining a reputation as a cyber bookstore, Amazon has gradually expanded its range of offerings into areas such as music, video, gifts and auctions. However, while Amazon has an impressive customer base, with over $1 billion in cash, and expanding sales, it has only just begun to make a profit (around £500000 in 2004).

In fact, Amazon has found that it faces many of the problems of traditional retailers. For instance it has had to build a vast infrastructure of warehouse and dis-tribution centres to house its burgeoning inventories of product lines, and has needed to spend heavily on off-line marketing to attract new customers.

Competition in the cyber book industry is also now very fierce with new com-petitors entering the market all the time. Barnes & Noble started to counterattack in 1997, and it quickly reached 15 per cent of the cyber book market share. Amazon also faces competition from software agents, such as BestBuyBooks.com and Buy.com, which offer to find the lowest prices available anywhere on the Net.

Nevertheless, Amazon still has many supporters. These argue that the lack of profits so far have arisen simply because the company has striven to build up a dominant position in e-commerce, and that triple-digit growth rates and expansion into new product lines will produce the increased sales needed to cross over into profitability. Also its rival on-line retailers lack scale. For instance, Barnes & Noble, Amazon's nearest rival, only attracts a third of Amazon's 14 million unique visitors a month.

Amazon has always shown an incredible ability to innovate and to diversify its product range. It has introduced ideas such as allowing customers to review books on its website, and publish rankings that assign a chart position to every book in print based on its sales. These ideas are now commonplace on other sites.

Amazon has also successfully patented its Associates programme that allows an on-line merchant to sell products through other websites by paying commissions for customer referrals. For instance, if you run a website selling rare coins, you can publish a website listing the best books available on rare coins. When visitors click on these titles they are transported (one-click) to the Amazon website, which will pay the referring website a commission, if the visitor buys a book. It is estimated that about $1 billion of Amazon's future sales (out of a total of $3.4 billion) per year could arise through this affiliate system.

To attract customers Amazon is also increasingly making special offers, such as free shipping, or further discounted prices, although critics claim this is financially unsound given the current lack of profitability.

Amazon though does have a number of opportunities to diversify and expand further. For instance, it has created partnerships with companies such as Toy 'R' Us, and Borders Groups Inc., which have found it difficult to operate their own on-line operations. What these companies are seeking is to share and benefit from Amazon's expertise in delivery. Bezos has made the point that while the distribu-tion centres of traditional retailers are good at shipping containers of products to stores, they are not designed to deliver single items direct to customers, something which requires very different capabilities, and in which Amazon specialises.

Second, there are a number of economic opportunities to expand the selling of additional higher-priced (if lower-margin) items on-line. Amazon is currently able to offer a selection of 25 000 electronic items on its site, compared with say 5000 in a big electronic store. Although gross margins in electronics are smaller than books, at only 10-15 per cent, the costs of storage, packing and shipping are roughly the same for a £300 digital camera as for a book. So overall the net profit per unit for these goods is actually higher.

Third, there are emerging makets such as China, which has an 86 per cent liter-acy rate and five times the population of the USA. Local companies, such as Dangdang.com, China's biggest online bookseller, are already becoming established but have less than 0.25 per cent of the Chinese book market. The problem with the Chinese market at the moment is not price but a lack of Web access, consumer trust and online banking services. So far, only 6 million of the 50 million Internet users in China have shopped online.

Fourth, Amazon continues to innovate. It has recently entered the DVD rental market. It delivers DVDs by first-class post with pre-paid envelopes provided for returns. As technology develops it will undoubtedly be able to supply DVDs virtu-ally in future, while it is able to use its current personalisation tools to recommend films to customers. In terms of technological improvements, by using sophisticated software tools to improve its internal operations management, it has managed to reduce distribution costs from 155 per cent of revenues in 1999 to 7 per cent today. Amazon was able to ship 1.4 million copies of *Harry Potter and the Order of the Phoenix* without a hitch on the day of its release in June 2003.

Postscript

Amazon's current sales were around $1.8 billion per quarter (October 2005), with 28 per cent of goods sold actually from third party sellers through its Associates Scheme.

Bibliography

Barnett, P.G.: *Survey of Research on the Impacts of Pesticides on Agricultural Workers and the Rural Environment*, Davis, CA: California Institute of Rural Studies, 1989.

Bryant, Bunyan and Paul Mohai: *Race and the Incidence of Environmental Hazards: A Time for Discourse*, Boulder, Westview Press, 1992.

Burch, William R. Jr.: *Human Ecology: An Environmental Approach*, Belmont, Duxbury Press, 1994.

Campbell, R. R., and Wade, J. L.: *Business and Environment: The Coming Collision*, Boston, Allyn and Bacon, 1972.

Daubenmire, R. F.: *Business Management and Environment*, New York, Wiley, 1947.

Kruvant, W.J.: *People, Energy, and Pollution*, Cambridge, Ballinger Publishing, 1975.

Meyer, Art: *Earth Keepers: Environmental Perspectives on Hunger, Poverty, and Injustice*, Scottsdale, Herald Press, 1991.

Sontheimer, Sally: *Business and the Environment: Crisis and Development in the Third World*, New York, Monthly Review Press, 1991.

Strahler, A. N., and Strahler, A. H.: *Introduction to Environmental Business: Santa Barbara*, New York, Hamilton Publishing Company; 1974.

Szasz, Andrew: *Ecopopulism: Toxic Waste and the Movement for Environmental Justice*, Minneapolis, University of Minnesota Press, 1994.

Vallette, J.: *The International Trade in Wastes: A Greenpeace Inventory*, Washington, Greenpeace, 1989.

Wenz, Peter S.: *Environmental Justice*, Albany, State University of New York Press, 1988.

Zupan, J.M.: *The Distribution of Air Quality in the New York Region*, Baltimore, Johns Hopkins University Press, 1973.

Index

□□□